RENÉ BOSEWITZ/ROBERT KLEINSCHROTH

GET TO GRIPS WITH COMPANY ENGLISH

WORTSCHATZTRAINING ON THE JOB

Rowohlt Taschenbuch Verlag

Impressum

Wir danken Frau Ortrud Grimm vielmals für ihre
Hilfe bei der Erstellung des Manuskripts.

Wir danken Herrn Gustav Gregor für das Scannen
von Bildern und Texten.

Originalausgabe
Veröffentlicht im Rowohlt Taschenbuch Verlag
GmbH, Reinbek bei Hamburg, November 1999
Copyright © 1999 by Rowohlt Taschenbuch Verlag
GmbH, Reinbek bei Hamburg
Umschlaggestaltung Barbara Hanke
(Illustration Cathrin Günther)
Layout Anne Drude und Alexander Urban
Zeichnungen Zarina Sheriff
Satz OCRA und Stone PostScript, QuarkXPress 3.32
Druck und Bindung Clausen & Bosse, Leck
Printed in Germany
ISBN 3 499 60845 6

Inhalt – Contents

Vorwort — 6

1. Rund um die Firma – Around the company — 7
2. Im allgemeinen Büro – At the General Office — 19
3. Die oberen Etagen – Rooms at the top — 27
4. Das Rückgrat der Firma – The company's backbone — 37
5. Einstellung und Entlassung – Recruitment and Dismissal — 47
6. Personalentwicklung – Personnel Development — 57
7. In der Einkaufsabteilung – At the Purchasing Department — 69
8. Forschung und Entwicklung – Research and Development — 81
9. In der Produktionsabteilung – At the Production Department — 91
10. Die Marketingabteilung – The Marketing Department — 103
11. In der Werbeabteilung – At the Advertising Department — 113
12. In der Verkaufsabteilung – At the Sales Department — 123
13. Im Warenlager – At the Warehouse — 135
14. In der Versandabteilung – At the Despatch Department — 141
15. Beim Kundendienst – At Customer Service — 151
16. Die Rechtsabteilung – The Legal Department — 163
17. Finanzen und Buchhaltung – Finance and Accountancy — 175
18. Gehälter und Löhne – Salaries and Wages — 187
19. Arbeitgeber und Gewerkschaften – Employers and unions — 199
20. Die Welt der Versicherung – The world of insurance — 213
21. Geschäfte mit der Bank – Bank business — 225
22. Das Geld arbeiten lassen – Making money work — 239

Job list — 253
Glossary: Understanding the jokes — 259
Key to the exercises — 265

Vorwort

Kill three birds with one stone! Schlagen Sie drei Fliegen mit einer Klappe. *Get to Grips with Company English* ist ein Nachschlagewerk, ein Lernwörterbuch und ein Übungsbuch für *business English around the company*.

Es ist ein **Nachschlagewerk**, dessen Wortfelder nach Abteilungen und Geschäftstätigkeiten Ihrer Firma geordnet sind. Es enthält *phrases* und *idioms* rund um die Firma – also keine Einzelwörter, sondern ganze Wendungen wie *run out of stock:* nichts mehr auf Lager haben oder *strike a balanced compromise:* einen ausgewogenen Kompromiß finden. So lernen Sie Englisch effektiver, so vermeiden Sie Fehler. Sie lernen Wortschatz statt Wörter: das Substantiv zusammen mit seinem treffenden Verb, dem passenden Adjektiv und den Präpositionen, denn diese sind die Hauptfehlerquellen für Deutsche. So lernen Sie Englisch auch leichter, weil sich unser Sprachengedächtnis eindeutige und sinnvolle Sachverhalte besser merkt als vieldeutige Einzelwörter. Das isolierte Wort ist ein schweres Wort!

Get to Grips with Company English ist ein **Lernwörterbuch** mit zahlreichen Lerntips zur Verbesserung Ihrer Lernleistung. Und es ist ein **Übungsbuch**. Anhand der vielen kurzen, abwechslungsreichen Tests, Kreuzwort- und Bilderrätsel können Sie Ihren Fortschritt messen.

Die genau auf das jeweilige Thema abgestimmten englischen Witze und ironischen Zitate sollen Sie immer wieder zum Weiterlesen motivieren. Auch mit diesen *business jokes* werden Sie Englisch lernen. Das Glossar sorgt dafür, daß Ihnen die Pointen nicht entgehen.

Zusammen mit seinem Pendant *Master your Business Phrases, Sprachmodule für den Geschäftsalltag* (rororo sprachen 60725) bietet *Get to Grips with Company English* eine wichtige Ergänzung zu den Standardthemen der Lehrbücher und Kursmaterialien. Mit beiden Werken können Sie sich gezielt auf Themen und Situationen des Geschäftslebens vorbereiten. Da immer mehr große Firmen dazu übergehen, in den höheren Etagen Englisch als Verkehrssprache einzuführen, gehören beide Bücher in Ihr Reisegepäck und auf Ihren Schreibtisch.

RUND UM DIE FIRMA

PART 1

AROUND THE COMPANY

What sort of companies are there? How are companies structured? There are so many different names for company structures. In this section you will find important vocabulary about founding, closing and changing company structures. The typical phrases for doing business can be found here, too.

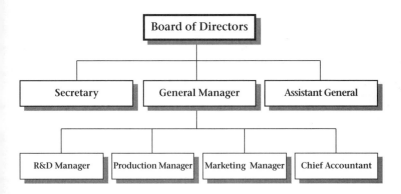

Incredible but true

In 1895 King C. Gillette had a wonderful idea. He was fed up with having to use a cut-throat razor every morning so he set about designing a wafer-thin, incredibly sharp blade that could be held together by a safety clamp. It took him eight years to perfect the design and when it went on sale in 1903, he thought he had been wasting his time, for in that year only 51 razors and 168 blades were sold. The following year, however, he knew it had been worthwhile: 90,000 razors were sold and 12,400,000 blades.

1 RUND UM DIE FIRMA

1. *Wo wir arbeiten* / Where we work

in einer freien Marktwirtschaft leben	live in a free enterprise economy
Geschäfte in einer Planwirtschaft machen	do business in a state-controlled economy
für ein Unternehmen / eine Firma / eine Gesellschaft arbeiten	work for an enterprise / firm / company
im öffentlichen Dienst arbeiten	work in the state / public sector
in einem verstaatlichten / staatlichen Unternehmen arbeiten	work at a nationalised / state-owned company
ein Familienunternehmen besitzen	own a family firm
ein Einzelunternehmen besitzen	have a sole-proprietorship
in der Produktions- / Finanz- / Dienstleistungsindustrie arbeiten	be employed in the manufacturing / banking / service sector
sich bei einem Großunternehmen / in einem Konzern / in einer Unternehmensgruppe bewerben	apply to a large-scale enterprise / concern / group
einem Unternehmen beitreten	join a company
Was für eine Gesellschaftsstruktur hat Ihre Firma?	What sort of corporate structure does your company have?

2. *Firmen gründen und schließen* / Founding and closing companies

Unternehmungsgeist haben	have entrepreneurial spirit
eine Firma gründen	create / establish / found a company
ein Geschäft / Firma / Unternehmen gründen	form / start / set up a business / firm / enterprise
ein Gemeinschaftsunternehmen gründen	establish / form a joint-venture
einen Alleinvertreter ernennen	appoint a sole-trader
eine Firma privatisieren / verstaatlichen	privatise / nationalise a company
eine Firma umstrukturieren	restructure a company
eine Umstrukturierung durchführen	do a restructuring
ein Unternehmen finanzieren	finance / fund an enterprise

AROUND THE COMPANY 1

Bankrott machen / pleite gehen — go bankrupt / broke
Aufgrund des schlechten Managements machte die Firma Bankrott. — Because of bad management the firm went broke.
Schlechtes Management war schuld, daß LOPY vor die Hunde ging. — Mismanagement caused LOPY to go down the drain.
Sie waren gezwungen, für immer dichtzumachen. — They were forced to close their doors permanently.
zahlungsunfähig sein — be in a state of insolvency
eine Gesellschaft auflösen — dissolve a company
eine Firma schließen — close down a company
Cash-flow-Probleme führten zur Schließung. — Cash flow problems resulted in closure.
Konkurrenten haben ihn dazu getrieben, in den sauren Apfel zu beißen. — Competitors forced him to bite on the bullet.
Wir müssen es verkaufen. — We have to sell it off.
an den Meistbietenden gehen — be up for grabs
Jetzt, wo sie Geld verlieren, geht die Firma an den Meistbietenden. — Now they're losing money the firm is up for grabs.
Wir haben aufs falsche Pferd gesetzt. — We've backed the wrong horse.
Sie sind pleite gegangen. — They've gone broke.
Fehlendes Interesse am Produkt hat sie gezwungen, das Geschäft zu schließen. — Lack of interest in the product made them shut up shop.
Nachdem sie TOM Ltd. gekauft hatten, ging es mit der Firma bergab. — After buying TOM Ltd. the company began to go downhill.
Drei Jahre finanzielles Mißmanagement, und sie sind pleite gegangen. — Three years of financial incompetence, then they went to the wall.
Dutch Bank sagte, der Verlust von einer Million Dollar ist "Kleingeld". — Dutch Bank said it was peanuts to lose a million dollars.
LOPY ging pleite nach einem schlechten Jahr. — LOPY went bust after a bad year.

1 RUND UM DIE FIRMA

A box of idioms (1)

vor die Hunde / den Bach hinuntergehen	go down the drain
an den Meistbietenden gehen	be up for grabs
in den sauren Apfel beißen	bite on the bullet
das Geschäft schließen	shut / close up shop
aufs falsche Pferd setzen	back the wrong horse
pleite gehen	go bust / go to the wall

Lerntip 1: Bite on the bullet

The bad news: Das Englische ist eine Sprache mit vielen Idioms. Wer sie nicht beherrscht, gerät in Gefahr, Situationen mißzuverstehen. Vorsicht beim Gebrauch von Idioms. Beherrscht man sie nicht exakt Wort für Wort, wird man als Ausländer belächelt. In den sauren Apfel beißen heißt (eben nicht *to bite into the sour apple*, sondern) *bite on the bullet* (Patrone).

And now the good news: Viele idiomatische Ausdrücke sind sprachliche Bilder, die sich gut einprägen, wenn man sie in mentale Bilder verwandelt. Zum Beispiel: *bite on the bullet*. Stellen Sie sich vor, wie Sie auf eine große *bullet* beißen, die sauer schmeckt. Je grotesker Ihr Bild, desto einprägsamer ist es.

3. *Partnerschaften* / Partnerships

Was für eine Personengesellschaft ist Ihr Unternehmen?	What sort of partnership is your company?
eine Handelsgesellschaft / offene Handelsgesellschaft / Kommanditgesellschaft haben	have a commercial / general / limited partnership
mit einem Partner assoziiert sein	be in partnership with a partner
einen stillen Gesellschafter / Hauptteilhaber / Juniorpartner haben	have a silent / senior / junior partner
einen Teilhaber abfinden	buy out a partner
Wer ist der geschäftsführende Gesellschafter / nicht aktiver Gesellschafter?	Who's the managing / nominal partner?

AROUND THE COMPANY 1

einen Gesellschaftervertrag unterschreiben	sign a partnership agreement
gemeinsam haften / allein haften	have joint / sole liability
am Gewinn beteiligt sein	participate in profit-sharing
Wie hoch ist der Gewinnanteil?	What's the share of profit?
Von außen betrachtet, scheint LOPY Ltd. nichts wert zu sein.	At face value LOPY Ltd. is worth nothing.
40 000 Mark als Eigenkapital einbringen	put in DM 40,000 as equity
100 000 Mark Fremdkapital bekommen	obtain DM 100,000 of borrowed capital
eine Gesellschaft auflösen	dissolve a partnership
als Gesellschafter ausscheiden	withdraw from a partnership

 ## Master your phrases

Task 1: Translate the German into English

1. go (*pleite*)
2. have (*Unternehmungsgeist*)
3. have a (*Kommanditgesellschaft*)
4. have joint (*gemeinsam haften*)

Task 2: Complete the idioms

1. go down the ....
2. The firm is up for ....
3. .... the bullet.

Task 3: Beef up your word power

Find a phrase that has almost the same meaning

found a company	e _ _ _ _ _ _ _ h a firm
form a business	s _ _ _ t an e _ _ _ _ _ _ _ _ e
shut up shop	c _ _ _ e d _ _ _
finance an enterprise	f _ _ _ an enterprise
go to the wall	go _ _ _ t

1 RUND UM DIE FIRMA

Task 4: Find the opposite

a free enterprise economy	a .... economy
privatise a company	.... a company
establish a company	.... a company
join a partnership	.... a partnership

Lerntip 2: Vernetzen Sie Ihren Wortschatz

Find the opposite – diese Übung ist besonders wertvoll. Lernen Sie zu einem Ausdruck sein Gegenteil mit. Ihrem Gedächtnis ist es tatsächlich gleich, ob Sie 3 Silben oder 12 Silben lernen. Gegensatzpaare stützen sich gegenseitig. Auf diese Weise vernetzen Sie Ihren Wortschatz.

---— **Picture your idiom** ———

"I'm afraid we've ...."
"Why?"
"The lira has collapsed. Our money is down the drain."

Time for a smile

Sign that can be found in almost all offices:
In our company all colleagues are equal -
only the salaries aren't.

AROUND THE COMPANY 1

4. Gesellschaften und Körperschaften/ Companies and corporations

als gemeinnützige Gesellschaft agieren	do business as a non-profit-making firm
eine eingetragene Gesellschaft gründen	establish a registered / incorporated (US) company
eine Aktiengesellschaft gründen	found a joint-stock company / public (limited) company / stock company (US)
Gesellschaft mit beschränkter Haftung gründen	set up a private (limited) company / close corporation (US)
für eine Kapitalgesellschaft / einen internationalen Konzern arbeiten	work for a corporation (US) / multinational
ein Kleinunternehmen / mittelständisches Unternehmen besitzen	to own a small / medium-sized company
eine Hierarchiestruktur / flache Struktur haben	have a hierarchical / flat structure
Wo sitzt Ihre Dachgesellschaft?	Where's your holding company?
Wie heißt Ihre Tochter- / Mutter- / Schwestergesellschaft?	What's the name of your subsidiary / parent / sister company?
Wir sind ein amerikanischer Mischkonzern.	We're an American conglomerate.
ein 100%ige Tochtergesellschaft / Niederlassung sein	be a wholly-owned subsidiary / branch
Aktienanteile an einer Firma besitzen	hold stock in a company
Gesellschaftsanteile kaufen / besitzen	buy / have shares in a company
Geschäftseigentum angeben	state the corporate assets / property of the company
im Handelsregister eingetragen sein	be in the Register of Companies
Wo ist Ihr Firmensitz?	Where's your headquarters located?
Wir wußten nichts von BWM. Wir haben die Katze im Sack gekauft.	We didn't know anything about BWM. We bought a pig in a poke.

1 RUND UM DIE FIRMA

5. Geschäftstätigkeiten / Business activities

Eigentümer eines Unternehmens sein	own an enterprise / be the proprietor of a company
eine Firma leiten / führen	run / manage / operate a firm
Geschäfte führen	conduct business
Preise festlegen	fix prices
ein Unternehmen vergrößern	expand / enlarge a company
ein Unternehmen gesundschrumpfen	slim down / delayer an enterprise
einen Konzern aufkaufen/übernehmen/erwerben	buy out / take over / acquire a concern
ein Angebot abgeben	launch a bid
eine Dividende ausschütten	distribute a dividend
das Geschäft ausweiten	diversify the business
fusionieren / zwei Unternehmen fusionieren	carry out a merger / merge two companies
ein Übernahmeangebot unterbreiten	make a take-over bid
ein sehr gutes Geschäft sein	be really big business
Aktien besitzen	hold shares
einen Unternehmenskauf tätigen	make an acquisition of a company
eine einvernehmliche / nicht einvernehmliche Übernahme tätigen	make a friendly / hostile take-over
ein raubgieriger Geschäftsmann / Unternehmer sein	be a predator / raider / corporate raider
Wer ist das Opfer?	Who's the prey?
ein Gebot / Angriff abwenden	ward / fend off a bid / attack
als „Retter" auftreten	"act as a white knight"
das Kern- / Randgeschäft darstellen	represent core / peripheral business
Mißlingt die Übernahme, müssen wir die Rechnung bezahlen.	If the take-over fails, we'll have to foot the bill.
Das neue Produkt hat sich als Fehlschlag erwiesen.	The new product has failed.
Sie sind Verlierer. Du verschwendest dein gutes Geld.	They're losers. You're throwing good money after bad.

AROUND THE COMPANY 1

Magic Squares

1. Match the phrases (A, B, C ...) ...

A. Do you really want to withdraw from the partnership?	B. What can we do to increase profits?	C. Where's your headquarters located?
D. Why do you want to buy your partner out?	E. Why did the firm go down the drain?	F. What sort of partnership is your company?
G. He's the typical corporate raider.	H. Shall we take over Rover?	I. Did you know? BM is up for grabs.

... with the phrases (1, 2, 3 ...).

1. It's a small family enterprise.	2. Well, I'm getting old, you know.	3. What? Throwing good money after bad.
4. Who's the prey this time?	5. We went bust after a bad year.	6. It's based in London.
7. Well, we could delayer the company.	8. Well, why not launch a take-over bid?	9. He's a complete failure.

2. Put the numbers in the magic squares.

A =	B =	C =
D =	E =	F =
G =	H =	I =

3. Check yourself.

When the answers are correct, all columns and rows will add up to the same number (15).

RUND UM DIE FIRMA

A box of idioms (2)

die Katze im Sack kaufen	buy a pig in a poke
lächerliche Summe / Kleinkram	it's peanuts
die Rechnung bezahlen / tragen	foot the bill
gutes Geld schlechtem Geld nachwerfen	throw good money after bad

Advice from the experts

Never put off till tomorrow what you can avoid altogether.

Better to be a coward for a minute than dead for the rest of your life.

Master your phrases

Task 5: Which phrase is the opposite?

1. let prices float .... prices.
2. keep your money safe .... with your money
3. sell a company .... a company
4. this contract is legal this contract is ....

Task 6: Which idioms could you use to mean ...?

1. You don't have much time left.
2. Buy something without knowing what it is.
3. That's nothing, no sum of money.

AROUND THE COMPANY 1

Lerntip: Außenseiter bleiben kleben

Lernen Sie Wortschatz in kleinen Gruppen, denn das erste und letzte Element einer Gruppe prägen sich besonders gut ein.
Wenn Sie 35 Ausdrücke in Gruppen von 7 (+/−2) aufteilen, erhalten Sie zehn Randelemente, also über 30 Prozent der Ausdrücke, die sich allein durch diesen Trick besser lernen lassen.

Task 7: Beef up your word power

Find a verb that has almost the same meaning.

1. *manage* a firm   .... a firm
2. *expand* a company   .... a company
3. *delayer* an enterprise   .... down an enterprise
4. *acquire* a concern   .... a concern

Task 8: Phrases in context

So what do we do when we want to get into business? The normal way is to f _ _ _ _ a company. But what sort of company? A p _ _ _ _ _ _ _ _ _ p can be a dangerous thing. If we get the wrong structure the whole business could go d _ _ _ the d _ _ _ _ . Then we'll have to sh _ _ up sh _ _ . And that's no good for anybody. And if you have a partner and even if the business is a s _ _ _ _ _ s, but he wants to leave anyway, you have to b _ _ him o _ _. It's not so easy to di _ _ o _ _ e a partnership.

RUND UM DIE FIRMA

Crossword power

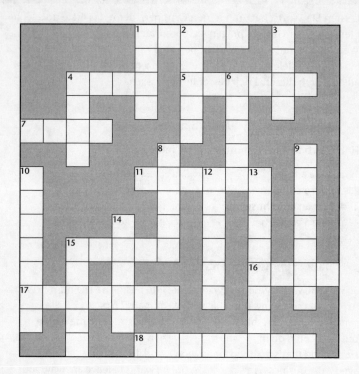

Across

1. What caused LOPY to go down the ✎?
4. Cash ✎ problems resulted in closure. 5. I work in the ✎ sector. 7. Another word for company. 11. We've ✎ the wrong horse. 15. What's our ✎ of profit? 16. Do you ✎ stock in your company? 17. The verb is *close*. What's the noun? 18. What's the opposite of *form* a partnership?

Down

1. Mismanagement caused LOPY to go ✎ the drain. 2. Did you ✎ to BMW for the job? 3. When did you ✎ the company? 4. What sort of corporate ✎ does your company have? 6. Because of bad management the firm went ✎. 8. At face ✎ LOPY Ltd. is worth nothing. 9. What's the opposite of a *friendly* take-over? 10. Another verb for *do* business. 12. Let's act as a white ✎. 13. After the take-over the firm went ✎. 14. He knows the ✎ of money. 15. Does he hold ✎ in the company?

IM ALLGEMEINEN BÜRO

PART 2

AT THE GENERAL OFFICE

Some companies still have a general office. This office supplies the other departments with all sorts of services and materials. It supplies stationery, general clerks and does the photocopying. Some general offices cover tasks from sorting the post to translating. Nowadays they are going out of fashion, however, the phrases can be used in all the offices around the company.

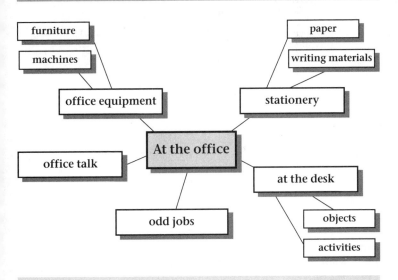

Rules of the office

If it's hand-written, type it.
If it's typed, copy it.
If it's copied, file it.
If it's Friday, forget it.

2 IM ALLGEMEINEN BÜRO

1. *Büroausstattung* / Office equipment

ein Großraumbüro gestalten	set up an open-plan office
Trennwände aufstellen	put up partitions
Büromöbel verrücken	move office furniture
verstellbare Drehstühle	adjustable swivel chairs
Dokumente im Reißwolf vernichten	shred documents
Papier in den Fotokopierer nachfüllen	put more paper in the photocopier
den Aktenschrank ausmisten	clear out the filing cabinet
eine Drehkartei anlegen	set up a rotary index
eine Hängekartei bestellen	order a suspension file

Time for a smile

The brain is a wonderful organ. It starts working the moment you get up in the morning and does not stop until you get into the office.
Robert Frost

2. *Telefax* / Fax

die Faxrolle auswechseln	change the fax paper
Toner einstellen	adjust the darkness / toner
ein Fax schicken	send a fax
ein Fax erhalten / empfangen	get / receive a fax
per Fax schicken	send by fax
den Termin per Fax bestätigen	confirm the appointment by fax
jemandem ein Fax schicken	fax someone
Ich faxe Ihnen die Liste mit den neuen Preisen zu.	I'll fax you the list with the new prices.

Food for thought

Since the introduction of computers at the workplace, I'm now the second smartest thing sitting at my desk.

AT THE GENERAL OFFICE

3. *Am Computer* / At the computer

eine Datei anlegen	create a file
eine Datei öffnen	open a file
Daten eingeben	key in / enter the data
Dokumente speichern	save / store files
ein Dokument ausdrucken	print a file out
Seitenformatierungen eingeben	set the page formats
Tabulatoren setzen	set the tabs
eine Software benutzen	use a software
Software aufrüsten	upgrade the software
am Computer korrigieren	make / do corrections on the screen
einen Brief gestalten	layout a letter
einen Serienbrief schreiben	write a standard letter
ein Dokument ausdrucken	print out a document
jemandem eine E-Mail (elektronische Post) schicken	e-mail somebody
ins Internet gehen	go on the Internet
Informationen herunterladen	download information
mit der Software zurechtkommen	manage with / handle the software

Time for a smile

They finally came up with the perfect office computer.
Whenever it makes a mistake, it blames another computer.
Milton Berle

4. *Büromaterial* / Stationery

Büromaterial bestellen	order stationery
eine neue Schreibtischgarnitur für den Chef	a new desk set for the boss
den Vorrat an Briefpapier mit Briefkopf überprüfen	check the quantity of headed paper
aus dem Katalog bestellen	order from the catalogue

2 IM ALLGEMEINEN BÜRO

Was für Büromaterial brauchen Sie?	What sort of stationery do you need?
Wir benötigen Tesafilm / Büroklammern / Ordner.	We require cellotape / paper clips / files / folders.
Was für Stifte benutzen Sie?	What sort of pens do you use?
Wir benutzen Kugelschreiber / Füllhalter / Filzstifte.	We use ballpoints / fountain pens / felt-tip pens.
Welche Art von Papier möchten Sie kaufen?	What type of paper do you wish to buy?
keine Schreibblöcke mehr haben	run out of writing pads
Wir brauchen Fotokopierpapier / Schreibpapier.	We need photocopy paper / writing paper.

Time for a smile

"How did the new office boy do today?"
"He had two tasks. One to get out and one to stay out."

5. *Die kleinen Dinge* / Odd jobs

die tägliche Arbeit eines Auszubildenden / Bürogehilfen	the daily routine of an apprentice / trainee / office boy
den Papierkorb ausleeren	empty the wastepaper basket
als Sachbearbeiter / Industriekaufmann arbeiten	work as a general / commercial clerk
Dokumente ablegen	file documents
die Post sortieren / verteilen	sort / distribute the mail
fotokopieren	do the photocopying
die Originale kopieren	photocopy the originals
Briefe auf der Briefwaage wiegen	weigh letters on the scales
Briefe frankieren	frank letters
Briefmarken auf die Umschläge kleben	put stamps on the envelopes
zur Post gehen	go to the post office
den Konferenzraum vorbereiten	prepare the conference room
Kaffee kochen	make the coffee
für andere Abteilungen arbeiten	work for other departments

AT THE GENERAL OFFICE 2

6. Am Schreibtisch / At the desk

den Schreibtisch aufräumen	tidy the desk
einen Bleistift anspitzen	sharpen a pencil
einen Bleistiftspitzer benutzen	use a pencil-sharpener
eine Linie mit dem Lineal ziehen	draw a line with a ruler
Der Kuli ist leer.	The pen / biro has run out.
Kugelschreibermine wechseln	change the refill of a ballpoint
Papiere zusammenheften	clip the papers together
eine Büroklammer benutzen	use a paper clip
die Blätter mit einem Hefter / Tucker zusammenheften	staple the sheets with a stapler
die Briefe mit einem Brieföffner öffnen	open the letters with a letter opener
den Briefbeschwerer auf die Papiere legen	place the paper weight on the paper
die Akten auf den neusten Stand bringen	bring the files up to date
die Kartei ergänzen	add to a card index
eine Kartei einrichten	set up a card index
das Papier lochen	punch the paper
die Eingangs- / Ausgangspost bearbeiten	deal with incoming / outgoing mail
ein Kundenkonto für ... einrichten	set up a customer's account for ...

A box of idioms

bis zum Hals in Arbeit stecken	be snowed under with work
bis zum Hals in Arbeit stecken	be up to one's ears in work
schwer schuften	keep one's nose to the grindstone
neue Besen kehren gut	new brooms sweep clean

Time for a smile

To make a long story short, there's nothing like having the boss walk in.

Doris Lilly

2 IM ALLGEMEINEN BÜRO

7. *Bürogespräch* / Office talk	
Wo ist meine Schere?	Where are my scissors?
Wer hat meinen Uhu genommen?	Who's taken my glue?
Das Tipp-ex ist ausgetrocknet.	The liquid paper has dried up.
Reich mir mal den Tesafilm rüber.	Pass me the cellotape, please.
Gehst du bitte ans Telefon?	Could you answer the phone for me?
Wer macht heute den Tee?	Who's making / brewing the tea today?
Wer ist diese Woche mit Brötchen-holen dran?	Whose turn is it to get the sandwiches this week?
Kannst du mir eine Essensmarke leihen?	Could you lend / let me have a food token?
Wir müssen noch den Urlaubsplan aufstellen.	We still have to draw up the holiday plan.
Kannst du mich für eine Stunde vertreten?	Could you cover for me for an hour?
Ich stecke bis zum Hals in Arbeit.	I'm up to my ears in work.
Der neue Chef möchte alle Abläufe ändern. Neue Besen kehren gut.	The new boss wants to change all the procedures. It's a case of new brooms sweep clean.
Keine Privatgespräche in der Dienstzeit.	No private calls during office hours.
Annette hat sich schon wieder krank gemeldet.	Annette's got a doctor's note again.

☛ Siehe auch *Das Rückgrat der Firma*, Seite 38 ff.

● ─────────── **Picture your idiom** ─────────── ●

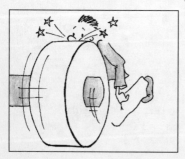

These girls do the typing
for the whole company.
They have to ....
their .... to the
....

AT THE GENERAL OFFICE 2

Master your phrases

Task 1: Let's go woggling

Replace the *woggles* with a suitable word.

1. We work in an open-*woggle* office.
2. Please *woggle* the appointment by fax.
3. Sorry, we haven't *woggled* your fax.
4. Clip the documents together with a *woggler*.
5. No private calls during *woggle* hours.

Task 2: Phrases in context

It's a bit old-fashioned, but never mind. They still do good work. Often the general office is o _ _ _ -p _ _ _ where all the desks are located in one room. One of the tasks of the general office is to o _ _ _ _ st _ _ _ _ _ _ _ _ y for the other offices.
They could probably order things such as b _ _ _ _ _ _ _ _ _ s, p _ _ _ _ c _ _ _ s etc.
So what goes on in the general office? People play with simple equipment. They sharpen their p _ _ _ _ _ s with a p _ _ _ _ _ sh _ _ _ _ _ _ _ _, st _ _ _ _ sheets of paper together, and put s _ _ _ _ _ on letters. If they want to survive as an office, they have to work hard. The general office must keep its n _ _ _ to the gr _ _ _ _ _ _ _ _ _.

Picture your idiom

"Can you spare me a minute, boss?" –
"Can't you see I'm busy, Dobson. I'm ....
...."

IM ALLGEMEINEN BÜRO

C Crossword power

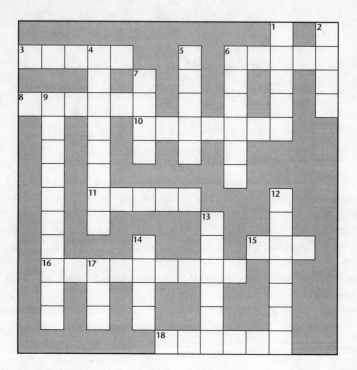

Across

3. R/E/T/E/N the data into a file. 6. What do you draw a line with? 8. Ein Drehstuhl is a ✎ chair. 10. Do it when the software is old! 11. Make two holes in a document. 15. Please ✎ me your price list. 16. Trennwand 18. Could you ✎ the phone for me, please?

Down

1. L/A/P/E/C an order for stationery. 2. Who's going to ✎ the tea today? 4. Put stamps on it. 5. ✎ letters on the scales 6. Eine Drehkartei is a ✎ index. 7. Klebstoff 9. Have you emptied the ✎ basket? 12. Staple the sheets with a ✎. 13. New ✎ sweep clean. 14. Do it with important documents! 17. We've ✎ out of fax paper.

PART 3

DIE OBEREN ETAGEN

ROOMS AT THE TOP

The top management. What do they really do for their – some would say – inflated salaries? They sit on the top floor, which has expensive carpets on it, at desks made of the finest woods, and make decisions. Well, they have to get the overall strategy right. Things like whether to expand, whether to acquire other companies and which direction to take the company in. They bear the responsibility in the final analysis.

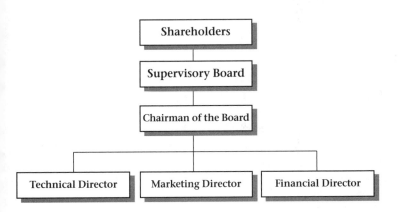

Time for a smile

The boss was addressing a meeting of the firm's senior executives and sales staff. "Now, when my son starts to work here tomorrow," he said, "I want you to treat him just as you would treat any other employee who was going to take over the company in two years' time."

3 DIE OBEREN ETAGEN

1. *Führungskraft sein* / Being an executive

Verantwortung tragen	have / bear responsibility
eine Führungsrolle übernehmen	assume a leadership role
den Posten als Vorstandsvorsitzender bekommen	get the post of Chairman of the Board
Vorstandsmitglied sein	be a Board Member
zum Firmenvorstand gehören	belong to the Board of Directors
Mitglied des Firmenvorstandes sein	be a member of the Board of Directors
zur Betriebsleitung gehören	be part of the managerial staff
dem Aufsichtsrat unterstellt sein	report to the Supervisory Board
als Vorstandsmitglied handeln	act as a member of the Board
als Unternehmensberater tätig sein	work as management consultant
an einer Vorstandssitzung teilnehmen	participate / take part in a board meeting
über Macht verfügen	have / possess power
für ein Unternehmen verantwortlich sein	be responsible for a company
als Geschäftsmann/-frau Erfolg haben	succeed as a businessman / woman
Sie sind nicht der Chef! Sie spielen hier nicht die erste Geige!	You're not the boss! You don't play first fiddle!
Ich muß zugeben, daß Herr Meggadorn allen weit überlegen ist.	I have to admit that Mr. Meggadorn is head and shoulders above the rest.
Er ist seit 40 Jahren im Geschäft. Was Hänschen nicht lernt, lernt Hans nimmermehr.	He's been in the business forty years. You can't teach an old dog new tricks.
Das ist Dr. Mirror. Er ist ein großes Tier bei uns.	That's Dr. Mirror. He's a big cheese around here.
Hier kommt der Vorstandsvorsitzende. Rollt schon mal den roten Teppich aus.	Here comes the Chairman of the Board. Better roll out the red carpet.

Food for thought
Lots of folk confuse bad management with destiny.

2. Aufgaben des Vorstands / Board activities

Kommunikation / Communication

den Aktionären Bericht erstatten	report to the shareholders
die Bilanz vorstellen	present the balance sheet
eine Besprechung / Hauptversammlung einberufen	convene a meeting / annual general meeting
eine Generalversammlung einberufen	call a general meeting
eine Besprechung verschieben	postpone / put off a meeting
eine außerordentliche Versammlung anberaumen	call an extraordinary meeting
Anweisungen geben	give instructions / orders
Leute mit Respekt behandeln	treat people with respect
die Belegschaft unterstützen	give assistance to the staff

Too old for the top job?

A journalist asked Ronald Reagan whether he thought it was right for a man of his age to be president. Reagan answered, "In this country, that's about the only job an old man can get."

Personalangelegenheiten / Personnel matters

jemanden zum stellvertretenden Vorsitzenden ernennen	nominate someone vice president
jemanden zum Geschäftsführer vorschlagen	propose someone for Managing Director
jemanden zum Vorstand ernennen	appoint somebody to the Board
jemanden zum Vorsitzenden des Aufsichtsrats ernennen	appoint somebody Chairman of the Supervisory Board
jemanden zum leitenden Angestellten befördern	promote someone to executive employee / senior manager / top manager
die Führungsrolle definieren	define leadership
Führungsqualitäten erkennen	identify leadership qualities
Aufgaben verteilen	distribute tasks

3 DIE OBEREN ETAGEN

Arbeit an die Chefsekretärin delegieren	delegate work to the executive secretary
als Geschäftsführer zurücktreten	resign as CEO
einen Mitarbeiter entlassen	fire / sack / dismiss an employee
Als Geschäftsführer darf man niemandem den Schwarzen Peter zuschieben.	There's no passing the buck when you're the Managing Director. Finally.
In Ordnung! Ich habe genug von dir. Pack deine Sachen und verschwinde bis Mittag.	Right! I've had enough of you. Pack your bags and be out of here by midday.

Firing the polite way

"Dobson," said the boss one morning, "I just don't know how we are going to get along without you – but starting Monday, we're going to try."

Entscheidungen treffen / Decision-making

Firmenpolitik entwickeln	develop corporate policy
die Unternehmenspolitik entwickeln	develop the management policy
die Firma umstrukturieren	restructure the company
ein Organigramm entwerfen	draw up an organisational chart
eine Situation geschickt beurteilen	judge a situation skilfully
Initiativen ergreifen	take initiatives
strategisch planen	do strategic planning
strategische Entscheidungen treffen	make strategic decisions
unternehmerische Risiken eingehen	take risks as an entrepreneur
auf Direktorenebene Entscheidungen treffen	decide at director level
Ziele entwickeln	develop objectives / targets
Ziele erreichen	achieve objectives

ROOMS AT THE TOP 3

Lerntip: Hard words

Der englische Wortschatz ist so reich an Synonyma (Wörter mit ungefähr gleicher Bedeutung), weil es zu den germanischen umgangssprachlichen Wörtern ein gleichbedeutendes Wort lateinischen Ursprungs gibt. Letztere gehören meist der Schriftsprache an. Sie tun Ihrem Gedächtnis einen Gefallen, wenn Sie diese Paare nicht getrennt lernen. Here we go.

Master your phrases

Task 1: Beef up your wordpower

Find the synonym. We've helped you with the first letters.

call a general meeting	c..................e a meeting
take part in a meeting	p................e in a meeting
go to a meeting	a..................d a meeting
put off a meeting	p....................e a meeting
have real power	p....................s real power
fire / sack an employee	d....................s an employee

Lerntip: Beef up your wordpower

Die Gesetze der Wortbildung kann man ins Gefühl kriegen, wenn man beim Nachschlagen im Wörterbuch die Ableitungen (Verb → Substantiv → Adjektiv und umgekehrt) notiert und lernt.

Task 2: Find the noun

resign as CEO	submit one's .... as CEO
promote an employee	give .... to an employee
delegate tasks	the .... of tasks
decide something	take a .... on something
develop strategies	the .... of strategies
be *responsible* for a company	have .... for a company
succeed as a businessman	have .... as a businessman

3 DIE OBEREN ETAGEN

3. *Geldangelegenheiten* / Money matters

ein Prämiensystem einführen	introduce a bonus system
an die Börse gehen	go public
Aktien auf den Markt bringen	float shares on the market
eine Bilanz vorbereiten	prepare a balance sheet
Teile des Unternehmens veräußern	sell off parts of the enterprise
Gewinn-und-Verlust-Rechnung überprüfen	check the profit and loss account
global / umfassend	across the board
Global gesehen sind die Zahlen schlecht.	The figures are poor across the board.
Eine halbe Million! Das ist nur eine Lappalie.	Half a million! That's only chicken feed.
Wenn wir zusammenlegen, können wir unsere Partner ausbezahlen.	If we club together we could buy out our partners.
Seit der neue Geschäftsführer von BWM zu uns gekommen ist, macht die Firma Geld en masse.	Since the new CEO came in from BWM the company is making money hand over fist.
Mit dem Gehalt eines Geschäftsführers hat man Geld wie Heu.	When you have a CEO's salary you have money to burn.

A box of idioms

allen anderen weit überlegen sein	be head and shoulders above the rest
die erste Geige spielen	play first fiddle
den roten Teppich ausrollen	roll out the red carpet
ein großes Tier sein	be a big cheese
(Geld) zusammenlegen	club together
den Schwarzen Peter weiterschieben	pass the buck
Geld wie Heu haben	have money to burn
Geld scheffeln	make money hand over fist
nur eine Lappalie sein	be small beer / chicken feed
Was Hänschen nicht lernt, lernt Hans nimmermehr.	You can't teach an old dog new tricks!
seine Sachen packen	pack one's bags

ROOMS AT THE TOP 3

Magic Squares

Match the phrases (A, B, C ...) ...

A. You're not the boss!	B. I've had enough of you.	C. We could buy out our partners.
D. Tom has deserved promotion..	E. We should go public.	F. You look overworked
G. The director has found some serious mistakes.	H. Here comes the chairman of the board.	I. Their new product is selling like hot cakes.

... with the phrases (1, 2, 3 ...).

1. Pack your bags and be out of here by midday.	2. They're making money hand over fist.	3. He is head and shoulders above the rest.
4. He told the clerk to pack his bags.	5. Then we float our shares on the market.	6. I agree. Let's club together.
7. You should delegate more tasks.	8. So don't try to play first fiddle!	9. Better roll out the red carpet.

2. Put the numbers in the magic squares.

A =	B =	C =
D =	E =	F =
G =	H =	I =

3. Check yourself. When the answers are correct, all columns and rows will add up to the same number (15).

3 DIE OBEREN ETAGEN

 Master your phrases

Task 3: What might you do with the following?

There's more than one solution.

1. prepare / s _ _ _ / c _ _ _ _ a balance sheet
2. call / c _ _ _ _ _ _ _ / p _ _ _ _ _ _ _ _ a meeting
3. perform / d _ _ _ _ _ _ _ / d _ _ _ _ _ _ _ _ _ tasks
4. r _ _ _ _ _ to the Supervisory Board

Task 4: What does the Board not do?

Please tick.

- ❏ appoint people to jobs
- ❏ report to the staff representative
- ❏ write the profit & loss account
- ❏ strategic planning
- ❏ nominate executives
- ❏ club together to buy things

--- Picture your idiom ---

You can't .... an .... new ....

ROOMS AT THE TOP 3

Task 5: Phrases in context

Dr Cautert was a.................d to the b................d at Low Valley Photocopiers. Now at last he had the chance to do some real s..................c p.....................g. He still had to r...................t to the s..................y board, but that was no problem. Now Dr. Cautert was really r.................e for the company. And there certainly were a lot of t..........s to complete. Cautert's first idea was to r........................e the company and even sell .... parts of it. And there were one or two employees who he wanted to get r........... of. They could p............ their b..........s in any case.

Picture your idiom

Tom's got money to burn.
Half a million is just ....
.... for him.

Task 6: Find the lively idioms

1. He's an important person (image of food).
2. He is able to make fire with banknotes.
3. Make sure this important person has the correct floor beneath his feet.
4. It's really very unimportant (image of food & drink).

Problem solving

When confronted by an impossible problem,
reduce it to the question:
"How would Groucho Marx have solved it?"

3 DIE OBEREN ETAGEN

C Crossword power

Across

3. We'd better invest in the ✎ market.
5. The boss is arriving. Roll out the red ✎.
6. *übernehmen* leadership role
8. Half a million! That's only chicken ✎.
10. ✎ your staff with respect.
12. When you lose money you make a ✎.
13. It's been a good year. We've made a big ✎.
14. Let's fire him. Tell him to pack his ✎.
15. Another word for *objectives*.

Down

1. English for *Befehl, Anweisung, Bestellung*
2. *give up one's post* as CEO
3. The board develops the corporate ✎.
4. Cautert will ✎ the meeting.
5. If we ✎ together we could buy out our partners.
7. move someone up in the hierarchy
9. *distribute* jobs
10. A good boss knows how to delegate a ✎.
11. *promote* someone to a post.
14. He's very rich. He's got money to ✎.

DAS RÜCKGRAT DER FIRMA

PART 4

THE COMPANY'S BACKBONE

The secretary – or personal assistant – and the secretarial pool in general are very important employees in the company. She – sometimes he – is in every department. Exactly what is a secretary? This can be best summarised by the comment that "the more effective the secretary, the more productive her boss". She deals with the routine and administrative matters. A true PA helps her boss to concentrate on his proper job. What does this include? What should she (or he) do?

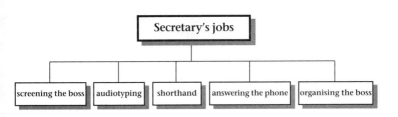

Tips for the boss on how (not) to get on with the secretary

- Never start work early in the morning – the secretary really prefers a terrific rush in the afternoon.
- Please smoke when dictating; it helps pronunciation.
- Hours for dictating: during the lunch hour or at any time between 4.30 and 5.30 p.m.
- If work is required urgently (a most unusual occurrence), it helps if you rush in at intervals of 30 seconds to see if it is done.
- When the secretary staggers out carrying a pile of files, please don't open the door for her. She has learned to open it with her teeth or crawl under it.

4 DAS RÜCKGRAT DER FIRMA

1. *Im Schreibbüro* / At the Secretarial Pool

zum Schreibbüro gehören	belong to the typing / secretarial pool
Sekretariatsarbeiten verrichten	do secretarial work
als Sekretärin arbeiten	work as a secretary
Notizen / ein Diktat aufnehmen	take down notes / a dictation
ein Interview stenographieren	take an interview down in shorthand
als Phonotypistin arbeiten	work as an audiotypist
die Korrespondenz überprüfen	check the correspondence
eine Besprechung protokollieren	take the minutes of the meeting
einen Entwurf erstellen	draw up a draft
einen Brief gestalten	layout a letter
Briefe tippen	type letters
die Briefe frankieren	frank the letters
Daten in den Computer eingeben	enter data in the computer
die Dokumente ausdrucken	print out the files
Dokumente korrekturlesen	proof-read documents
die Fehler korrigieren	correct the mistakes
ein Fax abschicken	send a fax
elektronische Post verschicken	send e-mail
Dank Frau Totchev funktioniert das Büro wie geschmiert.	Thanks to Mrs. Totchev the office works like clockwork.

☛ Siehe auch *Im allgemeinen Büro*, Seite 19 ff.

2. *Am Telefon* / On the phone

Die ersten Sätze / First phrases

ein Telefongespräch beginnen	start a phone call
ans Telefon gehen	answer the phone
Wer ist am Apparat bitte?	Who's speaking, please?
Kann ich Ihnen helfen?	Can I help you?
Wen möchten Sie sprechen?	Who would you like to speak to?
Können Sie mich mit ... verbinden?	Could you put me through to ... please?
Kann ich mit ... sprechen?	Can I speak to ...?
Darf ich fragen, worum es geht?	May I ask what it is concerned with?

THE COMPANY'S BACKBONE

Den Anrufer verbinden / Putting a caller through

Bleiben Sie bitte am Apparat.	Can you hang on / hold on a moment?
Ich sehe nach, ob sie da ist.	I'll see if she's in.
Ich verbinde Sie.	I'll put you through / connect you.
Es tut mir leid, Herr Biczo ist nicht in seinem Büro.	Sorry, Mr. Biczo is not at his desk / in his office.
Es tut mir leid, er hat heute einen freien Tag.	I'm afraid he's got a day off today.
Möchten Sie es später noch einmal versuchen?	Would you like to try again later?

Eine Nachricht aufnehmen / Taking a message

Nachrichten notieren	take down messages
Möchten Sie eine Nachricht hinterlassen?	Would you like to leave a message?
Können Sie etwas ausrichten?	Can you take a message?
Entschuldigung, könnten Sie das bitte wiederholen?	I'm sorry. Could you say that again / repeat that, please?
Könnten Sie bitte etwas langsamer sprechen?	Would you mind speaking a little slower?

Den Anruf beenden / Finishing the Call

Danke für Ihren Anruf. Auf Wiederhören.	Thank you very much for your call. Goodbye.
Auf Wiederhören und danke für Ihre Hilfe.	Goodbye and thanks for your help.

☛ Siehe auch *How to phone effectively, Business English am Telefon*, rororo sprachen 60146.

4 DAS RÜCKGRAT DER FIRMA

 Master your phrases

Task 1: Better phrases for the words in *italics*

1. Would you like to leave *a piece of information*?
2. Could you *prepare a rough version* of this report?
3. Please *write* these letters *by means of a dictaphone*.
4. The office is working *in a perfect way*, isn't it?

Task 2: Four verbs for the better letter

1. t ....   2. ....out   3. proof-.........   4. c..........

Task 3: What do you do?

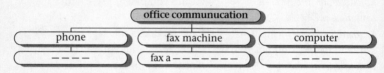

Read in a secretary's diary

Dear diary. This is day one of my first holiday on a cruise ship.
Day 1: While the cruise is nice there are an awful lot of men, including the stewards, making passes at me.
Day 2: I have been invited to sit at the captain's table.
Day 3: The captain made an improper suggestion last night. I refused.
Day 4: The captain says that unless I agree, he will sink the ship.
Day 5: Last night I saved the lives of 965 people.

3. *Aufgaben der Privatsekretärin* / The private secretary's tasks

die Stelle einer Privatsekretärin annoncieren	advertise for a private secretary
als Vorstandsassistent arbeiten	work as an assistant to the Board
einen Terminplan festlegen	fix a timetable / schedule

THE COMPANY'S BACKBONE 4

den Chef abschirmen	screen the boss
einen Bericht erstellen	compile a report
eine Besprechung vorbereiten	prepare a meeting
Es ist immer die Sache der Sekretärin, die Fehler des Chefs zu vertuschen.	It's always up to the secretary to paper over the cracks when the boss has made mistakes.
per du sein	be on first-name terms
Johns Sekretärin ist per du mit ihm.	John's secretary is on first-name terms with him.

Termine vereinbaren / Arranging appointments

einen Termin festlegen / vereinbaren / verlegen	fix / arrange / change an appointment
um einen Termin bitten	request an appointment
einen Termin vereinbaren	agree a date
ein persönliches Gespräch vereinbaren	organise a one-to-one appointment
eine mündliche Terminzusage geben	give a verbal confirmation of the date
einen Gesprächstermin verschieben	postpone a meeting
einen Termin vorverlegen	bring a date forward
Ich möchte einen Termin mit Herrn / Frau ... vereinbaren.	I'd like to make an appointment with Mr / Ms ....
Könnte ich wohl einen Termin bei ... bekommen?	I was wondering if it would be possible to make an appointment with ...?
Welcher Tag wäre für Sie am günstigsten?	What day would be the most convenient for you?

Reisevorbereitungen / Travel arrangements

beabsichtigen / planen, um ... Uhr abzureisen	intend / plan to leave at ... o'clock
einen Platz reservieren	reserve / book a seat on ...
eine Buchung/Reservierung bestätigen	confirm a booking / reservation
Ich möchte einen Flug für Herrn ... nach London buchen.	I'd like to book a flight to London for Mr ...
Und wann möchte er fliegen?	And when does he want to leave?

4 DAS RÜCKGRAT DER FIRMA

Erste Klasse oder Touristenklasse?	First class or economy?
Und wie sieht es mit dem Rückflug aus?	And what about the return flight?

Besprechungen / Meetings

ein Geschäftsessen / Rahmenprogramme / eine Kundenpräsentation organisieren	organise a business lunch / social events / client presentation
Teilnehmer anrufen	ring up participants
mit den Teilnehmern in Verbindung treten	contact participants
eine Projektliste für die Besprechung führen	keep a checklist for the meeting
die Einzelheiten erfassen	record the details
Erfrischungsgetränke bereitstellen	provide liquid refreshments

Master your phrases

Task 4: How would you react?

1. Is Brian taking the minutes?
   A. Yes, he's always on time.
   B. Yes, his shorthand is better than mine.
   C. Yes, he's already counting them.

2. May I ask what it is concerned with?
   A. Mr. Brain is concerned about the new copier.
   B. It's a multinational concern.
   C. It concerns the copier I bought the other day.

3. Miss Read is always papering over the cracks.
   A. Yes, she is a loyal secretary.
   B. Does she use liquid paper to do it?
   C. She had better type the entire letter again.

THE COMPANY'S BACKBONE 4

Task 5: What does a secretary do?

Put these verbs into the right place

| bring | handle | screen | act |
| organise | set | deputise | be |

1. .... the day of her boss so well that he can make the best use of his working day;
2. .... him from unnecessary callers and problems;
3. .... his priorities, but in a discreet way;
4. .... important matters to his attention when necessary;
5. .... those trivial and unimportant details in his life which become very important when not dealt with;
6. .... for him and handle his problems in a sensible way when he is out of town;
7. .... a valve when he is under pressure and needs to let off steam;
8. .... as a link between him and his staff so he does not get out of touch.

Just for fun

The chairman of the board had to make an important speech at a meeting of the shareholders, and as usual he delegated the job of writing the speech to his secretary.

"Miss Smith, just put something together for me, will you? You know all the facts and figures. And make it short and sweet – about twenty minutes should do."

When he returned to the office after the meeting, he was in a furious temper.

"What's the idea of writing me a one-hour speech?" he thundered. "Half of the audience walked out before I'd finished."

"With respect, sir, I wrote you a twenty-minute speech as you told me," replied the secretary. "However, you asked me to make two extra copies."

4 DAS RÜCKGRAT DER FIRMA

Lerntip: Die Ursachen des Vergessens

Das oberste Lerngesetz lautet: Lernen tut nur, wer lernen will. Aber auch der willigste Mensch lernt und vergißt, wenn er nicht wiederholt.

Verstrichene Zeit	Vergessen wird
20 Minuten	30 – 45 Prozent
1 Tag	50 – 65 Prozent
1 Woche	70 – 75 Prozent
1 Monat	80 Prozent

Wann müssen wir wiederholen?

Für das Wiederholen gilt wie für das Lernen: gestaffelt wiederholen. Also lieber acht Tage jeden Tag eine Viertelstunde üben als zwei Stunden an einem Tag. Eine Faustregel lautet:

Wiederholung nach

1. ein paar Stunden
2. einer Woche
3. einem Tag
4. einem Monat
5. spätestens einem halben Jahr

Das Wiederholen geht von Mal zu Mal schneller. Bei der dritten Wiederholung braucht man nur noch einen Bruchteil der Zeit. Wer mit Pinnwand und Haftzettel arbeitet, wiederholt im Vorbeigehen (Seite 89 und 101). Sekunden reichen für die tägliche Wiederholungsdosis en passant, für die wir keine Freizeit opfern müssen.

Was müssen wir wiederholen?

Gelernt werden soll nur, was vergessen wurde. Die Gefahr des Überlernens ist groß. Allein die Lernkartei (Seite 79 und 110) gibt zuverlässig Auskunft, welcher Teil des Wortschatzes zu wiederholen ist. Dadurch reduziert sich der Lernstoff von Schritt zu Schritt.

Was Sie beachten sollten

Wortschatz, der mehrmals nach derselben Methode wiederholt wird, ist beschränkt einsetzbar. Kreatives Wiederholen unter verschiedenen Gesichtspunkten kann auf vielfältige Art geschehen. Die wichtigsten Arbeitsformen sind:

Ordnen **Strukturieren**
Gruppieren **Schematisieren**

Unsere *Tasks* beruhen auf diesen Lerngesetzen.

THE COMPANY'S BACKBONE 4

The Executive Secretary

What's her claim to power? Well, evil tongues – they propagate gossip in every company – divide the executive secretaries into two categories:

Type A: The competent secretary is powerful because

- she manages his schedule
- she screens him off
- covers up his mistakes
- you reach him only over her dead body

Type B: The incompetent secretary is powerful because

- she knows too much
- she gives him alibis when he is at his girlfriend's
- she is young and has breathtakingly long legs
- the boss is not in a position to fire her

In other words the boss is in permanent quarantine.

Time for a smile

The chairman of a large company always asked his elderly secretary to write speeches for him. Although the speeches were normally a great success, he never congratulated her on her job. Shortly before she was going to retire, her boss asked her for a speech he was going to make at a congress attended by computer experts.

Everything went smoothly for the first five minutes. It was a brilliant speech full of hard facts, amusing jokes and snappy quotations that suited the occasion. When the chairman turned the third page of his manuscript he went pale. He read in big letters:
FROM NOW ON YOU ARE ON YOUR OWN, YOU OLD BASTARD.

4 DAS RÜCKGRAT DER FIRMA

Magic Squares

1. Match the words (A, B, C ...) ...

A. with   **B.** hold   **C.** through
D. minutes   **E.** forward   **F.** in
G. answer   **H.** leave   **I.** take

... with the phrases (1, 2, 3 ...).

1. Can you ✎ on a minute?
2. Can you ✎ a message?
3. Who's taking the ✎ of the meeting?
4. Is nobody going to ✎ the phone?
5. Is it possible to bring the conference ✎?
6. Could you put me ✎ to Ms. Brain, please?
7. I'll see if she's ✎.
8. May I ask what it is concerned ✎?
9. Would you like to ✎ a message?

2. Put the numbers in the magic squares.

A =	B =	C =
D =	E =	F =
G =	H =	I =

3. When the answers are correct, all columns and rows will add up to the same magical number (15).

Time for a smile

I think any man in business would be foolish to fool around with his secretary. If it's someone else's secretary, fine!
Senator Barry Goldwater

EINSTELLUNG UND ENTLASSUNG

RECRUITMENT AND DISMISSAL

PART 5

Hunting for the right heads – this is one of the vital tasks of personnel. And it's not so easy since the law gives employees lot of protection. If you get a bad one, your company may suffer for years. All this makes the job interview very important. Here the personnel manager has to discuss prospects, salary, conditions and, of course, responsibilities. Good luck!

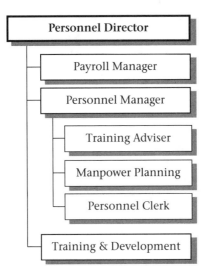

Time for a smile

Holidays is the spare time you grant your employees to remind them of the fact that the company can survive without them.

5 EINSTELLUNG UND ENTLASSUNG

1. *Personalplanung* / Personnel planning

über eine Belegschaft von 2000 Mitarbeitern verfügen	have a workforce / staff of 2,000
Die Personalabteilung hat Bedarf an Personal.	Human Resources has a need for personnel.
Personalbedarf haben	need human resources
Wir müssen die Mitarbeiterzahl verstärken.	We have to increase the workforce.
nach Mitarbeitern suchen	search for staff
neue Arbeiter einstellen	set on new workers
eine Beraterfirma heranziehen	use / commission a consultant
eine Refastudie	Organisation & Methods Analysis
Personalplanung durchführen	do manpower planning
200 Mitarbeiter einplanen	plan for 200 employees
Programmierer suchen	look for programmers
Die Personalabteilung sucht nach Arbeitskräften.	Personnel is looking for manpower.
Sachbearbeiter einstellen	employ clerical staff
ungelernte / angelernte Arbeiter einstellen	take on unskilled / semiskilled workers
die Zahl der Vorgesetzten erhöhen	increase the supervisory staff
einen Arbeitsvertrag anbieten	offer a contract of employment
Mitarbeiter / Arbeiter / Angestellte einstellen	employ staff / blue-collar workers / white-collar workers
auf der Lohn- / Gehaltsliste stehen	be on the payroll
abgespecktes Management einführen	introduce lean management
eine Firma verschlanken	slim down a company
ein Unternehmen rationalisieren	delayer an enterprise
einstellen und entlassen	hire and fire

2. *Die Stelle annoncieren* / Advertising the post

eine freie Stelle haben	have a vacancy
eine freie Stelle besetzen	fill a vacant post
eine Anzeige aufsetzen	draft an advert

RECRUITMENT AND DISMISSAL 5

den Inhalt besprechen	discuss the content
die Tätigkeit definieren	define the work content
Arbeitsplatzbewertung	job evaluation
eine Arbeitsplatzbeschreibung schreiben	write a job description
die Pflichten / Verantwortlichkeiten auflisten	list the duties / responsibilities
den Text für die Anzeige formulieren	word the text of the advertisement
die Formulierungen überprüfen	check the wording
Leistungsanreize erwähnen	mention the perks
die Anzeige inserieren	place the advertisement / advert / ad
die Stelle ausschreiben	make the post public
am Schwarzen Brett aushängen	put on the notice board
einen Personalberater für die Suche nach Führungskräften kontaktieren	contact a head-hunter
eine Stellenvermittlung beauftragen	commission an employment agency

Ads that went wrong

Wonderful opportunity for young woman to join fishing partners. Must be able to cook, wash. Please send photo of boat.

Man wanted to wash dishes and two waitresses.

3. *Arbeitsplatzbeschreibung* / Job description

einen Ingenieur / Techniker / technischen Angestellten benötigen	require an engineer / technician / technical clerk
eine Stelle als Sekretärin / Empfangsdame besetzen	fill a secretarial / receptionist vacancy / opening
einen Monteur / Mechaniker / Montagearbeiter suchen	look for a fitter / mechanic / assembly worker
einen Abteilungsleiter / Qualitätsprüfer ernennen	appoint a department leader / quality controller
Wir suchen nach einem Verkaufs- / Einkaufs- / Buchhaltungs- / Produktionsleiter	We are searching for a head of sales / purchasing / accounts / manufacturing

5 EINSTELLUNG UND ENTLASSUNG

die folgenden Eigenschaften besitzen: flexibel / fleißig / zuverlässig / ehrgeizig	have the following characteristics: flexible / conscientious / reliable / ambitious
verantwortlich sein für ...	be responsible for ...
Wir bieten ausgezeichnete Arbeitsbedingungen / einen sicheren Arbeitsplatz.	We offer excellent working conditions / job security.
außertarifliches Gehalt / Gehalt nach Vereinbarung	salary by negotiation
Gehalt nach Tarif	salary as per agreed salary scale
ein Jahresgehalt von £120 000 beziehen	receive an annual salary of £120,000
zur Altersversorgung beitragen	contribute to an old age provision
großzügige Altersversorgung	a generous pension scheme

4. Der Bewerber / The Applicant

eine Bewerbung einreichen	put in an application
sich um eine Stelle bewerben	apply for a post
sich als Kandidat für eine Stelle anbieten / bewerben	offer oneself as a candidate for a job
einen Lebenslauf einschicken	send a CV / curriculum vitae / resumé
den Inhalt seines Studiums beschreiben	describe the contents of one's course of study
in Cambridge / der Fachhochschule Worms studieren	study at Cambridge / the Politech of Worms
sich weiterbilden	continue one's education
Berufserfahrung haben	have professional experience / work experience
einen Universitätsabschluß haben	have a university degree
die Universität / das Gymnasium besuchen	attend university / high school
Abitur / mittlere Reife bestehen	pass A levels / O levels
ein Berufspraktikum machen	do a job placement
als Sekretärin / Manager / kfm. Angestellter arbeiten	work as a secretary / manager / commercial clerk

RECRUITMENT AND DISMISSAL 5

eine Stelle angeboten bekommen	be offered a job
Tom ist ein Faulenzer.	Tom's a lazy-bones.
Potential haben / Potentialträger sein	have / be a high potential

5. *Das Einstellungsgespräch* / The Interview

Bewerber überprüfen / sieben	check over / screen the applicants
die Bewerbungen sichten	screen the applications
eine Auswahl treffen	create a short list / short-list the applicants
ein Vorstellungsgespräch führen	conduct an interview
den besten Kandidaten auswählen	select the best candidate
Danke, daß Sie gekommen sind.	Thank you for attending.
Wir bedanken uns für Ihr Kommen.	We appreciate your coming.
den Bewerber beruhigen	put the applicant at ease
Bitte, nehmen Sie Platz.	Please take a seat.
ein Bewerbungsgespräch in einer entspannten Atmosphäre führen	conduct an interview in a relaxed atmosphere
nach dem Grund für die Bewerbung fragen	ask the reason why someone applied
Wann haben Sie bei LAMY begonnen?	When did you join LAMY?
praktische Erfahrung in ... haben	have practical experience in ...
Ausbildung am Arbeitsplatz erhalten	receive on-the-job training
eine Lehre / Ausbildung als ... machen	do an apprenticeship / training in ...
die richtige Person für die Stelle sein	be the right man for the job
der Stelle gewachsen sein	be up to the mark for the post
die richtigen Voraussetzungen für die Stelle mitbringen	have the right qualities for the job
ein Angebot annehmen	accept an offer
ein Angebot ablehnen	decline / turn down an offer
eine Probezeit vereinbaren	agree on a probationary period
den Vertrag unterschreiben	sign the contract
Wie ist Ihre Kündigungsfrist?	What's your period of notice?
in ein Unternehmen eintreten	sign on at a company (USA)
Durchhaltevermögen haben	have staying power
Ich glaube nicht, daß Tim das nötige Durchhaltevermögen für seine Arbeit hat.	I don't believe Tim has the necessary staying power for this work.

5 EINSTELLUNG UND ENTLASSUNG

LOPY Ltd. hat Bedarf an Übersetzern mit Erfahrung.

LOPY Ltd. requires experienced translators.

 Master your phrases

Task 1: Definition exercise

1. all the employees of the company: ....
2. job to be filled: ....
3. place for hanging information: ....
4. practical period at a company: ....

Task 2: Preposition time

Put the applicant	....	ease!
Would you agree	....	a probationary period?
Don't forget to put	....	your application!
I'm afraid Tom's not	....	the mark.
When did you sign	....	the company?

6. *Entlassung* / Dismissal

kündigen	give notice
an jemandes Stuhl sägen	undermine someone's position
Mitarbeiter entlassen	lay off staff
einen Mitarbeiter feuern	sack / fire / kick a worker out
jemandem kündigen	give notice / marching orders to somebody
jemandem seine Entlassungspapiere geben	give someone his / her walking papers
seine Papiere bekommen	get one's papers
eine gute / schlechte Abfindung bekommen	get the golden / leaden handshake
zu Unrecht entlassen werden	be unfairly dismissed
gefeuert / rausgeschmissen werden	get the axe / chop / boot

RECRUITMENT AND DISMISSAL 5

die Tür von außen zumachen	close the door from the other side
300 Leute entlassen	make 300 people redundant
arbeitslos / ohne Arbeit / ohne Job sein	be unemployed / out of work / jobless
Recht auf eine Mindestkündigungsfrist haben	have a right to a minimum period of notice
das Recht auf eine Abfindung haben	be entitled to redundancy
jemandes Dienste nicht mehr benötigen	not require somebody's services anymore
den Arbeitsvertrag beenden	terminate the contract of employment
das Arbeitsverhältnis mit oder ohne Kündigung beenden	terminate the working relationship with or without notice

Food for thought

Most young blokes stop looking for work
the moment they get a job.

7. *Karriere in der Firma* / Company career

auf der untersten Stufe der Leiter beginnen	start from / at the bottom of the ladder
die Stelle wechseln	change the job
Projektleiter werden	become project leader
zum Abteilungsleiter aufsteigen	rise to department leader
aufs Abstellgleis geschoben werden	get a dead-end job
jemandem einen Schreibtischjob geben	give some one a desk job
Geschäftsführer! Er hat seinen Weg nach oben gemacht.	Managing director! He's come up in the world.
Er ist unbezahlbar.	He's worth his weight in gold.
degradiert werden	get demoted / a demotion
seine Stelle verlieren	lose one's job
Tom ist ein Aufsteiger.	Tom's a social climber.
Zu viele Fehler. James wurde aufs Abstellgleis geschoben.	Too many mistakes. James was put on the back burner.

5 EINSTELLUNG UND ENTLASSUNG

Er wird niemals befördert werden.
Er hat den Zug verpaßt.
Aus einem Kieselstein kann man keinen Diamanten schleifen.
James ist immer noch an der untersten Stufe der Karriereleiter in der Firma.
Peter hat alle Trümpfe in der Hand.
Bildung und Geld in der Familie.
Er bekam nicht genügend Geld, deshalb hat er gekündigt.

He'll never get promotion. He's missed the boat.
You can't make a silk purse out of a sow's ear.
James is still at the bottom of the career ladder in the company.
Peter's holding all the aces. Education and money in his background.
He wasn't paid enough money so he gave notice.

A box of idioms

an seiner Karriere schnitzen	carve out one's career
die Trümpfe in der Hand haben	hold all the aces
jemandem seine Papiere geben	give someone his walking papers
Aus einem Kieselstein kann man keinen Diamanten schleifen.	You can't make a silk purse out of a sow's ear.
jemanden ins zweite Glied stellen	put someone on the back burner
den Zug verpassen	miss the boat

Finding the right man for the job

A construction company located in San Francisco won the contract for repainting the Golden Gate Bridge. The personnel manager had advertised for qualified painters and was interviewing the first of two hundred applicants, an Italian. "Do you know how to paint?" he asked.

"Not as professionally as Michelangelo, but I'll manage alright," answered the Italian.

The manager paused for a moment and then said, "Listen, I want this to be done as professionally as possible. Go back to the waiting room and send me that Michelangelo."

RECRUITMENT AND DISMISSAL 5

Master your phrases

Task 3: Guided Translation

1. He's a social (*Aufsteiger*), always wanting to move up.
2. £3,000? Not so good! That was a (*schlechte Abfindung*).
3. Jim got (*rausgeschmissen*) for being unreliable.

Task 4: Complete the idioms

1. No priority. Put it on the ....
2. Tom's not reliable. I'm going to give him his ....
3. You've got no problems. You're holding all the ....

Task 5: Phrases in context

Fill in the missing letters.

You've got to find the right man, but before that happens, personnel has to do some m _ _ _ _ _ _ _ pl _ _ _ _ _ _. The boss has to decide how many new men to t _ _ _ o _ . What do you do if you want to fill a v _ _ _ _ _ _ ? There are various tasks. For example, when we need a new man we have to pl _ _ _ an ad _ _ _ _ _ _ _ _ _ _ _ . In the advert we have to list his r _ _ _ _ _ _ _ _ _ _ _ _ _ _ _ . If we can't find anybody we should contact a h _ _ _ - h _ _ _ _ _ . His candidate will certainly have pr _ _ _ _ _ _ _ kn _ _ _ _ _ _ _ of the subject.

― Picture your idiom ―

He simply hasn't got the potential for this function. You can´t make a .... out of a ....

5 EINSTELLUNG UND ENTLASSUNG

Crossword power

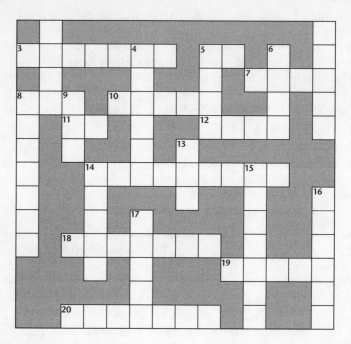

Across

1. We offer excellent working conditions and job ✎. 3. We have a ✎ for a wages clerk. 5. salary ✎ negotiation. 7. You can't make a ✎ purse out of a sow's ear. 8. I'm afraid we have to lay ✎ personnel. 10. ✎ an advert in a newspaper 11. BASF is going to take ✎ 200 employees. 12. hire and ✎ workers 14. all the workers of a company. 18. Organisation & ✎ Analysis 19. You can't make it out of a sow's ear. 20. ✎ education is a necessity nowadays.

Down

1. personnel, workforce 2. We're in the ✎ for salesmen. 4. White- and blue-✎ workers 5. You've got to ✎ up your word power. 6. ✎ and fire workers 8. another word for vacancy 9. We're searching ✎ staff. 13. Lay ✎ staff. 14. money a worker gets 15. Would you like to ✎ the interview for me? 16. be at or go to a university 17. Before inviting the applicants you create a ✎-list

PERSONALENTWICKLUNG

PERSONNEL DEVELOPMENT

PART 6

So the company has finally hired some staff. Now comes the problem of deciding who should get what sort of job in the future. Who are the high potentials? Who should get special training for more responsible jobs in the future? And what is the most efficient type of training to give them? It's not so easy.

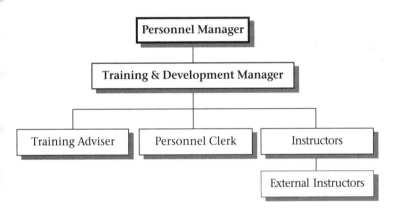

Time for a smile

"Education has failed the younger generation," said the personnel manager. "Our survey shows that as many as 40 per cent can't read properly, another 40 per cent can't write and the other 30 per cent can't add up."

PERSONALENTWICKLUNG

1. *Schulung anbieten* / Offering training

den Bedarf an Fortbildung ermitteln	determine / define training requirements
Ziele setzen	set goals / objectives
Stärken / Schwächen identifizieren	identify strong / weak points
ein Schulungssystem einrichten	put a training system in place
die Ausbildungseinrichtungen vergrößern	expand training facilities
ein offenes Lernzentrum einrichten	set up an open access centre
Fernunterricht ist zeitsparend.	Distance learning is time-saving.
Computergestütztes Lernen (CBT) kann effektiv sein.	Computer-based training can be efficient.
Kurse sollen nicht in der Kernzeit stattfinden.	Courses are not to take place in core time.
Kurse nur während der Gleitzeit abhalten	hold courses only in flexitime
Den Ausbildungsstand des Personals zu verbessern ist unser Ziel.	To improve the level of education of the staff is our goal.
in ein Schulungsprogramm investieren	invest in a training programme
Welche Ausbildungsmaßnahmen für Führungskräfte bieten Sie an?	What sort of management training do you offer?
Schulungen kosten eine Stange Geld – denken Sie an Gehalt, Hotel, verlorene Zeit.	Training costs a pretty penny – think of salary, hotel, lost time.
fortlaufende Schulungen abhalten	give ongoing training
Schulungen anbieten / durchführen	provide / give training
praktische Ausbildung anbieten	offer hands-on training
Ausbildungs- und Weiterbildungsmaßnahmen anbieten	offer further training / education
Schulungen für Anfänger / Fortgeschrittene durchführen	do basic / advanced training
einen Lehrgang abhalten	hold / conduct a training course
Seminarunterlagen bereitstellen	provide seminar documentation
Wer ist der Ausbilder?	Who's the trainer?
Wie hoch ist die Zahl der Abbrecher in Ihren Kursen?	What is the drop-out rate in your courses?

PERSONNEL DEVELOPMENT

2. *Ausbildung in der Firma* / In-house training

eine Stelle als Trainee bekommen	get a post as a management trainee
einen Auszubildenden einstellen	hire a trainee
ein Praktikum machen	do a placement
geschult werden	get training
Einzelunterricht bekommen	get individual tuition
Rotation am Arbeitsplatz	job rotation
die Aufgaben einer Abteilung lernen	learn a department's business
direkt mit jemandem zusammenarbeiten	work directly with someone
Aufgaben zuweisen	allocate tasks
Aufgaben erledigen	performs tasks
an internen Schulungen teilnehmen	participate in in-house training
an einem Seminar teilnehmen	attend a seminar
in der Praxis lernen	learn by doing
am Arbeitsplatz ausgebildet werden	do on-the-job training
eine gründliche Ausbildung bekommen	receive a thorough training
seine Erfahrung ausbauen	broaden one's experience
er befindet sich noch in der Ausbildung	he is still in training
seine Ausbildung abschließen	complete one's education / training / apprenticeship
Um die Wahrheit zu sagen, es ist reine Zeitverschwendung, diese Leute auszubilden.	To tell the truth, it's like flogging a dead horse trying to train these fellows.
Amy hat nicht die Spur einer Chance, die Deutschprüfung zu bestehen.	Amy doesn't have a snowball's chance in hell of passing that German exam.
das Gelernte an Kollegen weitergeben	pass on what you have learned to colleagues

Time for a smile

By the time a man learns to read women like a book,
he's too old to start a library.

6 PERSONALENTWICKLUNG

3. *Lernen nach der Arbeit* / Learning after hours

die Notwendigkeit lebenslangen Lernens	the necessity of life-long learning
etwas unternehmen, um sich zu verbessern	take steps to improve
sich fortbilden	do further education
sich für einen Posten qualifizieren	qualify for a post
Abendkurse besuchen	attend evening classes
sich an einer Universität einschreiben	enrol at a university
die Prüfungsunterlagen anfordern	request the examination documentation
sich für eine Prüfung anmelden	register for a test
auf eine Prüfung büffeln	cram for an exam
sich auf einen Test vorbereiten	prepare for a test
an mangelnder Motivation leiden	suffer from lack of motivation
Prüfungsangst bekommen	get the examination jitters
eine Prüfung ablegen	take / sit an exam
eine Prüfung bestehen	pass an exam
eine Prüfung nicht bestehen	fail an exam
überfordert sein	be unable to cope (with)
unterfordert werden	not to be challenged
ein Seminar abbrechen	drop out of a seminar
gute Fortschritte machen	make good progress
hervorragend abschneiden	pass with distinction
mit Leichtigkeit bestehen	pass hands down
ein gutes Zeugnis erhalten	get a good report
ein Diplom erhalten	get a diploma

Food for thought

Have you noticed how every prominent politician, even former prime ministers, decide to write books when they retire? It would have been better for the country if they had read one.

Education is the process of casting false pearls before real swine.
Irwin Edman

PERSONNEL DEVELOPMENT 6

Lerntip: Gegensätze ziehen sich an

Das isolierte Einzelwort ist ein schweres Wort. Versuche haben gezeigt, daß unser Gedächtnis das Einzelwort besser behält, wenn wir eine logische Beziehung mitlernen. Eine einfache logische Beziehung ist das Gegenteil, zum Beispiel *to pass a test* und *to fail a test*. Beide Wörter stützen sich gegenseitig. Versuchen Sie es gleich.

 Master your phrases

Task 1: Find the opposite

basic training	.... training
identify weak points	identify .... points
my weaknesses	my ....
he is lazy	he is ....
fail an exam	.... an exam

Lerntip: Bringen Sie Ordnung in Ihren Wortschatz

Führen Sie zusammen, was zusammengehört. Bilden Sie Gruppen, *clusters*. Sie bleiben, sagt die Lernpsychologie, länger haften als ihre einzelnen Elemente – vor allem die *clusters*, die man selber bildet. Hier ein Mini-*cluster* zum üben.

Task 2: Complete the cluster

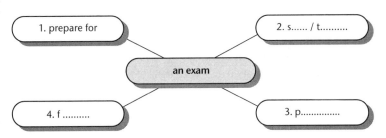

PERSONALENTWICKLUNG

4. Den Kandidaten beurteilen / Evaluating the candidate

einen Auszubildenden prüfen	test a trainee
Leistung analysieren	analyse performance
einen Mitarbeiter beurteilen / bewerten	appraise / assess / evaluate an employee
eine Leistungsbewertung durchführen	do / make a performance appraisal / rating
jemandes Leistung bewerten	evaluate someone's performance
eine Mitarbeiterbeurteilung durchführen	hold an employee appraisal
etwas von jemandem erwarten	expect something of somebody
auf der Höhe sein	perform up to par
die besten Kandidaten aussieben	sift out the best candidates
sich mit einem Personalproblem beschäftigen	handle a personnel problem
einen Schein in die Personalakte eintragen	add a certificate to the personnel file
Was ist sein Spezialgebiet?	What's his special area?
Er ist fleißig / faul.	He is hardworking / lazy.
Er ist ein gewissenhafter Schüler.	He's a thorough student.
Ich bin sicher, sie wird ihre Sache gut machen.	I'm sure she'll make a good job of it.
Er ist ein sehr fleißiger Schüler.	He's a hard-working learner.

Time for a smile

"My son Tom is so forgetful," complained a sales manager to his secretary, "I asked him to get me a packet of cigarettes on his way back from lunch, but I'm not even sure he'll remember to come back himself."

A few minutes later Tom dashed into the office, shouting: "Dad! At lunch I met old man Kelly, who hasn't bought a penny's worth from us in five years, and before we parted I talked him into a half-a-million-dollar order!"

"What did I tell you?" sighed the sales manager, "he forgot the cigarettes!"

PERSONNEL DEVELOPMENT 6

5. *Die Rolle des Personalchefs* / The role of Personnel manager

einen Mitarbeiter / Bewerber loben	praise an employee / candidate
die Qualifikation der Mitarbeiter verbessern	develop human resources / improve staff qualifacations
einen Mitarbeiter betreuen	coach a member of staff
Rückmeldungen bekommen	get feedback
jemanden aufmuntern	give somebody a pep talk
Erkenntnisse besprechen	discuss findings
eine Aufgabe zuteilen	give / allocate an assignment
Führungsfähigkeiten verbessern	improve managerial performance
Wissen vermitteln	convey / impart knowledge
Informationen weitergeben	transmit information
Informationen teilen	share information
sich verständlich machen	get something over / across
Potentialträger auswählen	select potentials
die Besten herausfiltern	sift out the best
technische Fertigkeiten fördern	demand technical skills
jemandes Fähigkeiten entwickeln	develop someone's abilities

Food for thought

A born executive is someone whose father owns the company.

Just when you think you've got the promotion in the bag, some new guy will come along and marry the boss's daughter.

6. *An seiner Karriere schnitzen* / Carving out a career

ein Karriere starten	embark on / launch a career
die Karriere vorantreiben	enhance career development
einen guten beruflichen Lebenslauf haben	have a good track record
er ist sehr ehrgeizig	he is very ambitious
sich gewaltig anstrengen	put one's best foot forward
in der Hierarchie aufsteigen	climb the career ladder
viele Stunden investieren	put in a lot of hours

PERSONALENTWICKLUNG

Überstunden machen	do overtime
sich freiwillig für Arbeit melden	volunteer for work
Arbeit annehmen	accept work
befördert werden	get promotion
die Karriereleiter aufsteigen	climb the ladder
seinen Weg machen	come up in the world
die Treppe hinauffallen	get unexpected promotion
es ernsthaft versuchen	make a go of it
Dr. Rautert war erfolgreich, deshalb wollte die Konkurrenz ihn abwerben.	Dr Rautert was successful so the competitors wanted to headhunt him.
Unser neuer Azubi hat wirklich Unternehmungsgeist.	Our new trainee certainly has get-up-and-go.
Jemand hat gesagt, Industriekaufleute gibt's wie Sand am Meer.	Someone said commercial clerks are ten a penny.
Herr Seba hat viel erreicht. Er hat gute Leistungen im Bereich Personalwesen erzielt.	Mr. Seba has achieved a lot. He has a good track record in personnel.
Die 20%ige Umsatzsteigerung war dein Meisterstück.	You did the job of your life to raise sales by 20%.
jemandes Karriere beenden	cut someone's career short
Er hat bei dieser Aufgabe versagt.	Jim really fell down badly on the job.

☛ See also *Einstellung und Entlassung*, Seite 53.

Carving out a career

Don't be irreplaceable.
If you can't be replaced,
you can't be promoted.

PERSONNEL DEVELOPMENT

A box of idioms

Perlen vor die Säue werfen	cast pearls before the swine
an seiner Karriere schnitzen	carve out one's career
eine Stange Geld kosten	cost a pretty penny / the earth
es gibt sie wie Sand am Meer	they are ten a penny / a dime a dozen
ein Meisterstück / Geniestreich liefern	do the job of one's life
Unternehmensgeist haben	have get-up-and-go
jemanden abwerben	head-hunt somebody
seine Sache gut machen	make a good job of something
nicht die Spur einer Chance haben	not to have a snowball's chance in hell
bei einer Aufgabe versagen	fall down on the job
tauben Ohren predigen	flog a dead horse

Master your phrases

Task 3: Fill in the missing prepositions

1. He didn't perform .... par.
2. We gave him hands .... training.
3. Daimler have invested millions .... their employees.
4. Twenty candidates. We have to sift .... the best.

Task 4: Fill in the missing letters

1. Further education costs a p_ _ _ _ y p_ _ _ y.
2. The company is holding an emp _ _ _ _ _ app _ _ _ _ _ _.
3. I've checked. He's got an excellent t _ _ _ _ r _ c _ _ _ d.
4. It's not a special job. Clerks are t _ _ a p _ _ _ _.

PERSONALENTWICKLUNG

Picture your idiom

Our books are so successful that Rowohlt's competitors have been trying to .... - .... us for years.

Task 5: Written versus spoken English

Written English	Spoken English
provide training	.... training
conduct a training course	.... a training course
attend a seminar	.... to a seminar
select the best	.... out the best
allocate an assignment	.... an assignment
embark on a career	.... a career

Education isn't everything

The young man was desperate for money and so on his holidays he decided to take a job in a local factory. "Now," said the foreman, "your first job is to sweep the floor."
"But I've got a BA," said the young man, "and I'm currently studying for a masters in business administration."
"Oh," said the foreman. "In that case I'd better show you how to hold the broom."

PERSONNEL DEVELOPMENT 6

Lerntip: Aktionsketten sind guter Gedächtniskitt

Was sind Aktionsketten? Tätigkeiten des täglichen Lebens werden in kleine logische Schritte zerlegt. Die Logik der Reihenfolge bildet die Eselsbrücken von Aktion zu Aktion, die man mühelos wie einen Film in der Vorstellung ablaufen läßt. Wortschatz, den Sie so ordnen, prägt sich besonders gut ein.

Unser Beispiel ist die Vorbereitung einer Prüfung bis zu ihrem erfolgreichen Bestehen.

Task 6: Step by step

Here are the German verbs to help you:

anfordern; sich einschreiben; vorbereiten;
pauken; ablegen; bestehen; erhalten.

1. .... the examination documentation
2. .... for the exam
3. .... the subject
4. .... for the exam
5. .... the exam
6. .... the exam with distinction
7. .... a good report

○──────────── **Picture your idiom** ────────────○

Bob Small hasn't got a .... chance .... of getting a professorship at university.

PERSONALENTWICKLUNG

Crossword power

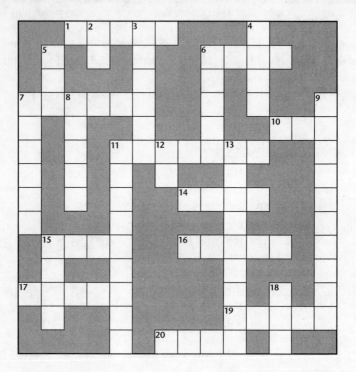

Across

1. Set someone ✎ to reach. 6. The opposite of *to pass* an exam. 7. Tim tries to ✎ his courses regularly. 10. I'm sure she'll make a good ✎ of it. 11. When do you ✎ the seminar documentation? 14. What is the drop-out ✎ in your courses? 15. Courses are not to take place in ✎ time. 16. He tried to ✎ at Harvard University. 17. ✎ out your career as long as you're young. 19. What are our training ✎? 20. He is unable to ✎ with the problems.

Down

2. Half of the trainees dropped drop out ✎ the seminar. 3. He climbed the career ✎ very quickly. 4. Have your certificate added to your personnel ✎. 5. They sifted ✎ the best candidates. 6. Courses are to be held in ✎ time. 7. They have set up an open ✎ centre. 8. She has a good ✎ record. 9. Another word for *goals* or *targets*. 11. English for *Praktikum* 12. Pass ✎ what you have learned. 13. Repair the word *renimeted* training needs. 15. ✎ for an exam. 18. He lacks motivation. So his boss gave him a ✎ talk.

IN DER EINKAUFSABTEILUNG

AT THE PURCHASING DEPARTMENT

PART 7

It's everywhere in industry. Save, save, save! And nowhere more so than in the Purchasing Department. Those poor fellows have to press down the prices of their greedy suppliers (or so it is said). The purchasing managers have to negotiate, discuss and calculate to explain to their partners (those evil suppliers) why they should supply at a price which might bankrupt them. Actually the truth is that it's all the law of the jungle. The big, strong one bullies the smaller boys.

Steps in purchasing

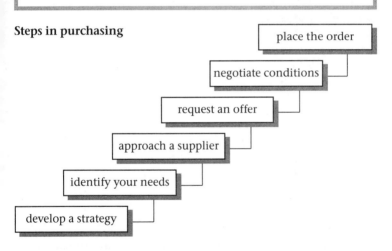

- place the order
- negotiate conditions
- request an offer
- approach a supplier
- identify your needs
- develop a strategy

The joy of buying

1. The Consumer Report on the item will come out a week after you've made your purchase.
2. The one you bought will be rated "unacceptable".
3. The one you almost bought will be rated "best buy".

7 IN DER EINKAUFSABTEILUNG

1. *Der Einkaufsleiter* / The purchasing manager

jemanden zum Einkaufsleiter / Direktor Einkauf ernennen	appoint somebody purchasing manager / director
als Angestellter in der Einkaufsabteilung arbeiten	work as a purchasing clerk
jemanden zum Haupteinkäufer befördern	promote someone to chief buyer
eine Ausbildung als Disponent / Einkäufer machen	train as a managing clerk / purchasing agent
Fachzeitschriften / Verbrauchertests durchsehen	go through trade journals / consumer reports
Fachmessen besuchen	attend trade fairs
eine Einkaufsstrategie entwickeln	develop the purchasing strategy
weltweite Einkaufspolitik	global sourcing
den Kauf im Budget einplanen	budget for the purchase
Bezugsquellen suchen	look for sources of supply
Geschäftsverbindungen anknüpfen	initiate business relations
Angebote einholen	solicit offers / invite quotations
die Preisentwicklung überprüfen	check the price development
eine Wertanalyse aufstellen	do a value analysis
vor Arbeit kein Bein mehr auf den Boden bekommen	be rushed off one's feet
Seit der Umstrukturierung stecken wir bis zum Kopf in Arbeit.	Since the restructuring we've been rushed off our feet.
Hand in Hand mit der Produktionsabteilung arbeiten	work hand in glove with the Production Department

The joy of shopping

1. When shopping, never look for something specific, you won't find it.
2. Always shop for nothing; you'll always come back with something.
3. After a tiring day's shopping, the perfect purchase is either in the first or the last shop you've been into.

AT THE PURCHASING DEPARTMENT 7

2. *Der Lieferant* / The supplier

potentielle Lieferanten finden	find potential suppliers
einen Lieferanten ansprechen	approach a supplier
Nachforschungen über die Zuverlässigkeit des Lieferanten anstellen	investigate supplier reliability
Lieferanten in die engere Auswahl nehmen	draw up a short list of suppliers
Lieferanten überprüfen	check out suppliers
Er ist absolut vertrauenswürdig.	He's safe as houses.
ortsansässige Lieferanten bevorzugen	prefer local suppliers
von einem Stammlieferanten kaufen	buy / purchase from a regular supplier
den Lieferanten Bedingungen auferlegen	impose conditions on the supplier
die Bezugsquelle wechseln	change the source / source of supply
Lieferzeiten / Mengen aushandeln	negotiate delivery dates / quantities
den Zwischenhändler / Mittelsmann ausschalten	eliminate the middleman / intermediary
Wenn wir eine positive Beziehung zu unseren Lieferanten aufbauen, wird das irgendwann Früchte tragen.	If we build up a positive relationship with our suppliers it will eventually bear fruit.

Why shoppers can't win

A sixty day warranty guarantees that the product will self-destruct on the sixty-first day.
If it can break, it will, but only after the warranty expires.
An item you need only goes on sale after you have purchased it at the regular price.

7 IN DER EINKAUFSABTEILUNG

3. *Einkaufen* / Purchasing

neue Artikel bestellen	place orders for new items
Waren beim Großhändler bestellen	order goods from the wholesaler
im Großhandel kaufen	buy wholesale
im Einzelhandel kaufen	buy retail
Waren in großen Mengen abnehmen	take bulk supplies
Rohstoffe im Ausland beziehen	source raw materials abroad
Materialien / Rohstoffe einkaufen	acquire material / raw materials
weltweit einkaufen	shop / source globally
Vorräte auf Lager nehmen	take supplies into stock
das Lager auffüllen	replenish / fill up stocks
billig einkaufen	buy cheap
einen guten Kauf machen	get a (good) bargain
eine Firma erwerben	acquire a company
einen Anlagekauf machen	make an investment
einen Einkaufsbummel machen	shop around
sofort bar bezahlen	settle promptly in cash
Zeit einplanen für ...	plan in time for ...

A box of idioms

Hand in Hand mit jemandem arbeiten	work hand in glove with someone
absolut vertrauenswürdig	safe as houses
vor Arbeit kein Bein mehr auf den Boden bekommen	be rushed off one's feet
nicht über den Tellerrand sehen können	not see beyond the end of one's nose
auf Kredit kaufen	buy on tick

Time for a smile

A bargain is something you buy that is cheaper than something you really want or need.

AT THE PURCHASING DEPARTMENT

4. *Angebote einholen und prüfen* / Soliciting and checking offers

Qualitätsstandard erreichen	reach quality standards
ein günstiges Angebot	a favourable offer
um ein verbindliches Angebot bitten	request a firm offer
ein schriftliches Angebot einholen	solicit a written offer
ein Angebot unterbreiten	send / submit an offer
Muster auf Verlangen schicken	send samples on request
Muster ziehen	draw samples
Muster prüfen	check samples
ein Preisangebot für ... machen	quote a price for ... / give a quotation for ...
ein verbindliches Angebot machen	give a firm offer
ein Angebot annehmen	accept an offer
ein Angebot bestätigen	confirm an offer
ein Angebot ablehnen	reject an offer
ein Angebot widerrufen	revoke an offer
mit niedrigeren / höheren Handelsspannen arbeiten	operate on lower / higher mark-ups
ein Gegenangebot machen	make a counter offer

☛ Siehe auch *In der Verkaufsabteilung*, Seite 123 ff.

Master your phrases

Task 1: Find the easier synonym

Latin word	Germanic word
attend trade fairs	.... to trade fairs
initiate business relations	.... business relations
replenish stocks	.... up stocks
grant a *quantity* discount	grant a .... discount
purchase from a regular supplier	.... from a regular supplier

7 IN DER EINKAUFSABTEILUNG

Task 2: Find the opposite

buy *retail*   buy ....
reject an offer   .... an offer
revoke a quotation   .... a quotation

Task 3: Fill in the prepositions

draw	....	a short list of suppliers
check	....	suppliers
operate	....	higher mark-ups
take supplies	....	stock
impose conditions	....	suppliers

5. *Preis aushandeln* / Negotiating the price

Preisauskünfte einholen	solicit price information
Preis nennen / angeben	quote a price
Preisangebot machen für ...	give a quotation for...
ein Angebot über 500 Stück machen	give a quote for 500 items
Preisvorteile anbieten	offer price advantages
ein konkurrenzloses Preisangebot	a quotation second to none
einen Preis aushandeln / vereinbaren	negotiate / agree a price
harte Verhandlungen führen	drive a hard bargain
Rabatte aushandeln	negotiate discounts
Gewähren Sie einen Mengenrabatt für ...?	Is there a quantity / bulk discount for ...?
einen Mengenrabatt gewähren	grant a bulk discount
Skonto bei schneller Bezahlung einräumen	allow / grant / give a prompt payment discount
Skonto bei Barzahlung gewähren	grant cash discount
Waren auf Teilzahlung kaufen	pay by instalments
das niedrigste Angebot	the lowest bid
Bitte nennen Sie Ihren niedrigsten Preis für ...	Please let us have your best / lowest price for ...
ein konkurrenzfähiger Preis	a competitive price

AT THE PURCHASING DEPARTMENT 7

Die Preise für Rohöl sind am Boden. — Prices of crude (oil) are at rock bottom.
Die Preise, die wir verlangen, richten sich nach Angebot und Nachfrage. — The prices we charge depend on supply and demand.
der Meistbietende — the highest bidder
Kosten und Fracht — cost and freight (C&F)

6. *Verträge schließen* / Concluding contracts

Lieferzeiten / -termine vereinbaren	agree delivery periods / deadlines
einen Termin verschieben / verpassen	postpone / miss a deadline
Kaufbedingungen angeben	state buying conditions
Es gibt keinen Kaufzwang.	There's no obligation to buy.
ein gutes Geschäft abschließen	strike a bargain
käuflich erwerben	acquire by purchase
nach Muster kaufen	buy according to sample
einen Kaufvertrag aushandeln	negotiate a purchasing agreement
ein Vertrag läuft ab	a contract expires
einen Vertrag erneuern	renew a contract
einen Vertrag verlängern	extend a contract
einen Vertrag unterschreiben	sign a contract
einen Vertrag widerrufen	revoke a contract
einen Vertrag brechen	break a contract
Das ist Vertragsbruch.	That's breach of contract.
den Vertrag kündigen	terminate the agreement
einen Kaufvertrag stornieren	cancel a buying contract
in beiderseitigem Einverständnis akzeptieren	accept in mutual agreement
Wie lange ist die Vertragsdauer?	What's the duration of contract?
den Verbraucher schützen	protect the consumer
einen Rahmenvertrag aufsetzen	set up a framework contract / skeleton agreement
Garantiezeit festlegen	fiix the warranty / guarantee period
einen Einkaufsvertrag unterzeichnen	sign a purchasing agreement

7 IN DER EINKAUFSABTEILUNG

Als wir diese Vereinbarung trafen, war es für beide Seiten ein Gewinn.	When we struck that bargain together, it was a win-win situation.
auf Kredit kaufen	buy on tick / credit
Wir kaufen nicht auf Kredit. Wir zahlen immer bei Lieferung.	We sure don't buy on tick. We always pay on delivery.

7. *Den Auftrag geben* / Placing the order

sich um einen Auftrag bewerben	tender for an order
ein Auftragsformular ausfüllen	fill out / in an order form
einen Auftrag schriftlich bestätigen	acknowledge an order in writing
ein Erstauftrag	an initial order
die technischen Angaben / das Lastenheft erfüllen	meet the specifications
ein großer Auftrag	a large order
Auftragsrückstand	backlog of orders
eine offene Bestellung	an outstanding order
eine Nachbestellung	a repeat order
nachbestellen	make a follow-up order
ein Dauerauftrag	a standing order
einen Auftrag übernehmen	take an order
einen Auftrag annehmen	accept an order
einen Auftrag ablehnen	reject an order
sich um einen Auftrag kümmern	attend to an order
die Bestellung stornieren	cancel the order
einen Auftrag bestätigen	confirm an order
einen Auftrag ausführen	execute / complete an order
den Auftrag bekommen	land the order
einen Auftrag verlieren	lose an order
einen Auftrag übersehen	overlook an order
einen Auftrag über ... geben.	place an order for ...
einen Auftrag bearbeiten	process an order
telefonisch / per Fax bestellen	order by phone / fax
Das Auto ist bestellt.	The car is on order.

AT THE PURCHASING DEPARTMENT 7

Wir können ihnen größere Aufträge geben. Sie sind absolut vertrauenswürdig.
We can place major orders with them. They're as safe as houses.

Wes Brot ich eß, des Lied ich sing!
He who pays the piper, calls the tune.

☞ Siehe auch *In der Verkaufsabteilung*, Seite 123 ff.

Master your phrases

Task 4: The verbs begin with the same letter

place an order	and	p............s it
accept an order	and	a............d to it
cancel the order	or	c............m it
land an order	or	l............e it

Task 5: Can you guess the verb?

The first one has been done for you

1. You can do it with Goethe and prices: quote
2. You can do it with glasses and contracts: ....
3. You can do it with ships and orders: ....
4. You can do it with a fast car and a hard bargain: ....

Task 6: Correct the idioms

1. The works council at the trade union is working hand in hand to trick management.
2. Put your money into S.U.P. The company is as safe as a bank.
3. The market is flooded. All our prices are at the bottom of the floor.

7 IN DER EINKAUFSABTEILUNG

Task 7: Phrases in context

Supplier: **S**, Thomas: **T**

S: So we thought we might n _ _ _ _ _ _ _ _ a new c _ _ _ _ _ _ t to fit the new co _ _ _ _ _ _ _ s.

T: Maybe you're right. When we s _ _ _ _ k our b _ _ _ _ _ n together last year things were different. This year we're buying a lot more from you. Let's talk about you g _ _ _ _ _ _ g us a b _ _ k d _ _ _ _ _ _ t.

S: But our costs have risen for all our _ _ w m _ _ _ _ _ _ _ _ s.

T: And where do you purchase?

S: All over Germany.

T: Aha ! Have you never heard of g _ _ _ _ _ s _ _ _ _ _ _ g? You can s _ _ _ _ e your r _ _ _ _ te _ _ _ _ s a _ r _ _ d . It's much cheaper.

Magic Squares

You know the rules of the game, don't you?

A. duration	B. breach	C. consumer
D. impose	E. instalments	F. mark-ups
G. rock bottom	H. obligation	I. according

1. There's no ✎ to buy.	2. Have you read the ✎ reports?	3. Don't ✎ conditions on buyers.
4. What's the ✎ of the contract?	5. Can we pay by ✎?	6. We'll buy ✎ to sample.
7. They operate on lower ✎.	8. Prices of crude oil are at ✎.	9. That's ✎ of contract.

A =	B =	C =
D =	E =	F =
G =	H =	I =

Check your solutions. The columns and rows should add up to 15.

AT THE PURCHASING DEPARTMENT 7

―――――――― Picture your idiom ――――――――

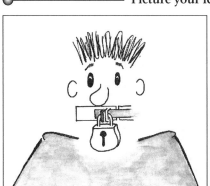

Bob: I wonder whether we still can trust this supplier.
Tom: Don't worry! I've known him for years. He's ..... as ....

Lerntip: Der Karteikasten als Wiederholungsmaschine

Auf Seite 110 finden Sie Tips zum Lernen mit Karteikarten. Wohin mit ihnen? Wie können Sie Ihre Kärtchen gehirngerecht verwalten? Nehmen Sie eine passende Pappschachtel. Unterteilen Sie den Karton von etwa 30 Zentimetern Länge in verschieden große Fächer.

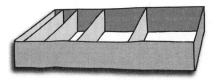

Die Karten mit dem Wortschatz eines behandelten Pensums wandern in das erste Fach. In ihm haben nur etwa 30 Karten Platz. Nach kurzer Zeit wird es in dem Fach zu eng. Dies ist das Signal für die nächste, größere Wiederholung. Wir nehmen den Packen heraus und wiederholen ihn: deutsche Seite anschauen und fremdsprachlichen Ausdruck ins Gedächtnis rufen.

Gekonnten Wortschatz legen wir auf die linke, Karten, die wir noch nicht können, auf die rechte Seite des Tisches mit der Fremdsprache nach oben. Den Wortschatz auf der linken beherrschen wir. Er wandert in die zweite, größere Abteilung des Kastens, wo er längere Zeit ruhen wird. Die Karten auf der rechten Seite schauen wir uns beim Einsammeln nochmals an und stecken sie zurück in das erste Fach, hinter etwaige neu angefallene, noch nicht wiederholte Karten.

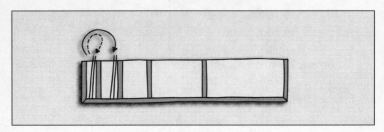

Nach einigen Wochen wird es auch im zweiten Fach zu eng. Platzmangel signalisiert uns: Zeit zum Wiederholen. Wir müssen Raum schaffen, indem wir die gewußten Karten in die dritte, noch größere Abteilung befördern. Auf die gleiche Art und Weise füllen sich im Laufe von Monaten Abteilung drei, vier und fünf. Der vergessene Wortschatz dagegen wandert zurück an den Anfang des Hürdenlaufs. Die Aufteilung des Kastens in verschieden große Fächer beruht auf dem Prinzip des Intervalltrainings. Je größer die Fächer, desto länger ist die Verweildauer der Karten.

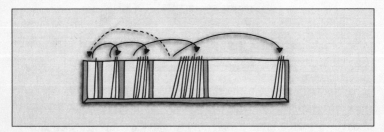

Die Abstände zwischen den einzelnen Wiederholungen werden auf diese Weise immer länger. Wortschatzkarten, deren Inhalt vergessen wurde, nehmen den umgekehrten Weg nach vorne, in das erste Fach. Sie werden öfter wiederholt. Unser Ziel ist es, die Karten vom ersten über die folgenden in das fünfte und letzte Fach zu transportieren. Dort angekommen, sind sie dauerhaft in unserem Langzeitgedächtnis gespeichert.

FORSCHUNG UND ENTWICKLUNG

RESEARCH AND DEVELOPMENT

PART 8

Some might say it's the power house of the company. The R&D Department should have ideas on how to improve products. Of course, they should get information from the marketing people, but often they think they themselves know what is better for the customers. From the outside we think of them as hundreds of men in white coats running around with devices strapped to their bodies. Nowadays, it's more a case of them sitting back and relaxing in front of computers.

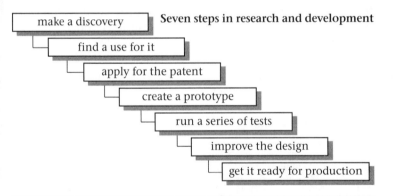

Seven steps in research and development

- make a discovery
- find a use for it
- apply for the patent
- create a prototype
- run a series of tests
- improve the design
- get it ready for production

Time for a smile

Engineers are the natural enemies of marketing people, always trying to inject their unwanted logic and knowledge into every situation. Often they'll make unreasonable demands. Sometimes they'll whine endlessly because the product maims customers. If it's not one thing it's another. You can minimise the problem by not inviting them to meetings.

Scott Adams, The Dilbert Principle

FORSCHUNG UND ENTWICKLUNG

1. *Wer ist wer?* / Who is who?

ein Ingenieurdiplom ablegen	qualify as an engineer
als Projektleiter arbeiten	work as project leader
als Konstrukteur beschäftigen	employ as a design engineer
jemanden zum technischen Betriebsleiter ernennen	appoint someone chief engineer
Er ist ein genialer Erfinder.	He is an ingenious inventor.
Versuchspersonen suchen	look for guinea pigs
Computerdesigner einstellen	hire computer designers

2. *Arbeitsplätze* / Work places

die Abteilung für Forschung und Entwicklung (F & E) leiten	run the Research and Development department (R&D)
für das Testlabor verantwortlich sein	be responsible for the testing plant
im Testlabor arbeiten	work in the test laboratory
im F-&-E-Labor testen	test in the R&D lab
in der Druckkammer testen	test in the pressure chamber
ein Auto auf der Teststrecke probefahren	test-drive a car on the test track
den Prüfstand überwachen	monitor the test rig
ein Versuchsgelände suchen	look for a test area

Time for a smile

The marvels of modern technology include the development of a soda can which, when discarded, will last forever and a $7,000 car which, when properly cared for, will rust in two or three years.

Paul Harwitz

RESEARCH AND DEVELOPMENT

3. *Geld für die Forschung* / Money for research

ein Budget für Forschung aushandeln	negotiate a research budget
das Budget für Forschung und Entwicklung ausarbeiten	work out the Research & Development budget
das Budget festlegen	fix the budget
das Budget einhalten	keep within the budget / adhere to the budget
das Budget übersteigen / überschreiten	go over / overrun / exceed the budget
Budgetüberschreitung rechtfertigen	justify budget excess / over spending
das Budget reduzieren / verringern	reduce / cut the budget back
seine Auslagen zurückerhalten	get returns on outlay
Fördermittel vom Staat erhalten	receive financial support from the State
Gelder / Finanzierung für ein Projekt erhalten	get funding / financing for a project
Gelder für das Projekt beschaffen	raise funds for the project
Forschungsgelder verschleudern	waste research funds
Unsere Investition in F & E macht uns schon nicht bankrott.	Our investment in R&D won't exactly break the bank.
Die Zeiten sind schwierig. Darum muß die Firma jeden Pfennig zweimal umdrehen.	Times are difficult. So the company has to watch every penny it invests.
Der Forschungsaufwand zahlt sich erst in 15 Jahren aus.	The research expenditure will pay off in 15 years.

Murphy's Law of discovery

All great discoveries are made by mistake.
The greater the funding, the longer it takes
to make the mistake.

FORSCHUNG UND ENTWICKLUNG

 Master your phrases

Task 1: Let's go woggling again

Replace the *woggles* with a suitable word.

1. Who is *woggling* the R&D department?
2. Who is in *woggle* of the project?
3. Have you already *woggled* funds for the project?
4. Our company *woggles* forward into the future.
5. We try to *woggle* up with the times.

Task 2: Say it in colloquial English

We mustn't *exceed* the budget.	We mustn't .... the budget.
We've got to *adhere* to the budget.	We've got to .... the budget.
I'm afraid they'll *reduce* the budget.	I'm afraid they'll .... the budget ..... .
When will you *generate* new ideas?	When will you .... with new ideas?

Task 3: Find the misprints

The first has been done for you.

Have you arised enough funds for the project?	*raised*
When will we get rerunts on our layout?	....
Who is sopsernible for the testing pnalt?	....
It's high time we reengeined a new ductrop.	....

Murphy's law of documentation

The project engineer will change the design
to suit the state-of-the-art.
The changes will not be mentioned in the service manual.

RESEARCH AND DEVELOPMENT

4. *Neue Gebiete erschließen* / Opening up new fields

forschen und entwickeln	carry out research and development
eine Erfindung machen	make an invention
zukunftsorientiert sein	look forward into the future / be forward-looking
auf dem neuesten Stand der Technik bleiben	remain state of the art
den technologischen Durchbruch erzielen	achieve the technological breakthrough
Wert auf Innovationen legen	place value on innovation
mit der Zeit gehen	keep up with the times
Wenn die Abteilungen nicht mit der Zeit gehen, sind die Produkte bald veraltet.	If the departments don't keep up with the times, the products will soon be out of date.
Forschung betreiben	undertake / do / carry out research
eine Ideenschmiede bilden	form a think tank
neue Ideen hervorbringen	generate / come up with new ideas
eine neue Idee beurteilen	assess a new idea
neue Methoden erforschen	research into new methods
zukünftige Produktionsmethoden erforschen	research future production methods
nach Produktinnovationen suchen	search for product innovation
neue Gebiete erschließen	open up new fields
Neuland beschreiten	enter a new field
die Forschungsvorgänge beschreiben	describe the research operations
ein Projekt aufbauen	set up a project
ein Firmenprodukt entwickeln	develop a company's product
ein Projekt planen / ausarbeiten	plan / work out a project
für das Projekt verantwortlich sein	be in charge of the project
die Grundkonzeption eines Projektes erstellen	draw up the outline of a project
einen Prototyp herstellen	produce a prototype
ein Produkt entwerfen	design / engineer a product
ein Patent umgehen	get round a patent
ein Produkt entwickeln	develop a product

FORSCHUNG UND ENTWICKLUNG

5. *Dokumentation* / Documentation

ein Patent anmelden	file a patent
technische Dokumentation zusammenstellen	compile technical documentation
eine technische Zeichnung erstellen	create / make a technical drawing
am Reißbrett arbeiten	work at the drawing board
die Normen erstellen / entwerfen	draw up / draft the standards
die technischen Daten überprüfen	check the specifications
das Pflichtenheft / Lastenheft ausarbeiten / beschreiben	work out / describe specifications
mit der Dokumentation übereinstimmen	conform to the documentation
ein Handbuch erstellen	produce a manual / handbook
eine technische Beschreibung drucken	print a specifications leaflet
das Handbuch überprüfen / auf den neuesten Stand bringen	review / update the manual

☛ Siehe auch *Die Rechtsabteilung*, Seite 169.

Murphy's Law of documentation

If you do not understand a particular word in a piece of technical writing, ignore it. The piece will make perfect sense without it.

6. *Arbeit im Laboratorium* / Work in the lab

im Testlabor arbeiten	work in the test lab
einen Prüfstand errichten	erect a test bed / rig
einen Prototyp zusammenbauen	set up a prototype
einen Versuch aufbauen	set up an experiment
eine Versuchsreihe planen	plan a test series
Versuche / Tests durchführen	carry out experiments / tests
Meßgeräte aufbauen	set up measuring equipment
Messungen vornehmen	take measurements
Meßwerte vergleichen	compare measuring values

RESEARCH AND DEVELOPMENT

technische Probleme lösen	solve technical problems
unter dem Mikroskop betrachten	observe / monitor under the microscope
Bauteile prüfen	test parts / components
die Oberfläche reinigen	clean the surface
die Eigenschaften eines Produkts untersuchen	investigate the qualities / properties / characteristics of a product
sicherstellen, daß die technischen Daten erfüllt werden	ensure specifications are kept / adhered to
sich auf die wichtigsten Aufgaben konzentrieren	concentrate on core activities
automatisierte / verbesserte Funktionen entwerfen	design automated / improved funtions
F & E ist mit diesem S21-Modell auf die Nase gefallen. Es hat die Marktanforderungen nicht erfüllt.	R & D certainly came a cropper with that S21 model. It wasn't up to market requirements.
Wir haben diese Technologie über ein Jahr erforscht und hatten kein Glück.	We researched this technology for more than a year and drew a blank.
Ich glaube, mit diesem Forschungsprojekt rennen wir gegen eine Wand.	With this research project, I think we're beating our heads against a stone wall.
Dieses Modell könnte ein ganz großer Wurf sein. Wir müssen es einführen.	This model could be real big-time. We've got to launch it.

A box of idioms

jeden Pfennig zweimal umdrehen	watch every penny
ins Leere rennen	beat one's head against a stone wall
ein großer Wurf sein	be real big-time
auf dem Holzweg sein	bark up the wrong tree
mit der Zeit gehen	keep up with the times
eine Niete ziehen	draw a blank
auf die Nase fallen	come a cropper

FORSCHUNG UND ENTWICKLUNG

 Master your phrases

Task 4: Find idioms for these definitions

1. be careful about what you spend
2. find no solution even though you tried
3. try to be up-to-date in what you do

Task 5: Complete the following idioms and phrases

1. The R&D department got their figures wrong.
   The company really c _ _ _ a c _ _ _ _ _ _ with that product.
2. R&D is building a new t _ _ _ _ _ _ to check the quality of their machinery.
3. You can't just spend money. You have to n _ _ _ _ _ _ _ _ e a b _ _ _ _ _ with the Board.
4. There's too much competition in this area. We have to o _ _ _ up new _ _ _ _ _ s if we want to survive.

Task 6: Phrases in context

Everybody's _ _ _ _ing costs and that applies to the R&D department, too. They have to k _ _ _ within certain b _ _ _ _ _ s. The company needs to get r _ _ _ _ _ s on o _ _ _ _ _ for any new products designed. The next problem is the documentation. For every product developed and sold the company is obliged to c _ _ _ _ _ e t _ _ _ _ _ _ _ _ l d _ _ u _ _ _ _ _ _ _ _ _ _. At the beginning of a project the engineers have to w _ _ _ _ _ t sp _ _ _ _ _ _ _ _ _ _ _ _ _. Later they will pr _ _ _ _ _ _ a pr _ _ _ _ _ _ _ _ which will be tested at a t _ _ _ _ _ g p _ _ _ t.

Murphy's law of research

Enough research will tend to support your theory.
If the facts do not conform to the theory, they must be eliminated.

RESEARCH AND DEVELOPMENT

Picture your idiom

If the departments don't .... the ...., the products will soon be out of date.

With this research project we're .... our .... against a ....

Lerntip: Haftzettel und Locitechnik

Erster Schritt: Schreiben Sie *phrases*, die Sie interessieren, mit der Übersetzung auf jeweils einen Haftzettel.

Zweiter Schritt: In Ihrer Wohnung gibt es Wege, die Sie mehrmals am Tag gehen. Heften Sie an markante Punkte dieses "Trampelpfades" je einen Merkzettel in Augenhöhe. Jedesmal, wenn Sie den Weg gehen, soll Ihr Auge auf einigen dieser Zettel verweilen. Sie lernen im Vorbeigehen, ohne eine Minute Ihrer Freizeit opfern zu müssen.

Dritter Schritt: Ihre ausgeschilderte Lernstrecke kennen Sie im Schlaf. Sie finden Ihren Weg also auch mühelos in Gedanken und können sich an die markanten Punkte erinnern. Die wohlbekannten Landmarken werden die "Mauerhaken" in Ihrem Gedächtnis, an denen Sie den Wortschatz festmachen.

Gleich, wo Sie sich befinden, Sie können den vertrauten Weg in Ihrer Wohnung jederzeit in Gedanken abschreiten. Jedesmal, wenn Sie einen Punkt aufrufen, wird sich der mit ihm verknüpfte Ausdruck einstellen. Gehen Sie den Weg abwechselnd vorwärts und rückwärts.

FORSCHUNG UND ENTWICKLUNG

C Crossword power

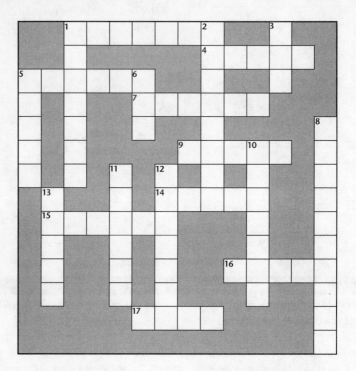

Across

1. Will we get sufficient ✎ for the project? 4. With this discovery we ✎ new fields. 5. We haven't finished the last test ✎ yet. 7. How am I to justify this budget ✎ again? 9. We have to ✎ every penny. 14. ✎ the surface. It's dirty. 15. We've got to test the prototype before we ✎ the product on the market. 16. *Set up* a test bed means to ✎ one. 17. My formula for success: '✎ up with the times'.

Down

1. Engineers must look ✎ into the future. 2. To ✎ ideas means to come up with them. 3. You can't sleep in a test ✎ . 5. Our products are ✎ of the art. 6. Let's ✎ up a new project. 8. The key to success in business is ✎ . 10. I'm afraid these tolerances do not ✎ to specifications. 11. A handbook is a ✎ . 12. Eureka! We'll ✎ a technological break-through. 13. A break-through? If you ask me, we've drawn a ✎.

IN DER PRODUKTIONSABTEILUNG

PART 9

AT THE PRODUCTION DEPARTMENT

We all like making things. But nowadays many things have to be produced as quickly as possible at the lowest possible cost. And production workers should be up-to-date with all sorts of technologies and especially with computer-aided tools. The factory has to react quickly to any changes in design. Another matter is the working conditions of the work. Nobody wants to get his hands dirty.

Seven steps towards production

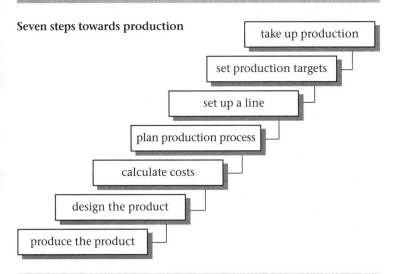

- take up production
- set production targets
- set up a line
- plan production process
- calculate costs
- design the product
- produce the product

Murphy's Law

If it were cheaper to buy a new unit,
the company would insist upon repairing the old one.

If it were cheaper to repair the old one,
the company would insist on the latest model.

IN DER PRODUKTIONSABTEILUNG

1. Aufgaben des Managements / Management tasks

Nachfrage decken	satisfy demand
eine Fabrik / Werk leiten	run a factory / plant / works
Produkte verarbeiten / fertigen	process / finish products
Produktionszahlen verbessern	improve production rates
Produktionseffektivität erhöhen	raise production efficiency
Produktion erhöhen	raise production
Bestände minimieren	minimise stocks
Warenbestände optimieren	optimise stock levels
Lagerfläche / Lagereinrichtungen reduzieren	reduce storage space / facilities
Überkapazitäten vermeiden	avoid excess capacity
die Produktion rationalisieren	streamline production
Ausfallzeiten erfassen	record down time
Arbeitszeit und Arbeitsmethoden untersuchen (REFA)	analyse time and methods, carry out a time and motion study
Waren herstellen / produzieren	manufacture / produce goods
Produkte einführen	phase products in
Produkte auslaufen lassen	phase products out
Ersatzteile lagern	store spare parts
den Produktionsablauf modernisieren	modernise the production process
die Produktion wiederaufnehmen	resume production
die Produktion steigern	step up production
freie Produktionskapazitäten haben	have idle plant capacity
Maschinen auslasten	use machines to capacity
Weihnachtszeit – und wir stecken wieder mal bis zum Hals in Arbeit.	Christmas season and we are up to our ears in work as usual.

Murphy's Law of production

1. Any tool, when dropped, will roll into the least accessible corner of the workshop.

2. On the way to the corner, any tool dropped will always strike your toes first.

3. The most delicate component will be the one to be dropped.

AT THE PRODUCTION DEPARTMENT

2. Menschen und Arbeitsplätze / People and workplaces

in einem Industriezweig arbeiten	work in a branch
dem technischen Bereich angehören	belong to the technical division
Montage im Ausland	offshore assembly
Produktion vor Ort	production on site
die Produktion einschränken	curb production
die Produktion auf die grüne Wiese verlagern	move production to a green-field site
jemanden in der Montagehalle einstellen	take someone on in the assembly shop
Geräte / Maschinen überprüfen	check on equipment / machinery
einen Leiter für Produktionsplanung und -kontrolle einstellen	employ a production planning & control manager
dem Aufsichtspersonal angehören	be part of the supervisory staff
einen Werksleiter einstellen	hire a works manager
den Prüfungsingenieur entlassen	dismiss the testing engineer
als Wartungsingenieur arbeiten	work as a maintenance engineer
jemanden zum Vorarbeiter befördern	promote someone to foreman
die Maschinen für eine neue Produktlinie umrüsten	tool up for a new line
Maschinen / Anlagen warten	maintain machinery / equipment
als angelernter Arbeiter anfangen	start as semi-skilled worker
sich als gelernter Arbeiter qualifizieren	qualify as a skilled worker
eine Ausbildung zum Schlosser / Monteur machen	train as a fitter / assembler
im Akkord arbeiten	do piece-work
am Fließband arbeiten	work on the assembly line
als Fräser / Werkzeugmacher arbeiten	work as a milling operator / toolmaker
in der Maschinenhalle arbeiten	work in the machine shop
am Förderband arbeiten	work on the conveyor belt
Sie stoßen täglich 200 Motoren aus.	They crank out 200 engines every day.
Montagearbeit ist eine Mordsarbeit.	Assembly work is a devil of a job.

9 IN DER PRODUKTIONSABTEILUNG

3. *Ein neues Produkt planen* / Planning a new product

das Sortiment erweitern	expand the range
eine Machbarkeitsstudie durchführen	do a feasibility study
eine Arbeitsstudie / Wertanalyse durchführen / machen	carry out / do a work study / value analysis
Arbeitsabläufe planen	plan work processes
ein Fabrikationsprogramm entwerfen	draw up a manufacturing schedule
Herstellungskosten kalkulieren	calculate manufacturing costs
Produktionsfunktionen aufteilen	divide up production functions
die Rahmenbedingungen für die Produktion aufstellen	provide / establish the framework for production
ein Produktionssystem entwickeln	develop a production system
Produktionszeitpläne vorbereiten	prepare production schedules
Zeitpläne einreichen	submit schedules
die Beschaffung von Material / Teilen / Komponenten planen	plan supply of material / parts / components
Produktionsziele setzen	set production targets

Time for a smile

Astronaut Gordon Cooper was about to start on his memorable flight into space when one of the reporters approached him and asked, "How do you feel?"

Cooper replied, "I'm worried."

The reporter said, "Why should you be worried when you think of what you are doing for your country?"

Cooper replied, "There are more than one thousand gadgets in this rocket and each has been made by the cheapest supplier."

☞ Siehe auch *The Way Things Work, Technisches Englisch für Business und Alltag* (rororo sprachen 60369).

AT THE PRODUCTION DEPARTMENT 9

 Master your phrases

Task 1: The first letter is an 'R'

eine Fabrik leiten	r............... a factory
die Produktion erhöhen	r............... production
Ausfallzeiten erfassen	r............... down time
Produktion wiederaufnehmen	r............... production
die Lagerkapazität verringern	r............... storage space

Task 2: Beef up your word power

Find the synonym.

work on the *conveyor belt*	work on the ....
supply *parts*	supply ....
streamline production	.... production
produce goods	.... goods

Task 3: What is the idiomatic phrase?

production *over the border*	.... production
production *at the customer's location*	production ....
production *out of town*	production on a ....-....... .....

4. *Das Produkt herstellen* / Producing the product

Produktion aufnehmen	take up production
Werkzeuge justieren	adjust tools
den Herstellungsablauf programmieren / steuern	program / control the manufacturing process
einen Prototypen fertigen	produce a prototype
ein Normteil herstellen	produce a standard part
Rohstoffe verwerten	exploit raw materials
Rohstoffe bearbeiten	process raw materials
Halbfabrikate bearbeiten	process semi-finished products

9 IN DER PRODUKTIONSABTEILUNG

Fertigwaren herstellen	turn out manufactured / finished goods
eine Fertigungsstraße errichten	set up a line
eine Maschine zusammenbauen	assemble / put together a machine
Instrumente einstellen	adjust the instruments
eine Werksnorm erstellen	create a works standard specification
für Serienfertigung freigeben	release for series production
Teile mechanisch herstellen	machine parts
Herkunftsland angeben	label the country of origin
Maschinen / Computer kombinieren	combine machines / computers
die Verfügbarkeit von Maschinen koordinieren	co-ordinate availability of machines
ständig mit der Marketingabteilung Verbindung halten	liaise with marketing department
eine Verbindung zwischen Marketing und Produktion herstellen	link up between marketing and production
Produktionsdokumente erstellen	draw up / prepare production documents
die Arbeitsrichtlinien befolgen	follow work rules

Murphy's Law

Hot glass looks exactly the same as cold glass.
No two identical parts are alike.

5. Einzel-, Serien und Massenproduktion / Jobbing, batch and mass production

zu Einzelproduktion übergehen	go into job / unique production
Einzelartikel herstellen	produce single / "one-off" articles
maßgeschneiderte / kundengerechte Teile fertigen	produce tailor-made / customised pieces
nach Maß fertigen	customise a product
Kundenanforderungen in Produktionsanweisungen umwandeln	translate customers' requirements into production instructions
Handarbeit machen	do handwork / manual work

AT THE PRODUCTION DEPARTMENT 9

Werthandarbeit anbieten	offer high-class manual workmanship
manuell / von Hand ausführen	do manually / by hand
Serienfertigung	batch production
Teile in Serie herstellen	make parts in series / in bulk
genormte Einheiten / Teile fertigen	turn out standardised units / parts
in großen Serien herstellen	make in large lots
systematisch produzieren	manufacture systematically
eine Serie maschinell bearbeiten	machine / process a lot
Massenproduktion	mass production
am Fließband arbeiten	work at the conveyor belt
von einem Arbeitsgang zum anderen übergehen	flow from one operation to another
strenge Produktspezifikationen beachten	follow rigid product specs
Spezialmaschinen nutzen	utilise specialised machines
Standardmethoden anwenden	apply standardised methods

Murphy's Law

Anything is easier to take apart than to put together.
That which cannot be taken apart will fall apart.

The work-bench is always untidier than last time.

6. *Werkzeuge und Maschinen* / Tools and machines

Maschinenbau studieren	study mechanical engineering
einen Maschinenantrieb bauen	build a machine drive
computerunterstütztes Design / computerunterstützte Herstellung einführen	introduce computer-aided design / computer-aided manufacturing
an einer Bohr- / Fräs- / Poliermaschine arbeiten	work at a drilling / milling / polishing machine
eine Drehbank installieren	install a lathe / turning machine
die Werkzeugmaschinen ersetzen	replace the tooling machines
ein Gerät auseinanderbauen / demontieren	dismantle / disassemble a device

9 IN DER PRODUKTIONSABTEILUNG

eine Störung in der Produktion / Werkstatt haben	have a hold-up in the production / machine shop
die Ausfallzeiten einer Anlage	the down time of a plant
Die Produktion ist in Gang gekommen, nachdem wir die neue Ausrüstung gekauft haben.	Production got into gear when we bought the new equipment.

> **Murphy's Law**
>
> When you try to prove to someone that a machine won't work, it will.

7. Ständige Kontrollen / Permanent checking

Qualitätskontrollen vornehmen	carry out quality control
die Stelle eines Qualitätsprüfers ausschreiben	advertise the post of quality manager
von minderwertiger / schlechter Qualität sein	be of inferior / poor quality
schlechte Qualität ablehnen	reject poor quality
fehlerlose / perfekte Qualität anbieten	offer flawless quality
Material / Werkstücke prüfen	test / check materials / workpieces
ein Lasten- / Pflichtenheft erstellen	draft / draw up a specifications list
dem Muster nicht entsprechen	show non-conformity with the sample
Proben ziehen	draw samples
eine Stichprobe machen	carry out a random sampling / make a random check
Teile untersuchen	inspect parts
vollautomatische Warenkontrolle einführen	introduce automatic testing of goods
eine 10%ige Ausfall- / Fehlerquote haben	have a 10% failure / defect rate
Diese Werkstücke entsprechen nicht den Spezifikationen.	These workpieces are not up to specs.
Mängel suchen	search for defects

AT THE PRODUCTION DEPARTMENT 9

versteckte Fehler suchen	search for hidden flaws
an ISO 9000, 9001 teilnehmen	take part in ISO 9000, 9001
die Normen erfüllen	fulfil the norms / standards
den ISO-Kriterien nicht genügen	fail the ISO criteria
Verfahren überprüfen	check on processes
schlampige Produkte aufdecken	detect shoddy products
den Ausschuß verringern	reduce spoilage
Ausschuß eliminieren / wegwerfen	eliminate / throw out rejects
Ausschuß verschrotten	scrap rejects
Die letzte Charge war verdorben.	The last batch was spoilt.
die Toleranzen einhalten	adhere to permissible limits / tolerances
ein Prüfzeichen geben	assign a test mark
Wenn unsere Firma schlechte Produkte auf den Markt bringt, muß die Qualitätsabteilung den Kopf dafür hinhalten.	If our company puts bad products on the market, it's the quality department that'll carry the can.
Der Chef hat bemerkt, daß ich ein paar defekte Artikel produziert habe, aber er hat ein Auge zugedrückt.	The boss noticed that I had produced some defective articles, but he turned a blind eye.

A box of idioms

eine Mordsarbeit sein	be a devil of a job
den Kopf hinhalten	carry the can
ein Auge zudrücken	turn a blind eye
einen Knüppel zwischen die Beine werfen / querschießen	throw a spanner in the works

Time for a smile

That component of any machine which has the shortest service life will be placed in the least accessible location.

9 IN DER PRODUKTIONSABTEILUNG

 Master your phrases

Task 4: Two words for one word

liaise with Marketing	.... with Marketing
a *problem* in the machine shop	a ....-........ in the machine shop
assemble a machine	.... a machine
finish a part	.... a part
start production	.... production

Task 5: They all begin with 're'

für Serienfertigung freigeben	re............ for series production
schlechte Qualität ablehnen	re............ poor quality
Ausschuß verschrotten	scrap re............
die Werkzeugmaschinen ersetzen	re............ the tooling machines

Task 6: Complete the phrases

1. How long does it take to a _ _ _ _ _ _ _ a m _ _ _ _ _ _ ?
2. The works manager has to plan the p _ _ _ _ _ _ _ _ _ n s _ _ _ _ _ _ _ s .
3. The m _ _ _ _ _ _ _ _ e e _ _ _ _ _ _ _ r is responsible for the repair of machines.

Task 7: What's the opposite of ...?

curb production	.... production
check every 20 items	do a .... sampling
produce it *by automation*	produce it ....
use *customised* methods	use .... methods

Murphy's Law

It works better if you plug it in.
When all else fails, read the instructions.

AT THE PRODUCTION DEPARTMENT 9

Picture your idiom

If our company puts bad products on the market,
it's our department that'll ....

Lerntip: Lernen im Vorbeigehen

Es gibt Wortschatz, der einfach nicht in den Kopf will. Wenn wir mit der Lernkartei arbeiten, sind es jene Karten, die immer wieder rechts auf unserem Tisch übrigbleiben und nicht in das zweite Fach wandern wollen. Sie nehmen diese harten Nüsse und heften sie in Gruppen von sieben an eine Pinnwand, so daß die fremdsprachliche Seite sichtbar ist. Jedesmal, wenn Sie vorbeigehen, werfen Sie einen Blick auf eines der Kärtchen. Sie erinnern sich, was auf der Rückseite der Karte steht, drehen sie zur Kontrolle um und heften sie wieder an. Jetzt ist Ihnen die deutsche Seite zugekehrt, und beim nächsten Vorbeigehen versuchen Sie, den fremdsprachigen Ausdruck zu finden. Es genügt, wenn Ihnen jedesmal nur eine Karte auffällt. Nach einigen Tagen werden Sie wissen, was da an der Wand hängt. So lernen Sie im Vorbeigehen ohne zusätzlichen Zeitaufwand. Die Pinnwand ist für einige Zeit Ihr externes Kurzzeitgedächtnis.

9 IN DER PRODUKTIONSABTEILUNG

C Crossword power

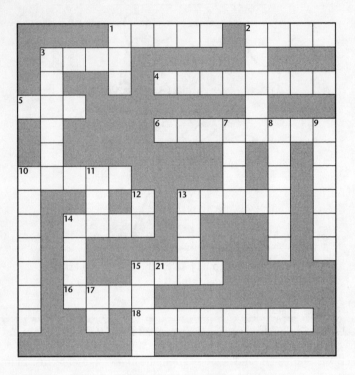

Across

1. These workpieces are not up to ◎. 2. We have a 10 percent defect ◎. 3. Could you assemble the machines on ◎? 4. Our aim is to offer ◎ products. 5. How do you process the ◎ materials? 6. Manufactured products are ◎ products. 10. It's not economical. Let's ◎ this product out. 13. The neighbours want us to move production to a green-◎ site. 14. It'll be Christmas soon. We should ◎ up production. 15. ◎ time on this production line beats all records! 16. Customers won't accept ◎ quality. 18. How long does it take to ◎ this machine?

Down

1. The production targets they've ◎ us are too high. 2. If you don't follow the work ◎ we'll have to fire you. 3. Let's ◎ for the hidden flaw. 7. It's not economical to have ◎ plant capacity. 8. Defects should not remain ◎. 9. A 10 percent ◎ rate is not acceptable. 10. Another word for *manufacture* 12. We'll soon have to tool ◎ for a new line. 13. Another word for *defect* 14. From genius to madness is often just a small ◎. 15. Let's do a random sampling and ◎ a sample out. 17. From time to time we should check ◎ our machinery.

PART 10

DIE MARKETINGABTEILUNG

THE MARKETING DEPARTMENT

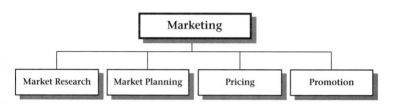

Schubert's Productivity

A company chairman was given double tickets for a performance of Schubert's 'Unfinished Symphony'. Being unable to go, he passed the invitations to the company's time-and-motion co-ordinator. The next morning the chairman asked him how he had enjoyed it and, instead of a few comments he handed him a memorandum which read as follows:

1. For considerable periods, the oboe players had nothing to do. Their number should be reduced, and their work spread over the whole orchestra, thus avoiding peaks of inactivity.
2. All twelve violins were playing identical notes. This seems unnecessary duplication and the staff of this section should be drastically cut. If a large volume of sound is required, this could be obtained through the use of an amplifier.
3. No useful purpose is served by horns repeating the passage that has already been handled by the strings. If all such redundant passages were eliminated, the concert could be reduced from two hours to twenty minutes.

In light of the above, one can only conclude that if Schubert had given attention to these matters, he would probably have had the time to finish his symphony.

10 DIE MARKETINGABTEILUNG

1. *Produktmanagement* / Product management

Marketing studieren	study marketing
jemanden zum Marketingdirektor ernennen	appoint somebody marketing director / director of marketing
als Abteilungsleiter / Angestellter im Marketing arbeiten	work as marketing manager / marketing clerk
zum Produktmanager befördert werden	be promoted product manager
für die Produktentwicklung verantwortlich sein	be responsible for product development
Dieser Posten ist genau mein Fall.	This position is right up my street.
eine Marktstudie in Auftrag geben	commission a market study
die Zielgruppe bestimmen	define the target group
ein Markenprodukt entwickeln	develop a brand
mit einem Warenzeichen versehen	brand a product
das Warenzeichen anmelden	apply for the brand name / trade mark
das Warenzeichen eintragen lassen	register the brand name
das Design verbessern	improve styling
eine Preisgestaltungsstrategie entwickeln	develop a pricing strategy
auf den Markt kommen	enter / come on to the market
Waren vermarkten	market goods
ein Markenprodukt einführen	launch a brand
den Absatz des Produkts fördern	promote the product
die Produktpalette diversifizieren	diversify the product range
eine Produktpalette haben	have a product portfolio / range
eine Produktmischung anbieten	offer a product mix
mit Verbrauchsgütern handeln	deal in consumer goods
Produkte weltweit vertreiben	market products on a world-wide scale
Dienstleistungen anbieten	offer services

THE MARKETING DEPARTMENT

2. *Marktforschung* / Market research

Marktforschung betreiben	do market research
den Markt analysieren	analyse the market
das Problem einkreisen	define / narrow down the problem
eine Hypothese testen	test a hypothesis
einen Forschungsplan erstellen / umsetzen	develop / implement a research plan
Ziele setzen	set objectives / goals / targets
Informationen sammeln	gather information
Marktpotential beschreiben	describe market potential
einen Fragebogen ausarbeiten	work out a questionnaire
den Bedarf ermitteln	identify needs / requirement
eine Verbraucherumfrage machen	do / carry out consumer research
die Bedürfnisse der Verbraucher ermitteln	identify consumer needs
Marktforschung zeigt, daß ...	market research proves that ...

Murphy's Law of market research

- The bigger the theory the better.
- Enough research will tend to support your theory.
- If the facts do not conform to the theory, they must be eliminated.

3. *Absatzplanung* / Sales planning

Es ist an der Zeit, daß wir unser Produktprogramm erweitern.	It's time to expand our product portfolio.
die Ergebnisse einer Marktuntersuchung vorlegen	present the results of a market investigation
eine Absatzplanung durchführen	carry out sales planning
einen Plan in die Tat umsetzen	put a plan into action
höhere Verkaufszahlen voraussagen	predict higher sales
eine Marktlücke entdecken	discover a market gap
eine Marktprognose erstellen	make a market forecast

10 DIE MARKETINGABTEILUNG

eine Strategie / Unternehmensmission / Pläne entwickeln develop a strategy / company mission / plans
die Mission / das Produkt bestimmen define the mission / product
das Produktprogramm festlegen decide on the portfolio
Verkaufe das Fell nicht, bevor du den Bären erlegt hast. Don't count your chickens before they're hatched.

 Master your phrases

Task 1: Fill in the missing words in the phrases

1. Your offer's very interesting. Could you show me your complete p _ _ _ _ _ _ p _ _ _ _ _ _ _ _ ?
2. If we want to survive, we have to e _ _ _ _ n _ _ m _ _ _ _ _ s .
3. A lot of variety. We must give the customer the correct p _ _ _ _ _ _ m _ _ .

Task 2: Find the correct preposition

1. carry .... marketing planning
2. decide .... the portfolio
3. apply .... a trade mark
4. deal .... consumer goods
5. sell .... a world-wide scale

4. *Den Markt erobern* / Conquering the market

Bedarf haben an	be in the market for
den Markt analysieren	analyse the market
den Markt beobachten	watch / observe the market
Kundenbedürfnisse befriedigen	satisfy customer needs
einen Markt beliefern	supply a market
eine Marktnische entdecken	discover a market niche
guten Absatz finden	meet with a ready market
in einen Markt eindringen	penetrate a market

THE MARKETING DEPARTMENT 10

einen Marktanteil gewinnen	obtain a market share
Märkte ausweiten	expand markets
ein Kampf um Marktanteile	a battle for market share
einen Marktsektor angreifen	attack a market sector
einen Markt erobern	conquer a market
einen Marktanteil an sich reißen	grab a market share
einen Markt zurückgewinnen	regain a market
zum Marktführer werden	become market leader
einen Markt kontrollieren / beeinflussen	control / influence a market
den Markt stärken / schwächen	weaken / strengthen the market
den Markt ankurbeln	push / stimulate / the market
den Markt sättigen	saturate the market
den Markt überschwemmen	congest / glut the market
den Markt aufteilen / segmentieren	slice up / segment the market
auf die Nachfrage reagieren	respond to demand
die Nachfrage sinkt	demand falls
vom Markt verschwinden	disappear from / drop out of the market
einen Marktanteil verlieren	lose a market share

5. *Preisgestaltung* / Pricing

eine Preisentscheidung treffen	take a pricing decision
einen Preis festsetzen	set a price
einen Preis für ein Produkt festsetzten	price a product
den Preis einer Ware erhöhen / senken	price an article up / down
die Preise senken	lower / reduce prices
einen Preis erhöhen	raise / increase a price
das Preisniveau / die Preisgrenze festlegen	fix the price level / limit
ein Produkt verteuern	mark up a product
ein Produkt verbilligen	mark a product down / cut the price
Preise unterbieten	undercut prices
jemandem einen Preis berechnen	charge someone a price

10 DIE MARKETINGABTEILUNG

die Preisbindung abschaffen	abolish retail price maintenance
Preise schießen in die Höhe, steigen stark an / fallen / gehen nach unten	prices sky-rocket / rocket / drop / decrease
durch überhöhte Preise nicht mehr konkurrenzfähig sein	price oneself out of the market
die Kosten / den Gewinn berechnen	calculate costs / profit
eine Gewinnspanne beibehalten / wiedererlangen	maintain / restore profit margin
den Gewinn erhöhen	increase profits
sich gut verkaufen	be a good seller
ein Renner sein	be a money spinner
Dieses Produkt ist unser Goldesel.	This product is our cash-cow.
Es bringt 70 % unseres Umsatzes.	It brings 70 % of our turnover.

6. Produkte im Markt plazieren / Placing products

ein Vertriebsnetz aufbauen	create a distribution / sales network
den Vertrieb planen	plan distribution
eine Kette von Einzelhändlern aufbauen	set up a chain of retailers
Generalvertreter	general representative / agent
ein Produkt im Markt plazieren	place / position a product
Franchising aufbauen / etablieren	set up / establish a franchise
einem Händler die Verkaufslizenz erteilen	license a dealer to sell
mit einem Großhändler zusammenarbeiten	work with a distributor
Es hat nicht funktioniert. Fangen wir noch mal von vorne an.	It didn't work. Back to the drawing board / back to square one.

Found in a newspaper

Stradivarius violin for sale. Almost new.

THE MARKETING DEPARTMENT 10

7. Internationales Marketing / International marketing

in einen ausländischen Markt eindringen	penetrate / enter a foreign market
in einen Markt exportieren	export to a market
einen Mittelsmann / Vertreter einsetzen	use a middleman / agent
direkt exportieren	export directly
ein Risiko mit einkalkulieren	involve risk
eine Exportabteilung aufbauen	establish an export department
Marktzugang erlangen	gain entry to a market
ein Image bekommen	gain an image
einen Markt auswählen	select a market
einen Marktanteil aufbauen	build (up) market share
Marktwachstum vorantreiben	push market growth

8. Verkaufsförderung / Promotion

für ein Produkt werben	advertise the product
den Verkauf fördern	promote sales
die Werbung aufbauen	organise the advertising
die Werbebotschaft formulieren	formulate the message
die Zielgruppe definieren	define the target group / audience
den Kunden ansprechen	appeal to the customer
Aufmerksamkeit erregen	attract attention
das Interesse wecken / halten	get / hold interest
Verlangen wecken	arouse desire
eine Werbekampagne starten	mount an advertising campaign
das einzigartige Verkaufsargument betonen	highlight the unique selling proposition
einen Bedarf schaffen	create a need
Produktvorzüge hervorheben	emphasise a product's benefits
eine Marketing- / Werbekampagne organisieren	organise a marketing / promotion campaign
das Werbemedium wählen	choose the advertising media
die Zielgruppen ansprechen	reach the target audience

10 DIE MARKETINGABTEILUNG

Hauptwerbezeit kaufen	buy peaktime
in Magazinen / Zeitschriften inserieren	put ads in magazines
Erstverkäufe tätigen	do initial sales
ein Markenimage etablieren	establish a brand image
Werbung einführen	launch advertising
den Verkauf vorantreiben	push sales
Computer verkaufen. Das ist genau mein Fall.	Selling computers. That's right up my street.
Die Vertreter müssen die Knochenarbeit tun.	The reps have to do the donkey work.

A box of idioms

noch einmal von vorne anfangen	go back to the drawing board / to square one
Man soll den Tag nicht vor dem Abend loben	Don't count your chickens before they're hatched.
sich / das Angebot vergrößern	branch out
das ist genau mein Fall	it's right up my street
Dieses Produkt ist unser Goldesel.	This product is our cash-cow.

Lerntip: Die Arbeit mit den Lernkarten

1. Übertragen Sie die fremdsprachige Wendung aus Ihrem Lehrbuch auf die Vorderseiten der Karten vom Format einer Zigarettenschachtel. Die Karten legen Sie (beschriftete Seite nach oben) in Siebenerkolonnen (siehe Seite 17) mit der deutschen Bezeichnung nach oben auf den Schreibtisch.
2. Versuchen Sie die deutschen Entsprechungen aus dem Gedächtnis auf die Rückseiten zu schreiben. Wenn nötig, werfen Sie dabei einen Blick auf das Buch. Dies ist eine erste Selbstkontrolle.
3. Sammeln Sie die sieben Karten einzeln ein. Mit einem kurzen Blick überprüfen Sie, ob Sie sich noch an die englische Übersetzung erinnern. Dies ist die zweite Selbstkontrolle. Karten, die Sie noch nicht beherrschen, legen Sie nach rechts auf den Tisch, die anderen kommen in das erste Fach des Karteikastens (siehe Seite 79).

THE MARKETING DEPARTMENT 10

4. Auf dem Tisch liegen nur noch die Karten, die Sie nicht auf Anhieb gewußt haben. Sie verfahren mit ihnen wie vorher, nehmen sie auf, übersetzen in Gedanken, kontrollieren mit einem Blick auf die Rückseite und stecken sie, wenn sie gekonnt wurden, in das erste Fach des Kastens. Dies ist ein dritter Lerndurchgang, der mit der geringen Anzahl Karten schon wesentlich schneller geht.
5. Unsere Hände sind dabei wie beim Patiencenlegen ständig beschäftigt, was besonders zappeligen Lernern wohltut. Die nun noch verbliebenen hartnäckigen Fälle stecken Sie in die Tasche oder an die Pinnwand, um später einen Blick darauf zu tun. Dafür benötigen Sie nur wenige Minuten.

Magic squares

1. Match phrases (A, B, C ...)

A. discover	D. identify	G. set up
B. register	E. analyse	H. define
C. develop	F. launch	I. discover

... with words (1, 2, 3 ...).

1. the brand name 2. a chain of retailers 3. an advertising campaign 4. a market gap 5. the market 6. a market gap 7. consumer needs 8. the product 9. the target group

2. Put numbers in the magic squares.

A =	D =	G =
B =	E =	H =
C =	F =	I =

3. Columns and rows will all add up to 15.

DIE MARKETINGABTEILUNG

 ## Master your phrases

Task 3: Find idioms for the words in *italics*

1. Okay, I'll deal with the question of advertising.
   It's exactly what I'm good at.
2. The plan's failed.
   We have to start all over again.
3. I think we have to *go into different areas*.

Task 4: Translate the German phrases

1. Sometimes I feel like I do the (*Knochenarbeit*) while others play sport.
2. With advertising from "Show It" I think we'll (*unsere Zielgruppe erreichen*).
3. MacRenRob have failed, so it's (*noch einmal von vorne anfangen*).

Task 5: Phrases in context

The danger of the marketing department is that they look into the future and make prognoses. They tend to think they have sold before they actually have. It's a question of don't c _ _ _ _ your ch _ _ _ _ _ _ before they're h _ _ _ _ _ _ _. Well, what does the marketing specialist have to do first? He has to id _ _ _ _ _ _ _ a pot _ _ _ _ _ l market and then a _ _ _ _ _ it. It's important to _ _ _ b a big market s _ _ _ _. To do this you've got to research the market, prepare the appropriate product and l _ _ _ _ _ it. Maybe if it's good it'll be a m _ _ _ _ sp _ _ _ _ _ _.

Time for a smile

When Anne finally brought her boss home her parents were relieved that this might be the right husband for her who would take her off their hands. But when they had a closer look they took Anne aside.
"He's not exactly a young man," whispered Mum to her daughter.
"He's fat, he's bald and he's pretty old isn't he?"
"There's no need to whisper, Mum," said Anne, "he's stone deaf too."

IN DER WERBEABTEILUNG

PART 11

AT THE ADVERTISING DEPARTMENT

The advertising department has to show potential customers why they should buy, but first of all it should make them aware that the products exist. Some of the tasks of the advertising department include writing about products, contacting advertising agencies, designing adverts and packaging and somehow communicating with the target group. It's not as easy as it sounds.

The AIDA-Formula

Four basic features of an advertising message:

Attention: attract them
    Instincts: appeal to them
        Decision: spark off a buying decision
            Action: trigger the customer's buying action

The psychology of advertising

Business without advertising is like throwing kisses to a girl in the dark. You know what you're doing, but nobody else does.
Edgar Watson Howe

Promoters are just guys with two pieces of bread
looking for a piece of cheese.
Evel Knievel

Advertising may be described as the science of arresting the human intelligence long enough to get money from it.
Stephen Leacock

11 IN DER WERBEABTEILUNG

1. *Die Werbeabteilung* / The Advertising Department

sich um den Posten des Direktors der Werbeabteilung bewerben	apply for the post of advertising director
als Kundenbetreuer arbeiten	work as an accounts manager
den Posten des Werbeleiters besetzen	fill the position of advertising manager
kundenorientiert sein	be customer-oriented
einen Werbetexter einstellen	employ a copy-writer
ein Marktsegment ansprechen	address a market segment
Kunden informieren	inform customers
Kunden auf dem laufenden halten	keep customers informed
Ausgaben für Werbung berechnen	calculate advertising expenditure
das Werbebudget einhalten	keep within the advertising budget
das Werbebudget überschreiten	exceed the advertising budget
einen Werbefeldzug starten	launch an advertising campaign
einen Werbefeldzug führen	run an advertising drive
für ein Produkt werben	advertise a product
eine Anzeige in die Zeitung setzen	put an ad in the paper
Anzeigen in einer Wochenzeitschrift / einem Magazin schalten	place ads in the weekly / periodical
etwas für sein Geld bekommen	get one's money worth
Diese Anzeigen sind teuer. Ich hoffe, wir bekommen was für unser Geld.	These ads are expensive. I hope we'll get our money's worth.
eine Werbefläche mieten	rent advertising space
einen Fernsehspot kaufen	buy a slot on TV
den Absatz fördern	promote sales
kommerzielle Werbung einsetzen	use commercial advertising
die Werbestrategie planen	plan the advertising strategy
Werbematerial entwickeln	develop advertising material
eine Testkampagne durchführen	do a test campaign

Advice from the expert

You can fool 88 percent of the public all the time, the rest haven't got any money.

AT THE ADVERTISING DEPARTMENT

2. *Die Werbeagentur* / The advertising agency

eine Werbeagentur leiten	run an advertising agency
in einer Werbeagentur / einem Grafikstudio arbeiten	work in an advertising agency / a graphic art studio
in der Kreativabteilung arbeiten	participate in the creative group
Medienforschung betreiben	carry out media research
die Zielgruppe bestimmen	define / identify the target group
die Zielgruppe analysieren	analyse the audience
eine Zielgruppenanalyse durchführen	do an audience analysis
eine Verbraucherumfrage in Auftrag geben	commission a consumer survey
Kunden befragen	interview customers
einen Fragebogen verschicken	send out a questionnaire
eine Fangfrage stellen	ask a leading question
den Befragten überprüfen	check the informant / interviewee respondent
einen repräsentativen Querschnitt wählen	choose a sample
Stichprobenerhebungen anwenden	use a sampling technique
das Kaufmotiv herausfinden	identify the buying motive
das Kaufverhalten der Verbraucher studieren	study the buying habits of consumers
Markenloyalität erwarten	expect brand loyalty
den Kunden erreichen	reach the customer
mit einem Werbeslogan werben	promote an advertising slogan
in der Presse / Fachzeitschriften inserieren	advertise in the press / specialist periodicals
Anzeigen in einer Wochenzeitschrift / einem Magazin schalten	place ads in a weekly / periodical
eine ganzseitige / doppelseitige Anzeige vorbereiten	prepare a full-page / double-page advert
eine Auflage von … erreichen	achieve a circulation of …
Wenn wir mit diesen Anzeigen keine Kunden aufrütteln, sind wir verloren.	If these adverts can't drum up some business / customers we're lost.

11 IN DER WERBEABTEILUNG

Mit unseren vielen Erfindungen sind wir der Konkurrenz voraus.
Our many innovations mean that we are ahead of the game.

die Konkurrenz überflügeln
gain an edge over one's competitors

die Konkurrenz bekämpfen
counter competition

Werbung gibt Anreize ...
advertising stimulates / arouses ...

Die erste Million wird eine klare Sache sein.
It'll be plain sailing to reach the first million.

Vergleichende Werbung in Deutschland – das ist eine komplizierte Geschichte.
Comparative advertising in Germany – that's opening a can of worms.

3. Werbung entwerfen / Designing an advert

die Eigenschaften des Produkts beschreiben	describe the properties of a product
einen Verkaufsvorteil gegenüber der Konkurrenz haben (einzigartiges Verkaufsargument)	have a U.S.P. (unique selling proposition)
die Medien einsetzen	use the media
ein Produkt anpreisen	promote a product
Waren der oberen / unteren Preisklasse anbieten	go up-market / down-market
eine Produkt vorführen	demonstrate a product
kostenlose Muster anbieten	offer free samples
einen Bilduntertitel gestalten	design a caption
Zielgruppenbewußtsein entwickeln	establish target audience awareness
Illustrationen entwerfen	design the illustrations
das Bildmaterial gestalten	do the artwork
die Ideen des Werbetexters interpretieren	interpret the copy-writer's ideas
eine Überschrift wählen	choose / select a headline
den Text einer Anzeige gestalten	layout the text of an advert
einen Werbeslogan / Schlagwort schreiben	write a slogan / catch-phrase
sich für eine Schriftart entscheiden	decide on the typography
das Firmenzeichen / Logo gestalten	create the logo

AT THE ADVERTISING DEPARTMENT 11

harte / weiche Verkaufsmethode anwenden use the hard / soft sell

marktorientierten Service anbieten offer market-driven services

ein namenloses Produkt anbieten offer a generic product

 Master your phrases

Task 1: Find a phrase that suits the definition

1. Ask potential customers questions to get necessary information.
2. Create the illustrations of an advertising page.
3. Write a short, attractive message which can be remembered easily.
4. Aim at part of a market with one's advertising.

Task 2: Let's go woggling again

Replace the *woggles* with a suitable word.

1. Lupy has to *woggle* new customers if it wants to survive.
2. If we want to survive on the market we have to *woggle* the competition.
3. Lupy has to hire a good *woggle*-writer for their advertising department.
4. *Woggle* advertising used to be forbidden in Germany.

Task 3: The verb that does the job

1. *sich bewerben* for the post of advertising director
2. *unterstellt sein* to the account director
3. *beschließen* the brand name
4. *starten* an advertising campaign
5. *berechnen* advertising expenditure
6. *einhalten* the advertising budget

11 IN DER WERBEABTEILUNG

4. *Verpackung* / Packaging	
Die Verpackung ist wichtiger als der Inhalt.	The packaging is more important than the contents.
eine Verpackung für Werbezwecke verwenden	use packaging for advertising
Verpackungen entwerfen	design packaging
Produkt und Marke sind auf der Verpackung gekennzeichnet.	Packaging identifies the product and brand.
das Produkt schützen	protect the product
das Aussehen des Produkts verbessern	enhance product appearance
die Aufmerksamkeit der Verbraucher wecken	catch consumers' attention
Annehmlichkeit für den Kunden bieten	offer convenience for the customer
die Identifizierung mit einem Produkt erreichen	achieve product identification

A box of idioms

eine glatte / klare Sache sein	be plain sailing
etwas für sein Geld bekommen	get one's money's worth
ein Überflieger sein	be a high flyer
der Konkurrenz voraus sein	be ahead of the game
die Werbetrommel rühren	drum up business
eine komplizierte Geschichte	a can of worms

Results of a consumer survey

In an effort to boost sales, British Airways announced that for two weeks only, any business executive who travelled on a midweek flight could take his wife along with him for only twenty per cent of the normal fare. In order to judge the success of this experiment, they wrote to all the wives concerned, asking them if they had enjoyed their flights. Eighty-five percent of the wives wrote back asking, "What flight?"

AT THE ADVERTISING DEPARTMENT

5. Ziele der Werbung / Aims of advertising

neue Marken ankündigen	announce new brands
ein neues Produkt einführen	launch a new product
das Produktimage verbessern	improve the product image
Interesse / Bedürfnisse wecken	arouse interest / needs
Aufmerksamkeit erregen	attract attention
Instinkte ansprechen	appeal to instincts
die Kundenvorteile hervorheben	highlight / emphasise customer benefits
zu einer Kaufentscheidung bewegen	induce someone to make a purchasing / buying decision
Markenbewußtsein entwickeln	develop product awareness
die Werbebotschaft vermitteln	communicate the advertising message
eine Marke / einen Namen bekannt machen	push a brand label / name
Händler unterstützen	support dealers
neue Kunden anziehen	attract new customers
neue Kunden gewinnen	capture new customers
abgewanderte Kunden zurückgewinnen	gain lost customers
Marktanteile hinzugewinnen	gain additional market shares
Gewinne erhöhen	increase profits
die Werbewirkung verstärken	stress the advertising appeal
Sonderangebote unterbreiten	make special offers

6. Öffentlichkeitsarbeit / Public relations

Verständnis aufbauen	establish understanding
Öffentlichkeitsarbeit informiert / beeinflußt	public relations inform /influence
den Stolz der Mitarbeiter stärken	enhance employees' pride
eine Pressemitteilung herausgeben	make a press release
Öffentlichkeitsarbeit aufbauen	establish public relations

11 IN DER WERBEABTEILUNG

einen Teil der Kommunikationsstrategie bilden	form a part of the communication strategy
ein Überflieger in Öffentlichkeitsarbeit sein	be a high flyer in PR

7. Direktwerbung / Direct advertising

per Telefon vertreiben	market by phone
Werbebriefe verschicken	send direct mailing
Massenwerbung einsetzen	use mass advertising
Werbung am Verkaufspunkt	point of sale advertising
eine Kleinanzeige inserieren	insert a classified ad
auf Plakaten werben	advertise on posters
auf Litfaßsäulen werben	advertise on poster pillars
eine Werbetafel / Anschlagtafel / Anschlagzaun anbringen	set up a billboard / panel / poster hoarding
eine Werbebroschüre / Prospekt zusammenstellen	compile a booklet
Werbebeilagen in Illustrierten	advertising inserts in magazines
ein Faltblatt gestalten	design a folder
Werbebriefe schreiben	write sales letters
einen nachfassenden Werbebrief schicken	send a follow-up letter
Rundschreiben / Flugblatt versenden	send a circular / leaflet / pamphlet
einen Versandkatalog erhalten	get a mail-order catalogue
Werbemuster bestellen	order a free sample
Einführungs- / Schleuderpreis anbieten	offer an introductory / knock-down price

Time for a smile

Two stores were engaged in bitter competition. Things reached a climax when one store flashed a notice saying: IF YOU NEED IT, WE HAVE IT. Whereupon the store across the street retorted: IF WE DON'T HAVE IT, YOU DON'T NEED IT.

AT THE ADVERTISING DEPARTMENT 11

   Master your phrases

Task 4: Beef up your word power

Find a synonym for the words in *italics*.

launch an advertising *campaign*	.... an advertising ....
select a headline	.... a headline
emphasise customer benefits	.... customer benefits
offer a *bargain* price	offer a .... price

Task 5: Phrases in context

To get the information, to potential buyers, the a _ _ _ _ _ _ _ _ _ _
department has to work out advertising c _ _ _ _ _ g _ s. This means
they have to get the right advertising _ _ x in order to g _ _ _
new _ _ _ _ _ _ _ s. To survive, a company must e _ _ _ _ d its
m _ _ _ _ _ s . Part of all this activity is to create a positive image of the
company among the general public. This is the area of p _ _ _ _ _
r _ _ _ _ _ _ s. And how should we do all this? We can go to an advertising a _ _ _ _ y and let them do it. But whatever strategy the company
chooses it should always remember to be c _ _ _ _ _ _ r-o _ _ _ _ _ _ d.

Picture your idiom

Bob: I think we should include these bench-marking tests in our advertising campaign.
Tom: Comparative advertising in Germany – that's .... a .... of .... Let's not wake sleeping dogs.

11 IN DER WERBEABTEILUNG

C Crossword power

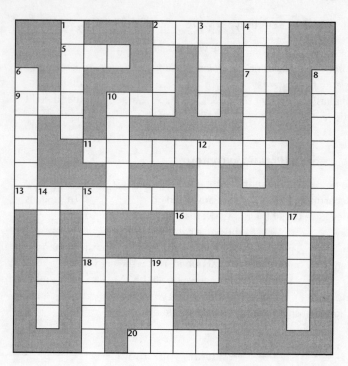

Across

2. Before you order ask for a free ✎.
5. Have you carried ✎ the media research?
7. Short for advertisement
9. I'd like to work in the graphic ✎ studio.
10. Shall we ✎ an ad in the paper?
11. Verpackung
13. They're breaking into our market ✎.
16. Find a synonym for *improve* product appearance
18. Another word for *catch-phrase*
20. Try to ✎ within the advertising budget.

Down

1. Will we ever get our money's ✎?
2. The opposite of *hard* sell.
3. When's our ✎-order catalogue ready?
4. I refuse to answer ✎ questions.
6. Know the buying ✎ of your customers!
8. Have you written the press ✎ for the trade fair?
10. Don't forget to ✎ an advert in the 'Zeit'.
12. Let's try to ✎ new customers.
14. Too expensive! We mustn't ✎ our budget.
15. Will the consumer understand our advertising ✎?
17. An ad should ✎ people's attention.
19. I'm afraid our competitor is ahead of the ✎.

PART 12

IN DER VERKAUFSABTEILUNG

AT THE SALES DEPARTMENT

This department has to get the product onto the market. Whatever they think of the product they have to find the best way of selling it with the most appealing advertising. They should also set up some sort of distribution system. Sometimes employees should be able to write advertising text, too.

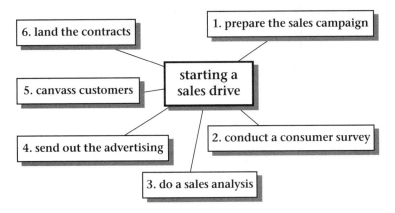

Small talk among salesmen

"We mustn't drink that much again," says Jones to Smith.
"Do you remember that last night you sold Tower Bridge?"
"Is that all?"
"No, I bought it."

12 IN DER VERKAUFSABTEILUNG

1. *In der Verkaufsabteilung* / At the Sales Department

für ein Absatzgebiet zuständig sein	be in charge of a sales territory
den Posten des Verkaufsdirektors innehaben	hold the post of director of sales
den Posten des Verkaufsdirektors annoncieren	advertise the post of sales director
die Stelle des Verkaufsmanagers innehaben	hold down the job of sales manager
einen Verkaufssachbearbeiter / Industriekaufmann beschäftigen	employ a sales clerk / commercial clerk
einen Verkaufsmanager / stellvertretenden Verkaufsmanager einstellen	hire a sales manager / assistant sales manager
eine Verkaufskampagne vorbereiten	prepare a sales campaign
einen Verkaufsfeldzug beginnen	start a sales drive
die Werbung verschicken	send out the advertising
mit einer Werbeagentur in Verbindung treten	contact an advertising agency
als Werbetexter arbeiten	work as a copywriter
die Fahnen korrigieren	correct the proofs
eine Verkaufsvereinbarung unterzeichnen	sign a sales agreement
eine Verkaufsanalyse erstellen	do a sales analysis
Waren führen	stock goods
Güter weiterverkaufen	resell goods
ein Angebot einreichen	submit a tender / bid
an einer Ausschreibung teilnehmen	participate in a tender

Time for a smile

"This car," said the salesman, "runs so smoothly you can't feel it, so quietly you can't hear it, so perfectly you can't smell it and so fast you can't see it."

Fred considered this for a moment, "Then how the hell do we know it's there?"

AT THE SALES DEPARTMENT 12

2. *Die Verkäufer* / The sales people

der Verkaufsmannschaft / Verkaufsbelegschaft angehören	belong to the sales force / sales staff
als Handlungsreisender arbeiten	work as a travelling salesman / sales representative / rep
eine Ausbildung als Verkäufer / Einzelhandelsverkäufer machen	train to be a salesman / sales person / shop assistant
an einer Verkaufsschulung teilnehmen	participate in a sales training course
ein großes Absatzgebiet haben	have a large selling area
auf harte Konkurrenz treffen	meet with fierce competition
im Außendienst sein	work in the field
auf Kundensuche gehen	canvass customers
Kundenbesuche machen	make calls / call on customers
Großkunden besuchen	visit major customers
das Produkt präsentieren	present the product
die Vorzüge beschreiben	describe the advantages
die Kundenvorteile hervorheben	highlight customer benefits
auf Referenzen verweisen	refer to testimonials
das Produkt vorführen	give a live demonstration of the device
ein System in vollem Betrieb vorführen	show a system in full action
Verkaufsgespräch	sales talk
aggressive Verkaufstaktik und diskrete Verkaufstaktik	hard sell and soft sell
eine Kaufentscheidung treffen	make a purchasing decision
Produkte absetzen	dispose of products
Produkte vertreiben	market products
Kauf mit Rückgaberecht	sale or return
Die Knochenarbeit müssen immer die Vertreter machen.	It's always the reps who do the donkey work.

Time for a smile

"Did you sell any of your paintings at the art show?"
"No, but I am encouraged," he replied. "Somebody stole one."

12 IN DER VERKAUFSABTEILUNG

3. *Produkteigenschaften* / Features of the product

ein typisches Merkmal des Produkts ist ...	a typical feature of the product is ...
eines der herausragenden Merkmale ist ...	one of the outstanding features is ...
wichtigste Eigenschaften sind ...	primary characteristics are ...
Neuerungen aufweisen	feature innovations
auf einem hohen Stand der Technik	highly sophisticated
widerstandsfähig und zuverlässig	tough and reliable
das neueste Modell	the latest design
kostensparend	cost-efficient
auf dem neuesten Stand der Technik sein	be state of the art
Testsieger in einer Verbraucherzeitschrift sein	be rated best in a consumer magazine
in vielen Tests bewährt	proven in many tests
einen Vergleichstest mit der Konkurrenz bestehen	pass a benchmarking test
unter extremen Bedingungen getestet	tested under extreme conditions
Den Verschleiß kann man vernachlässigen.	The wear and tear is negligible.

 Master your phrases

Task 1: Remember the prepositions

hold	....	the job of sales manager
meet	....	fierce competition
proven	....	many tests
tested	....	extreme conditions

AT THE SALES DEPARTMENT 12

Task 2: Find the missing twin

hire	and	....
supply	and	....
wear	and	....
buying	and	....
hard sell	or	....
sale	or	....

Task 3: Say it in other words

prepare a sales *campaign*	prepare a sales ....
submit a *bid*	submit a ....
call on major customers	.... major customers
attend a sales training course	.... in a sales training course

4. *Angebote machen* / Submitting offers

Wir könnten Ihnen ... anbieten.	We'd be able to offer you ... .
ein interessantes Angebot machen	make an interesting offer
einen Mengenrabatt gewähren	grant a quantity discount
einen Rabatt von 12 % auf den Katalogpreis gewähren	allow a discount of 12 % on the catalogue price
Wir gewähren einen höheren Rabatt bei Auftragswiederholung.	We give a better discount on a repeat order.
Bei einem Auftrag von mehr als $10 000 können wir einen Sonderrabatt gewähren.	If your order's over $10,000 in value, we can give you a special discount.
Die Preise verstehen sich ab Werk.	Price ex works.
ein Gegenangebot machen	make / give a counter-offer
Das Angebot versteht sich CIF München, im Preis sind also Fracht und Versicherung enthalten.	The quotation is CIF Munich, so the prices include freight and insurance.
Bei Barzahlung gibt es 2 % Skonto.	There's a 2 % discount for cash.

☛ Siehe auch *In der Einkaufsabteilung*, Seite 69 ff.

12 IN DER VERKAUFSABTEILUNG

5. *Der Verkaufsvertrag* / The sales contract

einen Vertrag entwerfen	write a draft agreement
eine Verkaufsvereinbarung aufsetzen	draft a sales agreement
einen Liefervertrag ausarbeiten	work out a supply contract
einen Vertrag abschließen	conclude a contract
einen Ratenzahlungsvertrag aushandeln	negotiate a hire-purchase agreement
einen Verkaufsvertrag unterschreiben	sign a sales contract
die Verkaufsbedingungen erfüllen	adhere to / keep the terms of contract
den Vertrag erfüllen	fulfil the contract
Vorauszahlung leisten	pay cash in advance
Zahlung bei Lieferung	cash on delivery (COD)
Zahlung bei Auftragserteilung	cash with order
einen Vertrag erneuern / verlängern	renew / extend / prolong a contract
die Vertragsparteien kommen überein ...	the contracting parties agree ...
die Vertragsbedingungen festlegen	stipulate the conditions of a contract
die Vertragsbedingungen aushandeln	negotiate the conditions of a contract
eine Vereinbarung eingehen	enter into an agreement
einen Vertrag stornieren / widerrufen / brechen	cancel / revoke / break a contract

Time for a smile

A tourist was asked what he thought about warm English beer. He said, "I think they ought to pour it back into the horse."

6. *Wie sich das Produkt verkauft* / How the product sells

den Verkauf ankurbeln	push / boost / promote sales
Winter- / Sommerschlußverkauf	winter / summer sale
Räumungs- / Totalausverkauf ankündigen	announce a clearance sale

AT THE SALES DEPARTMENT 12

ausverkaufen	sell out
Wie sind die Absatzperspektiven?	What are the sales prospects?
Der Verkauf steigt.	Sales are increasing.
sich gut / leicht verkaufen	sell well / briskly
ein Verkaufsschlager sein	be a best seller
Verkaufszahlen steigen.	Sales figures are rising.
Der Umsatz steigt.	Turnover is increasing.
Der Absatz schnellt in die Höhe.	Sales are rocketing.
gute Gewinne machen	make a good profit
Unsere Produkte verkaufen sich durch Mundpropaganda. Wir brauchen keine Werbung.	Our products sell by word of mouth. We don't need to advertise.
Taschenbücher gehen weg wie warme Semmeln.	Paperbacks are selling like hot cakes.
Das Geschäft ist ruhig.	Business is quiet.
eine Absatzstockung erleben	experience a stagnation
Der Umsatz stagniert.	Turnover is stagnating.
Die Verkaufszahlen sind rückläufig.	Sales figures are decreasing.
Der Verkauf ist zurückgegangen.	There's been a falling-off in sales.
ein Absatzproblem haben	have a sales / distribution problem
ein Verlustgeschäft machen	make losses
auf der Ware sitzen bleiben	get stuck with the goods
sich schlecht verkaufen lassen	sell badly
Dieses Modell ist ein echter Ladenhüter.	This design / model is a real shelf-warmer / non-seller.

Food for thought

Never simply say: "Sorry, we don't have what you are looking for."
Always say: "Too bad, I just sold the last one today."
Robert Skole

12 IN DER VERKAUFSABTEILUNG

7. *Die Lieferung* / The delivery

die Lieferbedingungen vereinbaren	negotiate the terms of delivery
Waren sind lieferbar.	Goods are available.
Unser Lagerbestand geht zu Ende.	Our stocks are running out.
auf Lager sein	be on stock
Ein Artikel ist ausverkauft.	An article is out of stock.
Ein Artikel ist nicht vorrätig.	An article is not available.
ab Lager liefern	deliver from stock
die Geräte ab Lager liefern	supply the equipment from stock
Lagerbestände abgeben	release supplies from stock
soweit lieferbar	subject to availability
die Ware versandfertig machen	get goods ready for despatch
Wohin soll die Ware gehen?	Where will the goods be delivered?
eine Lieferung versenden	despatch a consignment
Lieferung per Bahn, Straße oder per Luftfracht?	Delivery by rail, road transport or air freight?
die Waren umgehend zusenden	despatch the goods at once
Versanddatum	date of despatch
Termine einhalten	keep deadlines
den Liefertermin einhalten	meet the delivery date
eine Lieferfrist von drei Wochen	a three week delivery period
Lieferverzug	delayed delivery
die Lieferfrist überziehen	exceed the delivery period
Die Lieferung ist überfällig.	The delivery is overdue.
Lieferschein	delivery note

☛ Siehe auch *Im Warenlager*, Seite 135 ff., und *In der Versandabteilung*, Seite 141 ff.

The secret of success

A salesman with a phenomenal record finally revealed his secret to the new sales recruits. He said he put it down to the first seven words he invariably uttered when a woman answered his knock on a door," Miss, may I speak to your mother?"

AT THE SALES DEPARTMENT 12

Magic Squares

1. Let' draft a ...
2. These products sell ...
3. We give a better discount ...
4. Can you show me the system ...
5. There's been a falling-off ...
6. Let's negotiate the ...
7. We allow a discount of 12% ...
8. There's a 2% discount ...
9. The delivery of the items is ...

A. ... terms of delivery
B. ... on the catalogue prices
C. ... by word of mouth
D. ... sales agreement
E. ... in sales
F. ... overdue
G. ... for cash payment
H. ... on a repeat order
I. ... in action

Match the phrases. Put the numbers in the magic squares.
All columns and rows will add up to 15.

... = A	... = B	... = C
1 = D	5 = E	... = F
... = G	... = H	... = I

8. *Gründe für Reklamationen* / Reasons for complaints

Grund zur Reklamation haben	have cause for complaint
reklamieren	make / register a complaint
Das Problem ist ...	The problem / the trouble is ...
Die Lieferung ist unvollständig.	The shipment is not complete.
Folgende Artikel fehlen.	The following items are missing.
Waren sind beschädigt worden.	Goods have been damaged.
Die Artikel haben Fehler.	The articles are defective.
Der Preis entspricht nicht dem Angebot.	The price isn't the same as your offer.
Die Teile entsprechen nicht der Spezifikation.	The components are not up to specs.
Sie haben den Liefertermin nicht eingehalten.	You didn't meet the delivery schedule.

☛ Siehe auch *Beim Kundendienst*, Seite 157.

12 IN DER VERKAUFSABTEILUNG

 Master your phrases

Task 4: Beef up your word power

Find a word that has almost the same meaning as the one in *italics*.

1. The following *items* are missing.   a........................
2. Some of the *parts* are defective.   c........................
3. I have to *make* a serious complaint.   r........................
4. You have not *kept* the deadline.   m........................

Task 5: Say it the other way round

Use the opposite of the words in *italics*.
The first has been done for you.

1. The quality isn't *satisfactory*.
   The quality is *unsatisfactory*.
2. I can't *accept* this kind of thing again.
   This kind of thing is ....
3. The shipment is *not complete*.
   The shipment is ....
4. The printing press is *not reliable*.
   The printing press is ....

A box of idioms

den Löwenanteil bekommen	get the lion's share
IBM besitzt den Löwenanteil des PC-Marktes.	IBM have got the lion's share of the PC market.
die Knochenarbeit für andere tun	do the donkey work
Laßt uns das Eisen schmieden, solange es heiß ist.	Let's strike while the iron's hot.
durch Mundpropaganda	by word of mouth
Unsere Produkte verkaufen sich durch Mundpropaganda.	Our products sell by word of mouth.

AT THE SALES DEPARTMENT 12

9. *Was Sie dem verärgerten Kunden sagen* / What to say to the angry customer

Was haben Sie für ein Problem?	May I ask what the problem is?
Würden Sie mir bitte Ihr Problem schildern?	Would you be so kind as to describe your problem?
Ich verstehe Ihr Problem.	I can see your problem.
Es tut mir sehr leid, daß wir Ihnen Unannehmlichkeiten bereiten.	I'm very sorry for the inconvenience.
Tut mir leid, daß uns ein Fehler unterlaufen ist.	Sorry about the mistake on our part.
Bitte nehmen Sie unsere Entschuldigung an.	Please accept our apology.
Wir klären das Problem und rufen Sie sofort zurück.	We'll check the problem and call you back immediately.
Ich bin sicher, wir können das in Ordnung bringen.	I'm sure we can sort this out.
Ich werde mich sofort darum kümmern.	I'll see to it immediately.
Wir ersetzen natürlich die Ware.	We'll of course replace the article.

Picture your idiom

Bob: Anything wrong with you?
Tom: I'm fed up with this job. I'm afraid I've chosen the wrong career.
Bob: You are a real misery! Look at the bright side of things!
Tom: There aren't any bright sides in this job. It's always the reps who ...... the ...., don't they?

12 IN DER VERKAUFSABTEILUNG

 Master your phrases

Task 6: What do the following idioms mean?

1. strike while the iron's hot
   A. don't work too quickly
   B. wait until everything is ready
   C. act immediately

2. make a comeback
   A. try to start again
   B. begin over again
   C. go a few paces back

3. sell like hot cakes
   A. sell for a low price
   B. not sell very well
   C. sell extremely well

Task 7: Phrases in context

Terry: **T**, Jim: **J**

T: I've just heard they've ap _ _ _ _ _ ed James Dean s _ _ _ s d _ _ _ _ _ _ r . I hope he can _ _ _ _ the job down.

J: No problem there. He worked in sales and dis _ _ i _ _ _ _ _ _ n in Australia and our equipment is s _ _ _ _ ng like hot c _ _ _ _ there.

T: I've heard he'll probably h _ _ _ a new s _ _ _ _ m _ _ _ _ _ _ _ straight away. Actually did you know that sales have been f _ _ _ _ ng _ _f here in Europe ?

J: Of course I did. But I also know we've got something that's completely different from everything on the market. This Dean will help us to act quickly. We have to s _ _ _ _ _ while the i _ _ _'s hot.

A customer's revenge

I ordered a remote controlled helicopter for my son's birthday. It arrived in a kit which contained 123 pieces. The instructions said that it could be assembled in one hour. After a week, just in time for the birthday, I managed to fit the pieces together. I wrote a check, tore it into 123 pieces, and sent it to the company.

PART 13

IM WARENLAGER

AT THE WAREHOUSE

A few years ago companies kept large quantities of goods on stock waiting to be sold. Recently managers worked out that this costs a lot of money. And it takes up space. So they invented the J.I.T. (Just In Time) system. Now a minimum is kept and <u>conveyed to the factory or assembly area.</u> In some cases they even have suppliers deliver J.I.T. On the other hand, if anything goes wrong at the last minute (as it often does) then the workers are sitting around with nothing to do.

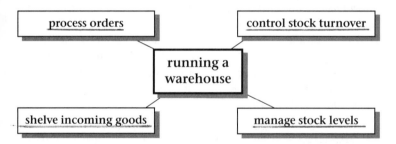

The price of packaging

John entered a store in the Bronx and asked the shopkeeper:
"What is the price of a herring?"
"Six cents a piece," answered Jacob, the shopkeeper.
In the meantime, John overheard the owner of the store opposite announcing his merchandise:
"Ladies and gentlemen, cheap! Five cents a herring!"
"Do you hear that?" John asked. "Why do you charge more?"
"Because," answered Katz, "I wrap the herring in today's newspaper and my neighbour uses week-old ones!"

13 IM WARENLAGER

1. *Lager und lagern* / Warehouse and warehousing

Lagereinrichtungen besitzen	own storage facilities
neue Lager einrichten	install new storage facilities
ein vollautomatisiertes Lager	a fully automated warehouse
Lagerkapazitäten anmieten	rent storage capacity
im Kühlraum lagern	keep in cold storage
als Lagerist arbeiten	work as a warehouse man / storekeeper
sich mit dem Lagerleiter in Verbindung setzen	contact the head storeman
einen Gabelstapler bedienen	operate / drive a forklift truck
die Europaletten stapeln	stack up Europallets
einen Bestand an Fertigprodukten haben	have a stock of finished goods / finished goods inventory (US)
Halbfabrikate / Ersatzteile auf Lager halten	keep in stock semi-finished goods / spare parts
Waren lagern	stock / store warehouse goods
einen Artikel führen	carry / stock an article
ein gut sortiertes Lager führen	keep a well-assorted stock
die Bestellnummer rausschreiben	note down the order number
ein zu großes / kleines Lager unterhalten	overstock / understock goods
den Bestand vom Computer abrufen	retrieve / call up stock levels from the computer
am Fließband arbeiten	work on the conveyor belt

2. *Das Lager verwalten* / Running the warehouse

für die Lagerbuchführung verantwortlich sein	be responsible for the warehouse bookkeeping
den Lagerbestand überprüfen	do the stock control
Inventur machen	take / draw up inventory
die Inventur vornehmen	do the stock-taking / inventory (US)
etwas ins Lagerbuch eintragen	enter something in the stock book
Wie hoch ist Ihr Lagerbestand?	What's your stock on hand?

AT THE WAREHOUSE 13

den Lagerumschlag kontrollieren	check the stock turnover
Lagerbestände auf die Produktion abstimmen	match stock levels to production
saisonale Schwankungen berücksichtigen	take into account seasonal fluctuations
Engpässe vermeiden	avoid bottlenecks
die Bestandskonten führen	manage stock levels
die Feuerlöscher warten	keep the fire extinguishers in good condition
die Waren versichern	insure the goods / products
Feuerversicherung abschließen	take out a fire insurance
gegen Einbrüche sichern	secure against break-ins
Wie hoch sind die Lagerhaltungskosten?	What are the costs for storage?
Wie hoch sind die Lagergebühren?	What are the storage charges?

3. Die Regale füllen / Filling the shelves

beim Wareneingang eintreffen	arrive at goods receiving / goods inward / incoming goods
auf Vollständigkeit überprüfen	check for completeness
die Lieferung mit der Bestellung vergleichen	compare the delivery against the order
den Erhalt bestätigen	confirm receipt
die Waren auspacken	unpack the goods
die Artikel einsortieren	shelve the articles
einen großen Bestand an ... haben	be well stocked in ...
einen geringen Lagerbestand haben	run low / short of stock
nichts mehr auf Lager haben	run out of stock
Bauteile für die Produktion nachbestellen	order some more components for production
die Lagerbestände erhöhen	increase stock
das Lager auffüllen	replenish / refill stock, restock
die Regale auffüllen	fill up the shelves
Nahrungsmittel kühl lagern	put foodstuffs into cold storage
Ersatzteile einlagern	place spare parts in a warehouse

13 IM WARENLAGER

4. *Die Regale leeren* / Clearing the shelves

beim Warenausgang arbeiten	work at goods outward / outgoing goods
das Lager räumen	clear the stock
die Lagerbestände verringern	decrease stock
ab Lager liefern	deliver ex warehouse
Bestellungen bearbeiten	process orders
ausverkauft sein	be out of stock
Waren aus dem Lager nehmen	take goods from stock
Artikel auslagern	withdraw articles from a warehouse
Waren versandfertig machen	get the goods ready for despatch
den Frachtbrief ausstellen	issue the consignment note
die Zollpapiere ausfüllen	fill in / out the customs documents
die Bedienungsanleitung beilegen	enclose the operating instructions
die Lieferwagen beladen	load the vans up

5. *Sicherheit geht vor* / Safety first

Transportschäden vermeiden	avoid damage in transit
die Artikel verpacken	pack the goods
stoßfest verpacken	pack things to be shockproof
das richtige Verpackungsmaterial wählen	select the correct packing material
transportsicher verpacken	pack safely for transport
empfindliche Meßgeräte polstern	pad sensitive measuring instruments
in Schaumstoff verpacken	pack with foam
einen Aufkleber anbringen	stick on a label
Diese Seite nach oben!	This side up!
Vorsicht! Glas!	Caution! Glass!
Vorsicht! Explosionsgefahr!	Caution! Explosives!
Vorsicht! Feuergefährlich!	Caution! Inflammable!
Kühl lagern!	Store in a cool place!
Verderbliche Waren!	Perishable goods!
Keine Haken!	No hooks!
Vorsicht! Nicht stürzen!	Caution! Don't tip over!

AT THE WAREHOUSE 13

A box of idioms

Vorsicht ist die Mutter der Porzellankiste.	An ounce of prevention is better than a pound of care.
sich klarwerden über / abschätzen	take stock
Ich schätze, wir sollten uns erst über die Situation klarwerden, bevor wir eine Entscheidung treffen.	I guess we'd better take stock of the situation before we decide.
am Ende seiner Kräfte / Geduld sein, sich nicht mehr zu helfen wissen	be at the end of one's tether
Keine Lastwagen. Die Leute im Versand sind am Ende ihrer Geduld / wissen sich nicht mehr zu helfen.	No lorries. The staff in despatch are at the end of their tether.

 Master your phrases

Task 1: Find a synonym

run *low* on stock	run .... of stock
replenish stock	.... stock
retrieve stock levels *from* a computer	.... stock levels from a computer

Task 2: Find the opposite

goods *outward*	goods ....
overstock goods	.... goods
fill the shelves	.... the shelves

Task 3: Improve the following idioms and phrases

1. Before we make a decision we'd better *check the situation out*.
2. We have our own *possibilities for storage*.
3. It's all too much stress. *I'm at the end of my rope.*
4. Bad management ! We've *kept too many* goods on stock.

139

IM WARENLAGER

Task 4: Phrases in context

Ron (R), Dave (D)

R: What does your work in the warehouse consist of ?

D: Well, it's not just a matter of st _ _ _ _ _ goods. There are other things. For example, every six months we have to do our st _ _ _ t _ _ _ _ _ _ .

R: Do you ever manage to c _ _ _ _ stock completely?

D: We certainly do, and then we have to r _ _ _ _ _ _ _ h stock so that we're always able to satisfy customers' wishes.

R: So it never happens that you _ _ n _ _ t of stock ?

D: Rarely. There is one bottleneck in the warehouse. That's where parts come in g _ _ _ _ i _ _ _ _ d . Then the boss is under pressure and shouts at me until I'm at the _ _ _ of my t _ _ _ _ _ , too.

Magic Squares

Head storeman McGregor has to despatch the following goods:

A. Perishable Goods	B. Test Tubes	C. Petrol
D. Antique Furniture	E. Acid	F. Bordeaux Wines
G. Live Animals	H. Gas	I. Chemicals

For each article McGregor has a special label:

1. Place no hooks!	2. Danger! Inflammable!	3. Caution! No naked flames!
4. Danger! Poison!	5. Don't tip!	6. Place in cold storage!
7. Fragile! Don't throw!	8. Handle with care!	9. Keep at room temperature!

Which label does he stick onto which carton?

A =	B =	C =
D =	E =	F =
G =	H =	I =

Rows and columns add up to the magic number 15.

IN DER VERSANDABTEILUNG

PART 14

AT THE DESPATCH DEPARTMENT

So the products have finally been manufactured, checked and tested. Now they must be collected together and sent out of the company to the various customers. This task is carried out by the despatch department. Not only must the articles be placed into the means of transport, normally some sort of lorry or container, their whole route has to be planned. Perhaps they need to go by sea or even air. Often it is necessary to call in a specialist firm called a forwarder. The whole process can be a real headache.

Handling the delivery

1. receive a shipping order
2. group the consignment
3. pack in crates
4. select mode of transport
5. commission a shipping agent
6. fill out a set of bills of lading

Selecting the mode of conveyance

"I personally don't believe in supersonic overseas transport."
"Why's that, is it because of the costs?"
"No, because I lisp."

☛ Siehe auch *Im Warenlager*, Seite 135.

14 IN DER VERSANDABTEILUNG

> **1. *Die Wahl des Transportmittels* / Choosing the means of transport**

in der Versandabteilung	at the Despatch Department
Versandart	mode of conveyance
Warentransport	carriage of goods
Welche Beförderungsart / Versandart wünschen Sie?	What mode of carriage / manner of shipment do you require?
öffentliche Verkehrsmittel benutzen	use public transport
per Schiene / Straße versenden	despatch by rail / road
Straßentransport	transport by road / land
verderbliche Waren mit einem Kühlwagen schicken	send perishable goods by refrigerator van
Gold im Panzerwagen liefern	deliver gold in an armoured van
Flüssiggas mit Tanklastwagen befördern	move liquid gas by tanker
Transportieren Sie feuergefährliche Fracht nicht auf der Straße.	Do not transport inflammable freight by road.
eine Ladung auf dem Landweg schicken	transport a shipment over land
Schienen- / Bahntransport	transport by rail
Gefahrengut mit Güterzügen versenden	send / despatch dangerous goods by freight / goods trains
weniger Umweltprobleme verursachen	cause less problems for the environment
Lufttransport	transport by air
Lufttransport ist ratsam für verderbliche Güter.	Air transport is advisable for perishable goods.
Transport auf dem Wasser	transport by boat / ship
Rohöl mit dem Tankschiff transportieren	convey crude oil by tanker
Produkte / Container verschiffen	ship products / containers
Sperrgut mit Lastkähnen befördern	convey bulky goods by barge
Frachtdampfer sind wirtschaftlich, aber langsam.	Cargo steamers are economical but slow.
eilige Dokumente mit Kurier schicken	send urgent documents by overnight courier
eine Sendung umleiten	reroute a shipment

AT THE DESPATCH DEPARTMENT 14

2. *Die Lieferung vorbereiten* / Preparing the delivery

in der Versandabteilung arbeiten	work in the delivery / shipping department
bei einer Transportgesellschaft arbeiten	work for a trucking / hauling company
einen Versandauftrag / Speditions-auftrag erhalten	receive a shipping order
Wir werden den Transport nach außen vergeben.	We'll outsource the transportation functions.
einen Spediteur beauftragen	commission a shipping agent / forwarding agent
den Transport bezahlen	pay for haulage
Frachtraum buchen	book freight space
Fracht abwickeln	handle freight
die Waren ab Werk / ab Fabrik versenden	despatch products ex works / ex factory
sofortige / prompte Lieferung anbieten	offer immediate / prompt delivery
eine Lieferung zusammenstellen	group a consignment
in Lattenkisten mit Dämmaterial verpacken	pack in crates with cushioning material
die Lieferung veranlassen	effect delivery
den Lastwagen / Container beladen	load the lorry / container
Waren liefern	deliver / supply / furnish goods
Waren verteilen	distribute goods
Güter befördern	haul goods
eine Lieferung senden / schicken	send a delivery / consignment / shipment
Produkte abschicken	convey / dispatch products
Produkte versenden / weiterleiten	forward the goods
Güter befördern	transport / convey / move / carry goods
den Transportweg planen	plan the route of transport
mit sperrigem Material arbeiten	work with bulky material
Ich wette meinen letzten Pfennig, daß der Transportplan nicht stimmt.	I bet my boots the transport schedule is wrong.

14 IN DER VERSANDABTEILUNG

 Master your phrases

Task 1: Can you complete the table?

By rail	By air	By water
goods train	freight plane	cargo steamer
railway	....	....
station	....	sea port / harbour
platform	....	....
....	pilot	captain

Task 2: Choosing the right transport

These goods should go ...

perishable food	by .... van
bulky goods	by ....
urgent documents	by ....
crude oil	by ....
diamonds	in an .... van

Task 3: Beef up your word power

Do you remember the synonym?

Latin English	Germanic English
What *mode* of *carriage* do you *require*?	What .... of .... do you ....?
Shall we *convey* the goods by air?	Shall we .... the goods by air?
I prefer using public conveyance.	.... use public ....
Please *despatch* the *consignment* by water.	Please .... the .... by water.

AT THE DESPATCH DEPARTMENT

3. *Die Fachsprache des Spediteurs* / Transport jargon

Was sind Incoterms?	What are Incoterms (International Commercial Terms)?
ab Werk	ex works
frei Waggon	F.O.R. (free on rail)
frei Waggon	F.O.T. (free on truck)
die Güter frei Kai anliefern	deliver the goods free quay
frei Längsseite Schiff	F.A.S. (free alongside ship)
frei an Bord	F.O.B. (free on board)
Kosten & Fracht	C&F (cost & freight)
Kosten, Versicherung, Fracht	C.I.F. (cost, insurance, freight)
frei Grenze	franco frontier

4. *Formulare und Formalitäten* / Forms and formalities

den Liefertermin / die Lieferzeit vereinbaren	agree the date of delivery / period of delivery
die Lieferbedingungen überprüfen	check through the terms of delivery
die Versanddokumente überprüfen	check the shipping documents
Exportdokumente / Verschiffungsdokumente vorbereiten	prepare export / shipping documents
den Frachtbrief ausfüllen	fill in / out the consignment note
ein vollständiger Satz Konnossemente	a full set of bills of lading
ein (See-)Konnossement ausstellen	issue an ocean bill of lading
Zolldokumente unterzeichnen	sign the customs documents
eine Importlizenz / Einfuhrgenehmigung beantragen	apply for an import licence / permit
eine Zollfaktura / Konsulatsfaktura ausstellen	raise a customs / consular invoice
eine Ausfuhrerklärung machen	make an export declaration
das Herkunftszeugnis anfordern	request the certificate of origin
die Übernahmebescheinigung des Spediteurs erhalten	receive the forwarders' receipt
einen Vertrag über die Beförderung von Waren abschließen	conclude a contract for the carriage of goods

14 IN DER VERSANDABTEILUNG

eine Versicherungspolice / -zertifikat vereinbaren	arrange an insurance policy / certificate
die Fracht versichern	insure the freight
das Transportrisiko versichern	insure the risk of conveyance
mit Frachtgebühren belasten	charge for carriage
eine Versandanzeige / Lieferschein schreiben	write an advice note / delivery note
dem Empfänger eine Versandanzeige schicken	send the consignee an advice despatch
Frachtkosten nachprüfen	check freight costs
die Frachtgebühr pro Kilometer beträgt ...	the freightage per kilometre is ...
die Versandkosten berechnen	calculate the costs of delivery

5. *Lieferprobleme* / Problems with delivery

Lieferverzug haben	have a delay in delivery
die Waren wurden fehlgeleitet	the goods were misrouted
die Sendung verzögert sich	the delivery will be delayed
die Lieferung ist unvollständig	the consignment is incomplete
vom Zoll beschlagnahmt werden	be confiscated by customs
im Zoll steckenbleiben	be held up at customs
Geräte sind beschädigt worden	equipment has been damaged
Kartons sind aufgerissen	boxes have been torn open
Wasserschäden aufweisen	suffer damage by water
Das haben wir nicht bestellt.	We didn't order that.
Das muß ein Mißverständnis sein!	There must be a misunderstanding!
Die Lieferung stimmt nicht mit dem Lieferschein überein.	The consignment does not conform to the delivery note.
Die Lebensmittel sind verdorben.	The foodstuff is spoiled / has gone bad.
Wieviel hat diese Armbanduhr gekostet? Das ist zu billig! Es muß Diebesgut sein.	What did that watch cost? It's too cheap! It must have fallen off the back of a lorry.
Diebstahl der Hafenpolizei melden	report a theft to the harbour police
Verlust während des Transports	loss in transit

AT THE DESPATCH DEPARTMENT 14

Beschädigung auf dem Transport	damage in transit
die Annahme verweigern	refuse to accept delivery
Schadenersatz fordern	claim damages
Der Möbelwagen hatte einen Unfall.	The furniture van had an accident.
Der Chef schlug vor, die Lastwagen in Zahlung zu geben. Sie sind nicht mehr verkehrstauglich.	The boss suggested we should trade in the lorries. They're no longer roadworthy.

6. *Die Ankunft der Lieferung* / The arrival of the delivery

Transport von Haus zu Haus	door-to-door transport
die Fracht umladen / umschlagen	transship the cargo
auf Abruf liefern	deliver on call
eine Lieferung an- / übernehmen	accept delivery
die Waren sind abholbereit	the goods are ready for collection
eine Ladung löschen	discharge a shipment
den Lastwagen / Container entladen	unload the lorry / container
Waren abholen	collect goods
die Vollständigkeit überprüfen	check for completeness
den Erhalt der Ware quittieren	sign for receipt of goods

7. *Menschen und Orte* / People and Places

Bestimmungsort / Bestimmungsland angeben	state the place of destination / country of destination
Verschiffungshafen	port of shipment
Bestimmungshafen	port of destination
die Fracht vom Güterbahnhof abholen	collect the freight at the goods station
Der Spediteur trägt die Risiken bei Frachtschäden.	The forwarding agent bears the risks of damage to cargo.
Absender / Versender	consignor
den Empfänger benachrichtigen	notify the consignee
in einen Hafen einlaufen	enter a port
aus einem Hafen auslaufen	clear a port
Umschlagplatz für Container	container handling facilities

14 IN DER VERSANDABTEILUNG

A box of idioms

Dieser Whisky muß Diebesgut sein.	This whisky must have fallen off the back of a lorry
Wir sollten weiterhin mit unserem Spediteur zusammenarbeiten. Er ist das kleinere Übel.	We should continue to work with our forwarder. He is the lesser evil.
bis zum Hals in Arbeit stecken	up to one's ears in work
Die Konkurrenz im Speditionsgeschäft ist hart. Die Konkurrenz ist mörderisch.	Competition is fierce in the forwarding business. It's dog eat dog.

 Master your phrases

Task 4: Fill in the missing words

Some tasks in the d _ _ _ _ _ _h department:
First you must d _ _ _ _ e on the mode of t _ _ _ _ _ _ _ _ _.
You might need to s _ l _ _ t a h _ _ l _ _ e c _ _ _ _ _ _y.
If it's going by sea or air, it will be necessary to b _ _ k some
f _ _ _ _ _ _ space. It's expensive.
Don't forget to c _ _ _ _ _ _ _ _e the costs of d _ _ _ _ _ _y.

Task 5: Guided translation

Paul: We've been asked to (*eine Lieferung schicken*) of electrical DXII components.

Fred: Well, we'd better be careful this time. They (*die Annahme verweigern*) of the last consignment.

Paul: They (*die Lieferbedingungen überprüfen*) and found we were late and there were other discrepancies as well.

Fred: Right, then we'd better (*die Lieferung zusammenstellen*) and (*beladen*) the lorry.

AT THE DESPATCH DEPARTMENT 14

Task 6: Phrases in context

I work in the sh_pp__g d_____t of a large manufacturing company in the sector of mechanical engineering. One of our tasks is to f_____d the g___s to customers as soon as they are ready. Sometimes we use private carriers but often we s___ goods by p____c c__v_____e. The job is difficult sometimes. It's not easy to h___ l_f____h_ which is b___y or heavy. Then there's the question of documents. In addition to dealing with carriage you have to f___ in the c_____ d_____ts.
And we need to watch costs. In this world it's d__ e__ __g!

Picture your idiom

I'm afraid we can't deliver the products before January. It's Christmas season and we are .... in work as usual.

Time for a smile

"You can take this consignment to Frankfurt," said the London forwarding agent to his new lorry driver.
"Couldn't somebody else do it, boss? I'm afraid of going to the Continent." – "Why?" – "Because they drive on the wrong side of the road." – What's wrong with that?" – "I tried it the other night," said the new man. "It's bloody dangerous."

14 IN DER VERSANDABTEILUNG

ⓒ Crossword power

Across

2. Another word for *despatch* 4. C.I.F. means *cost, insurance,* 🖋 7. despatch goods 🖋 works 9. We'll transport this shipment 🖋 land 10. We'd better send goods by 🖋. 11. Have we agreed the 🖋 of delivery yet? 12. Repair the word 'ra-geirac' 15. The forwarder 🖋 the risk of damage to cargo. 17. *Frei bis Grenze* heißt 🖋 *frontier*. 18. Dangerous goods should be despatched by 🖋 train. 19. Let's 🖋 the consignment and despatch it.

Down

1. Banknotes are delivered in 🖋 vans. 2. I bet my boots the transport 🖋 is wrong. 3. It's safer to 🖋 dangerous goods by rail 5. to plan the 🖋 of the transport 6. 🖋 delivery means prompt delivery 8. Have you filled 🖋 the consignment note? 13. 🖋 theft to the harbour police 14. Please add a full set of bills of 🖋 15. Conveying the 🖋 goods by barge is economical. 16. Why did they 🖋 to accept the delivery? 17. The goods are ready 🖋 collection.

BEIM KUNDENDIENST

AT CUSTOMER SERVICE

PART 15

When we buy something, we expect it to be perfect. Unfortunately when we get it home it doesn't work, a piece falls off, there are no batteries or an important cable is missing. Full of rage we rush to the telephone to call customer service. The staff in this department have to deal with angry customers, calm them down and generally make sure that there is service after the sale has taken place. That's the theory anyway.

Handling complaints

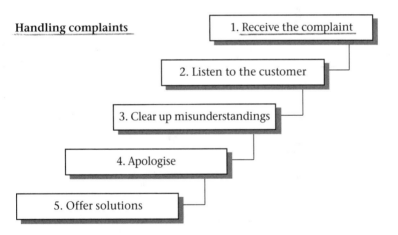

1. Receive the complaint
2. Listen to the customer
3. Clear up misunderstandings
4. Apologise
5. Offer solutions

Time for a smile

A telephone service girl received a call from an elderly lady: "My telephone cord," said the lady, "is too long. Would you please pull it back at your end?"

15 BEIM KUNDENDIENST

1. Kontakt zu Kunden halten / Keeping in touch with customers

in der Kundenbetreuung arbeiten	work at the hotline desk
den Kundendienst anrufen	phone / call customer service
Telefonarbeit erledigen	handle the phone calls
Anrufe beantworten	answer / handle calls
Kunde einer Firma sein	patronise a company
einen Kundenkreis aufbauen	build up a customer base
eine Kundenkartei / Kundenliste anlegen	create an index / list of customers
Stammkundschaft betreuen	deal with regular customers
seinen Kundenkreis halten	keep one's clientele
Kunden überprüfen	check customers
sich mit einem Kunden in Verbindung setzen	contact / get in touch with a customer
an Kunden in Übersee / im Ausland schreiben	write to customers overseas / abroad
Kunden besuchen	make calls on the customer / call at the customer's site
Kunden werben	canvass customers
neue Kunden anziehen	attract new customers
dem Kundenkreis angehören	belong to the clientele
einer Käuferschicht angehören	belong to a class of customers
den Kunden persönlich treffen	meet the customer face to face
den Kundenbedarf einschätzen	assess customers' needs
kundenorientiert sein	be customer orientated / driven
den Kunden gut / schlecht behandeln	treat the customer well / badly
die Kundenzufriedenheit überprüfen	check out customer satisfaction
einen Kunden zufriedenstellen	please a customer
den Kundenwünschen entsprechen	comply with the customers' wishes

Murphy's law about complaints

If you don't write to complain, you'll never receive your order.
If you write, you'll receive the merchandise before your angry letter reaches its destination.

AT CUSTOMER SERVICE 15

2. Kundenerwartungen / Customer expectations

Verständnis erwarten	expect sympathy / understanding
einen zuverlässigen Service benötigen / verlangen	need / demand a dependable service
die Lösung eines Problems	the solution to a problem
Service vor Ort	service locally / on site
schnelle Hilfe	fast support / quick assistance
schnelle Reparaturen	prompt repairs
Ersatz für defekte Geräte	replacement for defective devices
ein kompetenter Mechaniker	a competent / an able mechanic
die Ware zurücknehmen	take the product back
Entschädigung für Produktionsausfall	compensation for loss of production
Rückgaberecht bei Nichtgefallen	right to return unsatisfactory products
gleichbleibende Qualität erwarten	expect consistent quality
einen Rückruf erwarten	expect a call back
fachmännischer Rat	specialist advice
sachkundige Beratung	professional consultation
seine Produkte kennen	know one's products
Handbücher in deutscher Sprache	manuals / handbooks in German
präzise Dokumentation als selbstverständlich betrachten	take accurate documentation for granted

Time for a smile

The new girl is standing in front of the paper-shredder, looking very confused. Another secretary, walking by, asks, "Do you need some help?"
The new girl says, "Yeah, how does this work?"
"It's simple." The secretary takes the important report from the new girl's hand and starts feeding it into the shredder.
The new girl says, "Thanks, but where do the new copies come out?"

15 BEIM KUNDENDIENST

3. *Kundendienst* / After sales services	
Kundenbedürfnisse erfüllen	meet / fulfil customers' requirements
sich für den Verbraucher einsetzen	stand up for the consumer
Kundenrechte schützen	protect customers' rights
einen guten Kundendienst bereitstellen	provide good customer service
Kundendienst anbieten	offer after sales service
rund um die Uhr erreichbar sein	be available right round the clock
den Kundendienst ins Haus schicken	send the service team to the customer's company.
beschädigte Waren zurückschicken	return damaged articles
größere Reparaturen zum Hersteller einschicken	send it back to the manufacturer's for more serious repairs
defekte Geräte vor Ort reparieren	repair defective equipment on site
einen Wartungs- /Werksvertrag abschließen	conclude a service contract
seinen Garantieverpflichtungen nachkommen	fulfil / meet the guarantee
den Servicevertrag lesen / durchgehen	read / go through the service contract
die Garantiebedingungen nachlesen	look up the warranty / guarantee
einen Serviceeinsatz organisieren	fix up a service call
das Produkt zurückholen	call in the product

AT CUSTOMER SERVICE 15

 Master your phrases

Task 1: Where do these adjectives belong?

consistent	unsatisfactory
professional	damaged

1. The customer has the right to return ...
   .... products or
   .... articles.
2. The customer may expect ...
   .... quality and
   .... advice.

Task 2: Put the verbs in their places

provide	create
assess	comply

1. .... customers' needs
2. .... good customer service
3. .... a customer base
4. .... with the customers' wishes

Task 3: Find words that have the same meaning

Our company is customer-*orientated*. Our company is customer ....

We try to *meet* customers' *needs*. We try to .... customers' ....

We'll get in *contact* with you regularly. We'll get in .... with you regularly.

We have a team of *competent* mechanics. We have a team of .... mechanics.

We service your machines *locally*. We service your machines ....

15 BEIM KUNDENDIENST

4. *Kundenreklamationen* / Customer complaints

sich um Beschwerden kümmern	deal with complaints
mit einem anspruchsvollen / wählerischen Kunden reden	talk to a pretentious / choosy customer
reklamieren	make a complaint
Ich bedauere, daß ich reklamieren muß, aber ...	I'm sorry to complain, but ...
eine größere Reklamation melden	register a serious complaint
mit allem Nachdruck reklamieren	complain most strongly
seine Unzufriedenheit zum Ausdruck bringen	express one's dissatisfaction
das Problem ist ...	the problem / the trouble is ...
Artikel fehlen.	Items are missing.
Waren sind beschädigt worden.	Goods have been damaged.
Artikel haben Fehler.	Articles are defective.
Schund ablehnen	reject shoddy products
Teile entsprechen nicht der Spezifikation.	Components are not up to specs.
Die Qualität ist minderwertig.	The quality is below standard.
den Liefertermin nicht einhalten	fail to meet the delivery schedule
den Vertrag nicht einhalten	fail to fulfil the contract
Teile sind nicht eingetroffen.	Parts have not arrived.
total / völlig enttäuscht sein	be totally / extremely disappointed
Ihr Kundendienst entspricht leider nicht unseren Erwartungen.	I'm afraid your service hasn't met our expectations.
immer wieder die gleichen Ausreden hören	hear the same excuses every time
kein Wort davon glauben	not believe a word one hears
am Ende seiner Geduld sein	run out of patience
Kundschaft aufkündigen	withdraw one's custom
sich über den Service beschweren	complain about service
den Service nicht akzeptieren	not accept the service
Ich habe leider einige Probleme mit Ihren Bürorobotern.	I'm afraid I'm having problems with your office robots.
Um es kurz zu machen, Sie werden	To put it in a nutshell, you will not

AT CUSTOMER SERVICE 15

kein Geld von mir bekommen, wenn Sie nicht ...	be receiving payment if you don't ...
vollen Schadenersatz verlangen	ask for full compensation
eine Mahnung / letzte Mahnung verschicken	send a reminder / final reminder

5. Reklamationen entgegennehmen / Handling complaints

den Anrufer mit Namen ansprechen	address the caller by name
den Anrufer begrüßen	greet the caller
ruhig bleiben	stay calm
Einwände ernst nehmen	take objections seriously
einen freundlichen Ton anschlagen	use a friendly tone
verärgerte Kunden beruhigen	calm down angry customers
sich für den Anruf bedanken	thank someone for calling
die Gebrauchsanweisungen erklären	explain the instructions
auf das Handbuch verweisen	refer to the user manual
einen Nachfolgeanruf tätigen	make a follow-up call
gute Nachrichten überbringen	deliver good news
die Unterhaltung weiterführen	carry on a conversation
einen Anrufer in die Warteschleife stellen	place the caller on hold
einen Rückruf versprechen	promise a return call
prompt zurückrufen	return calls promptly
sofort zurückrufen	call back immediately
das Gespräch beenden	close the conversation

Zuhören und fragen / Listen and ask

den verärgerten Kunden beruhigen	calm the angry customer down
aufgeregte Anrufer beruhigen	placate excited callers
Wo liegt das Problem?	What seems to be the trouble?
Was haben Sie für ein Problem?	May I ask what the problem is?
Würden Sie mir bitte Ihr Problem schildern?	Would you be so kind as to describe your problem?
Ich mache mir ein paar Notizen.	I'll make a few notes.
Ich notiere mir das schnell.	I'm just taking this down.

15 BEIM KUNDENDIENST

Sich entschuldigen / Apologise

sich entschuldigen / sich beim Kunden entschuldigen	make an apology / apologise to the customer
sich bei jemandem entschuldigen müssen	owe someone an apology
Tut mir leid, daß uns ein Fehler unterlaufen ist.	Sorry about the mistake on our part.
eine Entschuldigung akzeptieren	accept an apology
höhere Gewalt	circumstances beyond our control

☛ Siehe auch *In der Verkaufsabteilung*, Seite 131 und 133.

Time for a smile

A lady wrote this to her laundry:
Dear Sirs,
You have just sent back some buttons with no shirts on them. Would you please return the shirts as well?

Lösungen anbieten / Offering solutions

Wie können wir Ihnen helfen?	How can we help you?
ein Problem lösen	solve a problem
ein Problem klären	sort a problem out
ein Mißverständnis klären	clear a misunderstanding up
sich sofort darum kümmern	see to it immediately
das Produkt zurücknehmen	take the product back
sein Geld zurückbekommen	have one's money returned
die Ware ersetzen	replace the article
die Dinge so schnell wie möglich in die Wege leiten	get things moving as quickly as possible
einen Fachmann schicken, um es zu reparieren	send a specialist to fix it

---

Time for a smile

"Madam, this handkerchief is perfect. Why the complaint?" –
"It was a sheet before I sent it to your laundry."

AT CUSTOMER SERVICE 15

A box of idioms

so tun, als ob	go through the motions
Die Firma tut nur so, als ob sie ihren Service verbessern würde.	The company's just going through the motions of improving its service.
Kurz gesagt, ...	To put it in a nutshell ...
nicht mehr weiterwissen	be at the end of one's tether
schmutzige Wäsche in der Öffentlichkeit waschen	air / wash one's dirty linen in public
Ich möchte die schmutzige Wäsche unserer Firma nicht in der Öffentlichkeit waschen.	I don't wish to air our company's dirty linen in public.
herziehen über	sound off
Der Kunde hat über unsere schlechte Qualität hergezogen.	The customer was sounding off about bad quality.
im Klartext	in plain English
Im Klartext, Ihr Produkt ist ein Stück Dreck.	In plain English your product is a pile of rubbish.
leicht verdientes Geld	money for old rope
Ihr Seminar war schlecht vorbereitet. Das war leicht verdientes Geld für Sie.	Your seminar was badly prepared. You got money for old rope.

Lerntip: Phrases statt words

Ob Sie sich unsere *phrases* dauerhaft merken, hängt davon ab, wie Sie lernen. Ein Beispiel: Lesen Sie folgende Zahlenreihe dreimal durch. Testen Sie anschließend Ihr Gedächtnis.

2-4-1-2-1-9-8-7-3-1-1-2-1-9-9-0

Fast unmöglich, nicht wahr? Bei mehr als 7 +/- 2 Einheiten ist das Kurzzeitgedächtnis überfordert. Wenn Sie aber bemerken, daß es sich um Weihnachten 1987 (24.12.1987) und um Sylvester 1990 handelt, haben Sie keine Probleme mehr, denn Sie haben die Zahlen zu sinnvollen Einheiten zusammengefaßt. Wörter machen erst in *phrases* Sinn. Und noch eins: Verbinden Sie beim Schreiben und Lesen den jeweiligen Ausdruck mit einer Situation, in der Sie ihn hätten anwenden können.

15 BEIM KUNDENDIENST

Master your phrases

Task 4: Find the opposite

patronise a company	.... one's custom
accept a shoddy product	.... a shoddy product
start a conversation	.... a conversation

Task 5: Fill in the prepositions

1. Calm the angry customer.................. .
2. Take the complaint ....
3. Clear misunderstandings ....
4. Try to sort the problem ....
5. Fix .... a service call, if necessary.

Task 6: Explain the following phrases

1. assess customers' needs
   A. deliver what the customer needs
   B. check what the customer wants
2. place the caller on hold
   A. ask the caller to wait
   B. put the caller in a queue
3. placate the customer
   A. calm him down
   B. return the money
4. register a complaint
   A. take a complaint down
   B. make a complaint

Task 7: Spot the mistakes

1. Our company takes accurate documentation for understood.
2. I don't believe a word I listen to.
3. That was easy money. Cash for old rope.
4. In simple English we're looking at bankrupt.

AT CUSTOMER SERVICE 15

Task 8: Complete the idioms

1. We don't want to air our d _ _ _ _ linen in p _ _ _ _ _ _ .
2. The personnel department doesn't really mean it.
   They're just g _ _ _ _ through the m _ _ _ _ _ _ .
3. We've got so many problems. I'm at the e _ _ of my t _ _ _ _ _ .

Task 9: Phrases in context

Jan: Customer service is quite a good department to work in, but I don't like working on the h _ _ _ _ _ _ d _ _ k .

Tom: Why not? I find the work okay.

Jan: That's because you're an extrovert and your English is better than mine. Nowadays it's difficult to c _ _ _ y with all the c _ _ _ _ _ _ _ s' w _ _ _ _ _ , so they often c _ _ _ _ _ _ n about the s _ _ _ _ _ _ .

Tom: Don't worry, Jan. They're people too, you know. The hotline is one way of k _ _ _ _ ng in t _ _ _ h with customers. And h _ _ _ _ _ ng people is more interesting than filing documents. Whatever happens, s _ _ y _ _ _ m!

--- Picture your idiom ---

I have to register a serious complaint: The components are not up to specs. Some items are defective, others are missing.

....
....................., we're totally disappointed with your service.

How to handle complaints

An elderly lady entered a pet shop and said to the shop assistant, "I'm rather disappointed with this canary you sold me yesterday. I've found out that it's a little lame."

"What do you want," replied the shop assistant, "a singer or a dancer?"

15 BEIM KUNDENDIENST

C Crossword power

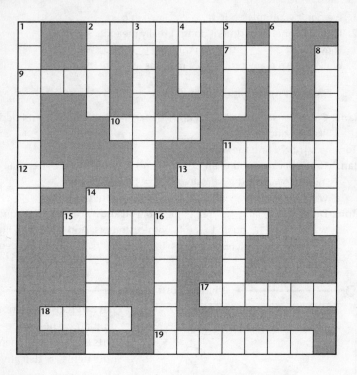

Across

2. Thank you for coming. This was really fast ✎. 7. I don't wish to ✎ our company's dirty linen in public. 9. The company has to ✎ the guarantee. 10. Tom knows how to ✎ with complaints. 11. I'm sorry to say that the components are not up to ✎. 12. I'm afraid we'll have to call ✎ all the products. 13. Well, we ✎ someone an apology. 15. We demand replacement for ✎ goods. 17. I'm at the end of my ✎. 18. I want my money ✎. 19. The company's just going through the ✎ of improving service.

Down

1. I want to ✎ most strongly. 2. In this case we'll repair the defective equipment on ✎. 3. You will not be receiving ✎. 4. The customer was sounding ✎ about bad quality. 5. We ✎ all objections very seriously. 6. Accurate documentation is taken for ✎. 8. I have to ✎ a serious complaint. 11. I'm afraid your ✎ hasn't met our expectations. 14. We will of course ✎ the article. 16. If you don't apologise we'll withdraw our ✎.

DIE RECHTSABTEILUNG

PART 16

THE LEGAL DEPARTMENT

A difficult job. This is the department which prepares all the contracts and agreements regarding employment, purchasing and sales. These people have mostly studied law. They should advise the company on any legal matters affecting the company. The legal department has to pay a great deal of attention to detail.

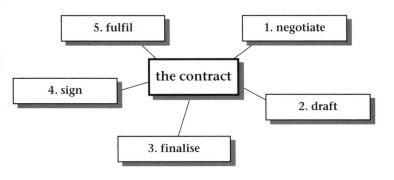

Business ethics: a lesson in honesty

A young man who was just about to embark on a business career went to see his grandfather, who had founded the family firm. "Remember, my boy, that in business honesty is still the best policy." – "Right, grandfather," said the grandson.

"But before you do anything else, read up on company law," the old man went on, "You'd be surprised at the kind of things you can do in the name of business and still be honest."

16 DIE RECHTSABTEILUNG

Activities in the Legal Department

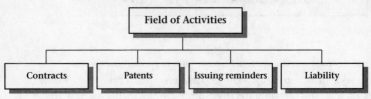

1. *Die Rechtsabteilung* / The Legal Department

Jura studieren	do a degree in law
in Jura promovieren	do a PhD / doctorate in law
zum Chef der Rechtsabteilung ernannt werden	be appointed head of the legal department
mit rechtlichen Angelegenheiten zu tun haben	deal with legal matters
als Patentanwalt arbeiten	work as a patent agent / attorney (US)
sich auf das Patentrecht spezialisieren	specialise in patent law
die Firma vor Gericht vertreten	represent the company at court
vor Gericht gehen	go to court
Prozesse führen	conduct cases
Verträge entwerfen, aufsetzen	draft contracts
Geschäftsbedingungen vereinbaren	agree terms of business
Verträge bearbeiten	process contracts
Verträge schließen	conclude contracts
die rechtliche Seite prüfen	check out the legal side
Uns sind die Hände durch einen früheren Vertrag gebunden.	Our hands are tied by a previous contract.
die rechtlichen Folgen abklären	research / investigate the legal implications
Mahnungen verschicken	issue reminders
Lizenzen vergeben / entziehen	grant / withdraw licences

THE LEGAL DEPARTMENT

> **Business ethics: a lesson in honesty**
>
> The company director was giving some advice to his son. "There are two things you must remember if you're going to succeed in business, my boy," he said. "The first is honesty and the second is wisdom."
> "What do you mean by honesty?" asked the son.
> "I mean that you should always keep your word once you've given it, no matter what the consequences." The boy nodded.
> "And wisdom, father?"
> "Never give your word."

2. *Verträge schließen* / Concluding contracts

Vereinbarungen / Verträge ausarbeiten	work out agreements / contracts
einen Vertrag überarbeiten	revise / rework a contract
die Vertragsbedingungen festlegen	stipulate the conditions / terms
einen Vertrag erstellen	draw up a contract
die endgültige Fassung eines Vertrags ausarbeiten	finalise a contract
eine Vereinbarung schließen	conclude make an agreement
ein Dokument unterschreiben	sign a document
eine Vereinbarung aushandeln	negotiate an agreement
ein Dokument gegenzeichnen	countersign a document
jemandem einen Vertrag erteilen	award somebody a contract
einen Vertrag / Staatsvertrag ratifizieren	ratify a contract / treaty
einen Vereinbarung umsetzen	carry out / execute an agreement
seine Seite der Abmachung einhalten	keep one's side of the bargain
einen Vertrag erfüllen	fulfil a contract
einen Vertrag buchstabengetreu erfüllen	fulfil a contract to the letter
eine Vereinbarung auf Treu und Glauben treffen	make a gentleman's agreement
einen Verkaufsvertrag / Vertretungsvertrag entwerfen	draw up a sales / agency agreement
einen Dauerauftrag vereinbaren	arrange a standing order

16 DIE RECHTSABTEILUNG

eine Vertrag formulieren	formulate a contract
einen Vertrag in Kraft setzen	put a contract into force
Vereinbarungen mit den neuen Angestellten sind alle schon festgelegt.	Agreements with the new employees are all cut and dry.
zu einer Übereinkunft kommen	reach / come to an agreement
eine Verpflichtung eingehen	enter into an obligation

3. *Verträge ändern* / Amending contracts

eine Klausel / einen Paragraphen modifizieren / abändern	modify / amend a clause / paragraph
Vertrag erneuern / verlängern	renew / prolong a contract
vom Vertrag zurücktreten	withdraw from the contract
einen Vertrag kündigen	terminate a contract
einen gültigen / ungültigen Vertrag anfechten	contest a valid / void contract
einen Vertrag für nichtig erklären	invalidate a contract
einen Vertrag nicht anerkennen	repudiate a contract
einen Vertrag aufheben	abrogate / cancel a contract
einen Vertrag annullieren	rescind / annul / revoke a contract
gegen einen Vertrag verstoßen	violate a contract
einen Vertrag brechen	break / breach a contract

Business ethics

It horrifies me that ethics is only optional at
Harvard Business School.
Sir John Harvey, former chairman of ICI

It is not the crook in modern business that we fear,
but the honest man who doesn't know what he is doing.
Owen D. Young

THE LEGAL DEPARTMENT 16

4. *Die Sprache der Verträge* / The language of contracts

ein Vertragsentwurf	a draft contract
Zweck des Vertrags	purpose of the contract
die Bedingungen einer Vereinbarung	the terms of an agreement
der Vertragsgeber / Vertragsnehmer ist berechtigt zu ...	the licensor / licensee shall be entitled to ...
die Firma X mit Sitz in ...	company X located in ...
Firmensitz	seat of business
im folgenden als Firma bezeichnet	hereafter the Company
im Namen von	for and on behalf of
im folgenden als Kunde bezeichnet	referred to hereafter / hereinafter as the customer
der Obengenannte	the aforesaid
der oben erwähnte Kunde	the above-mentioned customer
Die Laufzeit dieser Vereinbarung beträgt zwei Jahre.	The term of this agreement is two years.
eine Klausel aufnehmen	include a clause
wie in Klausel 4 festgelegt	as stated / stipulated in clause 4
Die Klauseln in dieser Urkunde sollen gelten für den Fall, daß ...	The stipulations in this document shall apply to ...
Die Klauseln dieses Vertrags haben Gültigkeit von ... bis ...	The stipulations of this contract are valid from ... till ...
Vertragszusätze	extensions to a contract
Ergänzungen zu diesem Vertrag bedürfen der schriftlichen Form.	Amendments to the contract require the written form.
Ergänzungen müssen schriftlich erfolgen.	Amendments must be in writing.
für den Fall, daß ...	in the event of ...
wenn der Kunde in Verzug gerät	if the customer is in arrears
Der Vertrag schließt eine Vertragsstrafe mit ein.	The contract includes a penalty clause.
eine Vertragsstrafe zahlen müssen	be obliged to pay a penalty
jemanden mit einer Vertragsstrafe belegen	levy a penalty on someone
Der Preis ist (nicht) Gegenstand von Abmachungen.	The price is (not) negotiable.

16 DIE RECHTSABTEILUNG

Zahlung erfolgt innerhalb von 90 Tagen.	Payment is within 90 days.
Zahlung 30 Tage nach Erhalt der Ware.	Payment 30 days after receipt of goods.
beginnend mit dem 15. August	commencing 15 August
Zahlung im voraus	payment up front / in advance
Auftraggeber / Vertreter	principal / agent
gültig nur bei Vertragsabschluß	subject to contract
seine Verpflichtungen aus dem Vertrag erfüllen	conduct and perform one's tasks

Time for a smile

When a person with experience meets a person with money, the person with experience will get the money. And the person with money will get some experience.

Leonard Lauder

 Master your phrases

Task 1: Verbs around a contract

a _ _ _ d   a _ _ _ _ _ e
            (a contract)
a _ _ _ l   a _ _ _ d

c _ _ _ _ l   c _ _ _ _ _ _ e
            (a contract)
c _ _ _ _ _ t   c _ _ _ _ _ _ _ _ _ n

THE LEGAL DEPARTMENT 16

Task 2: Word builder's corner

The first has been done for you.

The verb	and its noun
amend a contract	make an *amendment*
extend the contract	add an ....
penalise someone	levy a ....
sign a contract	put a .... to a contract

5. *Patente & Lizenzen* / Patents & Licences

ein Patent beantragen	apply for a patent
Patent anmelden	file a patent / take out a patent
eine Erfindung patentieren	patent an invention
ein Patent schützen	protect a patent
eine Erfindung durch Patent schützen	put an invention under patent
an das Patentamt schreiben	write to the Patent Office
ein Patent beanspruchen	claim (right to) a patent
den Patentgegenstand beschreiben	describe the object of a patent
ein Patent / eine Lizenz verletzen	infringe on a patent / licence
ein Patent umgehen	get round a patent
einen Patentstreit verlieren	lose a patent litigation
eine Patentgebühr bezahlen	pay a patent fee
zum Patent angemeldet	patent pending
zum Patent angemeldet sein	have a patent pending
der Patentinhaber sein	be the patentee
ins Patentregister eintragen	enter in the Patent Register
Patent erteilen	issue / grant a patent
ein Patent erhalten	obtain a patent
eine lizenzierte Erfindung verwenden	use an invention under licence
Lizenzgebühren zahlen	pay royalties
eine Lizenz erneuern	renew a licence
eine Lizenz entziehen	revoke a licence
ein eingetragenes Warenzeichen beantragen	apply for a registered trademark

16 DIE RECHTSABTEILUNG

ein Warenzeichen herausgeben	issue a trademark
ein Warenzeichen erhalten	receive a trademark
ein Warenzeichen eintragen lassen	register a trademark
gegen ein Warenzeichen verstoßen	infringe a trademark
ein Warenzeichen tragen	bear / display a trademark

6. *Haftung* / Liability

für ein Produkt haftbar sein	have liability for a product
für etwas haften	be liable for something
Haftung übernehmen	accept liability
wirklichen Grund zur Klage haben	have real cause for complaint
Waren beweisen sich als unbefriedigend.	Goods prove defective.
beträchtliche Unannehmlichkeiten bereiten	cause considerable inconvenience
eine Reklamation anerkennen	approve a claim
den Schaden wiedergutmachen	make amends
einem Kunden entgegenkommen	meet a customer halfway
Teile umtauschen	exchange parts
nicht zufriedenstellende Ware zurücksenden	return unsatisfactory goods
Geld erstatten	refund money
eine unberechtigte Reklamation ablehnen	refuse an unjustified claim
sich von jeder Haftung frei fühlen	feel free of any liability

☞ Siehe auch *Beim Kundendienst*, Seite 156 ff.

Advice from the expert

Experience teaches you that the man who looks you straight in the eye, particularly if he adds a firm handshake, is hiding something.

Clifton Fadiman

THE LEGAL DEPARTMENT

7. *Vor Gericht gehen* / Going to court

gerichtlich gegen jemanden vorgehen	bring a legal action against somebody
jemanden verklagen	prosecute / sue somebody
wegen Entschädigung prozessieren	litigate for indemnification / compensation
auf Entschädigung verklagen	sue for damages
einen Prozeß anstrengen	bring a law suit against somebody
gerichtliche Schritte unternehmen	take legal steps / proceedings
aus dem Gerichtssaal geworfen werden	be thrown out of court
einen Anwalt beauftragen	engage a lawyer / an attorney / solicitor
auf Zahlung drängen	press for payment
gegen einen Schuldner gerichtlich vorgehen	proceed against a debtor
eine Forderung anfechten	contest a claim
eine Vorladung zustellen	serve notice / a summons
vor Gericht bringen	take to court
vor Gericht erscheinen	appear in court
einen Vergleich aushandeln	negotiate a settlement
gerichtlich und außergerichtlich	in and out of court

Master your phrases

Task 3: Guided translation

1. After two years the patent finally (*erteilen*).
2. Our competitor refused to (*Lizenzgebühren zahlen*).
3. They tried to (*das Patent umgehen*).
4. However, they didn't succeed. They (*unser Patent verletzen*).
5. We had to (*rechtliche Schritte unternehmen*).
6. But nevertheless we (*Patentstreit verlieren*).

16 DIE RECHTSABTEILUNG

Picture your idiom

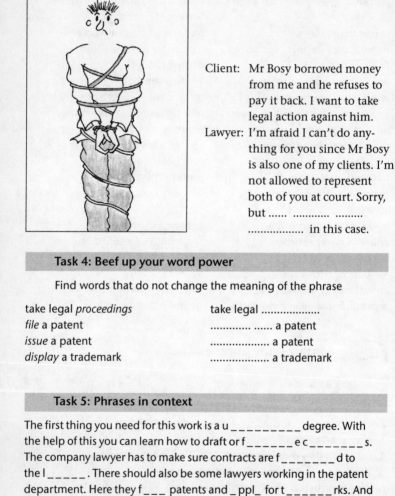

Client: Mr Bosy borrowed money from me and he refuses to pay it back. I want to take legal action against him.

Lawyer: I'm afraid I can't do anything for you since Mr Bosy is also one of my clients. I'm not allowed to represent both of you at court. Sorry, but .... in this case.

Task 4: Beef up your word power

Find words that do not change the meaning of the phrase

take legal *proceedings*	take legal ....
file a patent	.... a patent
issue a patent	.... a patent
display a trademark	.... a trademark

Task 5: Phrases in context

The first thing you need for this work is a u _ _ _ _ _ _ _ _ _ degree. With the help of this you can learn how to draft or f _ _ _ _ _ _ e c _ _ _ _ _ _ _ _ s. The company lawyer has to make sure contracts are f _ _ _ _ _ _ _ d to the l _ _ _ _ _ . There should also be some lawyers working in the patent department. Here they f _ _ _ patents and _ ppl_ for t _ _ _ _ _ _ rks. And when a competitor i _ _ _ _ _ _ es on a p _ _ _ _ t they must fight a patent l _ _ _ _ _ _ _ _ n. It's very tiring and detailed work.

THE LEGAL DEPARTMENT 16

Lerntip: Vorteile der Lernkartei

1. Gelernte Karten stecken wir in das nächste Fach des Kastens. Wo immer wir das Lernen unterbrechen, wir nehmen es genau dort auf, wo wir stehengeblieben sind. Wir machen weiter mit der ersten Karte des jeweiligen Kartenpäckchens.
2. Die Kartei gibt uns Rückmeldungen über unsere Fortschritte. Der Lernerfolg ist optisch sofort sichtbar.
3. Karteikarten sind klein und handlich. Phrases, die nur schwer in den Kopf wollen, können wir in der Tasche überall mitnehmen.
4. Mit den Karteikarten wehren wir uns gegen Zeitverschwendung. Wann immer man versucht, uns die Zeit zu stehlen, greifen wir zu einem kleinen Päckchen Karten.
5. Die Lernkartei meldet, wann es für uns Zeit zum Wiederholen wird. Wiederholung ist angesagt, sobald ein Fach gefüllt ist.
6. Durch die Abmessungen der einzelnen Fächer wiederholen wir in sinnvollen, immer größer werdenden Abständen.
7. Mit der Kartei arbeiten wir rationell. Es wird immer nur der Wortschatz wiederholt, der vergessen wurde. Das Überlernen des bereits gekonnten Stoffes wird vermieden.
8. Schwerer Wortschatz, den wir vergessen haben, wandert in das erste Fach. Er wird so oft wieder vorgelegt, bis auch er beherrscht wird. Dies ist vielleicht einer der größten Vorteile der Kartei.
9. Durch gezieltes Ordnen entsteht die "On-the-job-Kartei" für den Schreibtisch Ihres Arbeitsplatzes. Sie enthält die "Learning-by-doing-Kärtchen". Hier sammeln Sie die Fachausdrücke Ihrer Branche.

Business ethics

Nothing is illegal if 100 businessmen decide to do it.

Buying and selling is essentially antisocial.
Edward Bellamy

16 DIE RECHTSABTEILUNG

C Crossword power

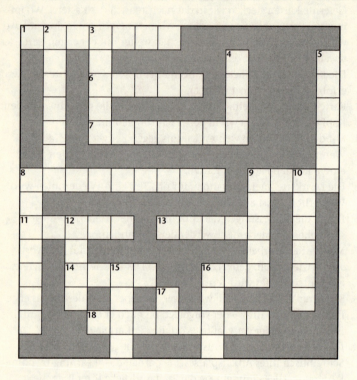

Across

1. If a complaint is justified you should 🖉 the claim 6. 🖉 a contract means to change it. 7. Strike a compromise and meet your customer 🖉. 8. A contract is safer than a gentleman's 🖉. 9. To 🖉 a patent means to apply for one. 11. A 🖉 contract is the opposite of a void one. 13. It's not easy to put an invention 🖉 patent. 14. This contract is null and 🖉. 16. I'm afraid we'll have to 🖉 you for damages. 18. He's trying to arrange a 🖉 order with us.

Down

2. Renew a contract is almost the same as to 🖉 it. 3. It's a pity we didn't 🖉 agreement. 4. If you break the contract we'll have to 🖉 a penalty on you. 5. The company is 🖉 for defective goods. 8. Payment up front is payment in 🖉. 9. Contracts are useless if they aren't put into 🖉. 10. Contracts must be fulfilled to the 🖉. 12. Do you remember? They do it with taxes and penalties. 15. Check all the clauses before you enter 🖉 an obligation. 16. If you break our patent, we'll bring a law 🖉 against you. 17. We won't infringe 🖉 your patent.

PART 17

FINANZEN UND BUCHHALTUNG

FINANCE AND ACCOUNTANCY

We all know that without our accountants we would all be in the red. A good budget helps to make our business run more smoothly and profitably and that's what we all want, isn't it? A company should keep within its budget, but there are other important financial matters: investing in stocks and shares, currency exchange rates and knowing what to do with the profit we hopefully make. Some people think that accountants are dry and boring like the figures they work with. Well, some "men of figures" are even the life and soul of the party.

Time for a smile

It's a socialist idea that making profits is a vice;
I consider the real vice is making losses.
Winston Churchill

Capitalism without bankruptcy is like Christianity without hell.
Frank Borman

17 FINANZEN UND BUCHHALTUNG

1. *Die Wirtschaftsprüfung* / The external audit

staatlich geprüfter Wirtschaftsprüfer sein	qualify as a certified accountant
als Buchprüfer arbeiten	work as a certified Public Accountant
die Wirtschaftsprüfer erwarten	expect the auditors
die Revision einer Firma arrangieren	arrange for the auditing of the company
Handelsbücher überprüfen	check the commercial books
die Revision einer Firma durchführen	do a company audit
einen Wirtschaftsprüfungsbericht erstellen	write an audit report
die Bücher prüfen	audit the books
Rechnungsprüfung durchführen	audit the accounts
einen Steuerberater konsultieren	consult a tax adviser

Time for a smile

Said the auditors sadly, "It looks
As if you've been hoodwinked by crooks.
We've discovered the ruse,
We have proof and accuse
Your accountant of cooking the books."

2. *In der Finanzabteilung arbeiten* / Working in Accountancy

Die Buchhalter sind dem Finanzdirektor unterstellt.	The accountants report to the finance director.
Kostenrechnungswesen studieren	study cost accounting
die Bücher führen	keep the books
die finanziellen Angelegenheiten einer Firma regeln	deal with the company's financial affairs
Geld beiseite legen	set money aside
Der Chefbuchhalter hat ein wachsames Auge auf die Bücher.	The chief accountant keeps a watchful eye on the books.
die Finanzen verwalten	manage the finances

FINANCE AND ACCOUNTANCY

Preispolitik entwickeln	develop a pricing policy
die Statistiken analysieren	analyse the statistics
eine Aufstellung machen	make a statement
die Zahlen präsentieren / zusammenstellen	present / compile the figures
mit der Finanzbehörde verhandeln	negotiate with the tax authorities
flüssige Geldmittel	cash-in-hand
von der Steuer absetzen	deduct from tax
steuerlich abzugsfähig	tax deductible
die Steuererklärung ausfüllen	fill in the tax forms
die Mehrwertsteuer abführen	pay value added tax
Mehrwertsteuer ist ein Durchlaufposten	value added tax is a transitory item
etwas abschreiben	write something off
Du kannst deinen Wagen über 4 Jahre abschreiben.	You can write your car off over 4 years.

What an accountant should not do

get into the red	rote Zahlen schreiben
manipulate figures	die Zahlen manipulieren
cook the books	die Konten frisieren
fiddle the taxes	Steuern hinterziehen
go bankrupt	Bankrott machen

The accountant ...

... is a man whom we hire to explain to the tax authorities that we haven´t made the money they think we have.

What an accountant should do

watch the cash flow	den Kapitalfluß beobachten
audit the books	die Bücher prüfen
balance the books	die Bücher abschließen
pay debts	Schulden bezahlen
get into the black	schwarze Zahlen schreiben

17 FINANZEN UND BUCHHALTUNG

3. *Das Budget verwalten* / Controlling the budget

ein Budget aufstellen	prepare a budget
die Budgetziele diskutieren	discuss the budget targets
das Budget verwalten	control the budget
das Budget beläuft sich auf ...	the budget amounts to ...
das Budget überprüfen	examine the budget
das Budget zuweisen	allocate the budget
im Budgetrahmen bleiben	keep within the budget
das Budget überziehen	exceed the budget
die Budgetabweichung erklären	explain the budget variance

4. *Rechnungsstellung* / Invoicing

Zahlungsmittel vereinbaren	agree the means of payment
eine Rechnung erstellen	raise an invoice
einem Kunden etwas in Rechnung stellen	bill / invoice a customer
eine Rechnung / Quittung ausstellen	make out an invoice / a receipt
auf die Rechnung setzen	enter on the invoice
pünktlich innerhalb der vereinbarten Zeit bezahlen	pay promptly within the agreed time
einen Betrag / eine Summe überweisen	transfer / remit an amount / a sum
Zahlungen einstellen	suspend payments
mit seinen Zahlungen im Rückstand sein	be in arrears with payments
seinen Zahlungsverpflichtungen nachkommen	meet one's payment obligations
Zahlungen wiederaufnehmen	resume payments
Skonto einräumen	grant / allow a cash discount
Skonto abziehen	deduct a cash discount
um Zahlungsaufschub bitten	ask for an extension
einen Kredit eröffnen / gewähren	open / allow a credit
die Bank mit ... beauftragen	instruct the bank to ...
eine Mahnung / letzte Mahnung schicken	send a reminder / final reminder

FINANCE AND ACCOUNTANCY

eine Rechnung abstempeln / unterschreiben	stamp / sign an invoice
Rechnungen begleichen	pay invoices / accounts
Rechnungsdatum notieren / eintragen	note / register the date of invoice
einen Mengenrabatt gewähren	grant a bulk / quantity discount
bar/ per Scheck bezahlen	pay cash / by cheque
eine Anzahlung machen	put down a deposit
Rabatt / Skonto gewähren	grant a discount
einen Scheck einlösen	honour a check
Inlungia hat ihren letzten Barscheck nicht eingelöst.	Inlungia didn't honour their last pay check.

The Balance Sheet
Incest with figures.

5. *Bilanzen* / Balance Sheets

die Bücher abschließen	close / balance the books
eine Vermögensaufstellung anfertigen	draw up a financial statement
die Bilanz erstellen / vorbereiten	do / prepare the balance sheet
die Bilanz konsolidieren	consolidate the balance sheet
den Bilanzwert angeben	state the balance sheet value
die Bilanz prüfen	audit the balance sheet
die Bilanzen analysieren	break the balance sheet down
Vermögenswerte erscheinen in der Bilanz	fixed assets appear in the balance sheet
Posten aktivieren	enter values in the book / enter on the asset side
die Abschlußbilanz erstellen	prepare the final balance
die Vermögenswerte neu bewerten	revalue / re-evaluate fixed assets
den ideellen Firmenwert berechnen	calculate goodwill value
die Bücher abschließen	balance the books
Wenn Sie die Bücher nicht ordentlich	If you don't balance the books,

17 FINANZEN UND BUCHHALTUNG

abschließen, bekommen Sie Probleme mit den Behörden.	you'll have problems with the tax authorities.
die Bilanz fälschen	falsify the balance sheet
die Bilanz veröffentlichen	publicise the balance sheet
die Bilanz prüfen	check the balance sheet
Schauen Sie mal diese Ergebnisse an.	Look at these results. We're in a real stew.
Wir sitzen in der Tinte.	

Finance

Finance is the art of passing money
from one hand to the other
until it finally disappears.
Robert Sarnoff

Lerntip: Lernen Sie Wortschatz statt Wörter

Prägen Sie sich stets
- das Verb mit seinen Präpositionen (Task 1),
- das Substantiv mit den treffenden Verben (Task 2) und
- Vorgänge in ihrer chronologischen Reihenfolge ein, und Sie lernen effektiver.

Time for a smile

The managing director called for a meeting because the company was in serious financial trouble. The secretary came in, tiptoed up to the director and whispered into his ear, "The accountant wants to have a word with you, sir. I think it's urgent."
"Not now!" replied the director angrily. "Can't you see that we're in the middle of an important meeting?" – "But he is phoning from the Bahamas, sir."

FINANCE AND ACCOUNTANCY 17

 Master your phrases

Task 1: Fill in the preposition

1. write something .... after five years
2. keep .... the budget
3. apply .... a loan
4. fill .... the tax forms
5. arrange .... the auditing of the company

Task 2: The A, B, C of books

Books should (not) be

a _ _ _ _ _ d   b_ _ _ _ _ _ d   c _ _ _ _ d

Ein Auge auf die Finanzen haben / Controlling finance	
das Betriebsvermögen erfassen	record the assets / business assets
verfügbares Kapital verwalten	control available funds
eine Gewinn-und-Verlust-Rechnung aufstellen	create a profit&loss account
den Umsatz vorhersagen	forecast sales
Gewinne voraussagen	predict profits
Gemeinkosten kürzen	reduce the overheads
die Herstellungskosten berechnen	calculate production costs
Preise knapp kalkulieren	cut prices fine
Wie hoch sind die Ist-Kosten?	What are the actual costs?
Inflation mit einkalkulieren	allow for inflation
eine Preiskontrolle einführen	establish control over prices
die Verbindlichkeiten überwachen	monitor the liabilities
Verbindlichkeiten begleichen	settle liabilities
Rechnungen ausstellen	invoice customers
In unseren Bedingungen steht, daß der Kunde im voraus bezahlt.	Our conditions state that the customer must pay in advance.
Mahnungen verschicken	send out reminders

17 FINANZEN UND BUCHHALTUNG

im voraus bezahlen	pay in advance
bar bezahlen	pay cash in hand
sofort bezahlen	pay as you go
Zahle direkt und du wirst keine Schulden machen.	Pay as you go then you won't get in debt.

> ### Time for a smile
>
> A famous English entrepreneur once said to an applicant for the job of senior accountant:
> "In your references it says you are an extremely dull fellow, without imagination, afraid of life and a 'yes-man' with no sense of humour at all. In most professions all these things would be a great drawback. In accountancy they are a positive asset."

6. *Schwarze oder rote Zahlen schreiben* / Be in the black or in the red

schwarze / rote Zahlen schreiben	be in the black / red
Unter dem Strich sind wir in den roten Zahlen.	The bottom line is that we're in the red.
an Wert verlieren / gewinnen	lose / gain value
einen Kredit beantragen	apply for a loan
kostendeckend arbeiten	break even
Das Wichtigste ist, daß wir kostendeckend arbeiten.	The important thing is that we break even.
Eine Währung verliert an Wert.	A currency depreciates.
Das Pfund sackt ab / purzelt nach unten / stürzt.	The pound dives / nosedives / plunges / tumbles.
Die Lira ist eingebrochen / abgebröckelt / abgestürzt.	The Lira has collapsed / crashed / crumbled / slumped.
Der Dollar gewinnt an Wert.	The dollar is gaining value.
Preise tendieren nach oben.	Prices are edging ahead.
Preise sind fest.	Prices are firm.
Unser Geld ist futsch.	Our money is down the drain.
Ein solch morsches Haus zu kaufen heißt Geld zum Fenster hinauswerfen.	Buying such a rotten house is money down the drain.

FINANCE AND ACCOUNTANCY

The way prices go up / increase and go down / decrease

kräftig anziehen	soar, surge	*nachgeben*	edge down, ease
sprunghaft steigen	jump, leap	*abrutschen*	slip, dip
jäh ansteigen	shoot up	*abstürzen*	slump
in die Höhe schnellen	rocket / sky rocket	*im Keller sein*	be at rock bottom

Time for a smile

"I heard the company was looking for an accountant."
"But didn't they take on a new accountant just a month ago?"
"Yes. That's the one they are looking for!"

7. *Investitionen* / Investment

Geld investieren	invest money
ein Investitionsprogramm entwickeln	develop a capital expenditure programme
die Wirtschaftlichkeit überprüfen	check on profitability
Investitionen finanzieren	finance capital projects
ausländische Investitionen kürzen	reduce foreign investments
um jeden Preis	at all costs
Die Firma muß um jeden Preis rationalisieren.	The company must rationalise at all costs.
auf dem Spiel stehen	be at stake
Bei diesem Geschäft steht eine Menge auf dem Spiel.	There's a lot of money at stake in this venture.
Viel zu teuer. Wir haben uns dumm und dämlich für das Gebäude gezahlt.	Much too costly. We paid an arm and a leg for this building.
Kapital einsetzen	employ capital
Kapitalerträge erhalten	get a ROCE (return on capital employed)
an die Börse gehen	go public
Aktien in Umlauf bringen	float shares
Anteilsscheine / Aktien kaufen	buy stocks / equities

17 FINANZEN UND BUCHHALTUNG

lahme Enten erkennen	identify the lame ducks
Investieren Sie nicht in schwache Unternehmen. Sie müssen lahme Enten erkennen können.	Don't put money in weak companies. You must be able to identify the lame ducks.
leicht verdientes Geld	easy money
Der Verkauf dieser Bücher ist leicht verdientes Geld.	Selling these books is real easy money.

A box of idioms

ein wachsames Auge haben auf	keep a watchful eye on
in der Tinte sitzen	be in a stew
bei der Steuer betrügen	fiddle the taxes
die Bücher frisieren	cook the books
rote / schwarze Zahlen schreiben	be in the red / black
pleite gehen	go bust
sich dumm und dämlich zahlen	pay an arm and a leg / pay through the nose
den Schlüssel zur Kasse haben	control the purse-strings
die Preise sind im Keller	prices are at rock bottom

A reminder

Dear customer,
If I were you
And you were me,
a different story this would be.
If you were me
And I were you,
This bill would not be overdue.
Since I am I
And you are you,
Please send your cheque in
P.D.Q.[1]

[1]Pretty damn quick

FINANCE AND ACCOUNTANCY 17

 Master your phrases

Task 3: Find opposites for the following

prices *shoot up*   prices ....
increase fixed costs   .... fixed costs
keep within the budget   .... the budget
gain value   .... value

Task 4: Find the words for the following definitions

1. do a course involving working out costs of things
2. send customers a bill
3. the value of a country's money goes down
4. check the accounts of a company

Task 5: Fill in the missing words

1. Customers must pay in ....
2. First rule in finance: don't .... the budget.
3. A bad purchase: It was money down the ....

---— Picture your idiom ———

"Did you know that we're expecting the auditors tomorrow?"
"God heavens! We'd better start ...."

FINANZEN UND BUCHHALTUNG

Task 6: Fill in the missing letters:

The financial men in the company have to know where to invest the p_ _ f _ _ _ . They can take the capital to the s _ _ _ _ /m _ _ _ _ _ in order to i _ _ _ _ _ in s _ _ _ _ s or e _ _ _ _ ies . It's a risky business. The company itself may go p _ _ _ _ _ . In order to create more liquidity, more available money, the Board may decide to f _ _ _ _ the company's s _ _ _ _ s. But who is it that checks the company's business? This, of course, is done by a new, unloved tribe of c _ _ _ _ _ _ _ _ _ _ _ . They m _ _ _ _ _r everything. Some people argue they have no vision.

Time for a smile

The company's personnel department had carefully interviewed thirty-eight people for the job of assistant to the financial director. The chief executive thought that one candidate – Charles – seemed ideal. Charles had been to a major public school. Not only was he a qualified accountant, but Charles also had a masters degree in business administration. He seemed fully aware of the latest creative accountancy techniques. "Charles," said the chief executive, "we've decided to offer you the job. And as you're so well qualified we've decided to start you off on a slightly higher salary than the one advertised. We'll pay you £48,000 a year."
"Thank you," replied Charles. "How much is that per month?"

Lerntip: Gehirngerechtes Lernen

Ihr Kurzzeitgedächtnis hat Platz für sieben Sätze von etwa zwölf Silben. Lernen Sie Wortschatz deshalb in Gruppen von 7+/−2. Festigen Sie eine Gruppe, bevor Sie zur nächsten übergehen.

GEHÄLTER UND LÖHNE

SALARIES AND WAGES

PART 18

> Well, we all want to get money and holidays for the work we do. The personnel department prepares our wage slips and pays us our salaries every month. What the employee expects and what he gets do not always match up. And there are a whole lot of legal issues involved with all of this.

Payroll Procedure

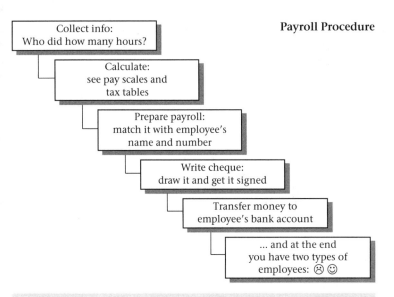

- Collect info: Who did how many hours?
- Calculate: see pay scales and tax tables
- Prepare payroll: match it with employee's name and number
- Write cheque: draw it and get it signed
- Transfer money to employee's bank account
- ... and at the end you have two types of employees: ☹ ☺

Time for a smile

My husband once worked for a company where they had a merit pay system. After six months they told him that he owed the company money.

Phyllis Diller

18 GEHÄLTER UND LÖHNE

1. Schlüsselwörter / Key-phrases

Lohn- / Gehaltspolitik	payment / wage policy
Lohngefüge	wage structure
Wie viele Mitarbeiter stehen auf unserer Gehaltsliste?	How many employees do we have on our payroll?
Tarifpolitik einführen	introduce a wage policy system
Was für eine Gehaltsstruktur haben Sie?	What sort of salary structure do you have?
außertarifliches Gehalt beziehen	get a negotiated salary
die Löhne einfrieren	introduce a wage freeze
auf der Gehaltsliste einer Firma stehen	be on the payroll of a company
In welcher Lohngruppe bin ich?	Which pay bracket am I in?
Welcher Gehaltsgruppe gehören Sie an?	Which salary group / pay bracket are you in?
eine Gehaltsüberprüfung fordern	demand a salary review
einen Lohn- / Gehaltsstreifen bekommen	get a salary / wage slip
einen Lohnvorschuß erhalten	get an advance
angemessene Vergütung anbieten	offer adequate remuneration
im Akkord arbeiten	do piece work
als Lohnsachbearbeiter arbeiten	work as a wages clerk
zum Leiter der Lohn-und-Gehalt-Abteilung ernennen	appoint head of Wages & Salary
Leistungszulagen und Vergünstigungen erhalten	receive incentives and benefits
die Lohnsteuerkarte sicher aufbewahren	keep the tax card safe
Einkommensteuererklärung einreichen	hand in one's tax return
Lohnsteuerfreibetrag beantragen	apply for tax allowance
seine Steuererklärung unterschreiben	sign one's tax sheet
Lohnsteuer bezahlen	pay income tax

SALARIES AND WAGES 18

2. *Ein Gehalt aushandeln* / Negotiating a salary

den Mindestlohn erhalten	get the minimum standard of pay
den Mindestlohn ablehnen	refuse the minimum wage
Tariflohn/-gehalt zahlen	pay the collective agreement
Wie hoch ist der Tariflohn?	What's the agreed wage?
einen Stundenlohn vereinbaren	agree an hourly wage
in der Gehaltstabelle nachsehen	check in the salary scale
das Gehalt aushandeln	negotiate the salary
um Gehaltserhöhung bitten	ask for a raise / rise / wage increase
Spitzenlöhne verlangen	demand top wages
den Umzug bezahlen	pay for / bear the costs of relocation
Gehalt und Extras in einem Paket anbieten	offer a salary package
eine Bonusvereinbarung treffen	negotiate a bonus agreement
einen Lohnanreiz anbieten	offer a wage incentive
Lohn / Gehalt erhöhen	raise a wage / salary
Lohn / Gehalt kürzen	lower a wage / salary

Time for a smile

Sir Harry Lauder, one of Scotland's most famous sons, was once interviewed by a reporter who asked him how he had managed to amass such a large fortune.
"Well, it's a long story," he replied, "and since we have no need of light while I'm telling it, let me blow out the candle."
"I don't think you need to tell me any more," replied the reporter.

3. *Die rechtliche Seite* / The legal side

einen Anstellungsvertrag aufsetzen	draft / draw up an employment contract
etwas im Vertrag festlegen	stipulate something in the contract
einen Vertrag abändern	make a change / amendment to the contract
die Gehaltsgruppe festsetzen	fix / set the salary grade / bracket

18 GEHÄLTER UND LÖHNE

Brutto- / Grund- / Anfangsgehalt in den Vertrag aufnehmen	state gross / basic / initial salary in the contract
einen befristeten / vorläufigen Arbeitsvertrag erhalten	get a limited / temporary contract of employment
zu Geheimhaltung verpflichtet werden	be pledged to secrecy
sein Gehalt geheimhalten	keep one's salary secret
eine Kündigungsfrist von 3 Monaten	a period of notice of 3 months
auf Probe eingestellt werden	be on a probationary period
die Vertragsbedingungen akzeptieren	accept the terms of the contract
eine Vereinbarung erfüllen	fulfil an agreement
seinen Verpflichtungen nachkommen	fulfil one's obligations
vor ein Arbeitsgericht gehen	go to an industrial tribunal

4. Große Erwartungen / Great expectations

Das Gehaltspaket beinhaltet ...	The salary package includes ...
soziale Leistungen	welfare benefits
Nebenleistungen / zusätzliche Leistungen bekommen	receive fringe benefits
eine Firmenwohnung erhalten	get a company flat
Unterkunft bezahlen	pay accommodation
einen Firmenwagen zur Verfügung stellen	provide a company car
Weihnachtsgratifikation gewähren	award a Christmas bonus
bezahlte Überstunden	overtime pay
bezahlter Urlaub	paid holiday
ein dreizehntes Monatsgehalt	a thirteenth salary
Leistungszulagen, Prämien	bonus rates
Prämienplan	bonus / merit system
eine Prämie verdienen	earn a bonus
Leistungsanreize motivieren die Belegschaft.	Perks motivate the workforce.
Sonderleistungen anbieten	offer extras
Gewinnbeteiligung für leitende Angestellte	profit-sharing for executives
in die Betriebskrankenversicherung eintreten	join the company's medical insurance

SALARIES AND WAGES 18

Bezahlung im Krankheitsfall	payment in the case of sickness
eine Altersvorsorgung haben	belong to an old age provision scheme
Firmenrente beziehen	receive / draw a company pension
Überstunden bezahlt bekommen	get paid for overtime
Was für Bonussysteme gibt es?	What sort of benefit schemes are there?
ein Arbeitsplatz mit geregelter Arbeitszeit	a nine to five job
Wenn er ein Manager bei Lopy sein will, muß er das Zeug dazu haben.	If he wants to be a manager at Lopy he must have what it takes.
eine gute Vergütung erwarten	expect a good remuneration
um Gehaltserhöhung bitten	ask for a raise / rise / wage increase

Lerntip: Was man nicht in Sekunden lernt, lernt man überhaupt nicht.

Die meisten Menschen glauben, sie prägen sich einen Ausdruck ein, wenn sie ihn mehrmals lesen. In Wirklichkeit nehmen sie ihn nur zur Kenntnis. Wie erreicht man eine optimale 'Verarbeitungstiefe' des Gelesenen?

Stellen Sie sich vor, Ihre Augen seien eine Kamera. So gebrauchen Sie Ihre Kamera:

1. Auf einen Ausdruck zoomen!
2. Abphotographieren!
3. Vor dem geistigen Auge sehen!
4. Kontrollieren und vergessen!

Keine Angst! Sie 'vergessen' nicht. Sie machen Ihr Gedächtnis nur bereit für die nächste Aufnahme. Die vier Schritte sollen nur Sekunden dauern, denn ein Lerngesetz lautet: "Was man nicht in Sekunden lernt, lernt man überhaupt nicht."

GEHÄLTER UND LÖHNE

5. *Complaints* / Klagen

sich unterbezahlt fühlen	feel underpaid
Angst vor der Zukunft haben	fear for the future
die Belegschaft in den Betriebshallen diskriminieren	discriminate against the workforce on the shop floor
über seine Verhältnisse leben	live beyond one's means
sich krank melden	take time off sick
einen Krankheitsurlaub nehmen	go on sick leave
eine Belohnung für seine Arbeit erwarten	expect a reward for one's work
Ein Arbeiter bei VMW muß bis zum Umfallen arbeiten.	A worker at VMW must work his fingers to the bone.
Du mußt dich zerreißen, um deine Kunden zufriedenzustellen.	You have to bend over backwards to satisfy your customers.
Der durchschnittliche Arbeiter hat keinen Pfennig in der Tasche.	The average worker doesn't have a penny to his name.
Mit all dieser Rationalisierung ist Paul angst und bange vor der Zukunft.	With all this rationalisation Paul fears for the future.
Dienst nach Vorschrift machen	work to rule
in einen wilden Streik treten	come out on a wild-cat strike

Words of wisdom

If work were such a splendid thing, the rich would have kept more of it for themselves.
Bruce Grocott

6. *Die Arbeitgeberseite* / The employer's side

Grundlohn bezahlen	offer basic rates of pay
einen Mindestlohn garantieren	guarantee a minimum wage
jemanden für überbezahlt halten	consider someone overpaid
Der Belegschaft von Lopy ging es noch nie so gut.	The workforce at Lopy has never had it so good.
Unsere Löhne liegen über dem Durchschnitt.	Our wages are above average.
das Weihnachtsgeld streichen	cancel the Christmas bonus

SALARIES AND WAGES 18

angemessene Vergütung anbieten	offer adequate remuneration
etwas von Gehaltsempfängern erwarten	expect something of salaried staff
Fehlzeiten abbauen	reduce absenteeism
schwarz arbeiten	to moonlight / go moonlighting
Die jetzige Arbeitergeneration ist nicht auf Zack.	This current generation of workers is not up to scratch.
einen Lohnstopp einführen	introduce / bring in a wage freeze
Löhne kürzen	cut / reduce wages
eine jährliche / automatische Lohn- / Gehaltshöhung anbieten	offer an annual increase / increment
ein reizvolles Gehalt / Lohn / Vergütung bezahlen	pay an attractive salary / wage / remuneration
nach Leistung bezahlen	pay according to performance
einen Bonus streichen / kürzen	cancel / reduce a bonus
harte Arbeit und Loyalität verlangen	expect hard work and loyalty
Akkordarbeit mit Zulage anbieten	offer piece work with bonus

A box of idioms

Wir sind kein Füllhorn. / Die Firma ist kein Goldesel.	We're not a horn of plenty.
kein Geld in der Tasche haben	be out of pocket
ohne einen Pfennig sein	not have a penny to one's name
sich zerreißen	to bend over backwards
Öl ins Feuer gießen	add fuel to the flames
sich am Riemen reißen	pull one's socks up
ein Zusage / Versprechen zurücknehmen	eat one's words

Proverbs

Geld ist die Wurzel allen Übels.	Money is the root of all evil.
am falschen Ende sparen	be penny wise, pound foolish

Time for a smile

He told her he was a self-made man.
She said she would accept that as an apology.

18 GEHÄLTER UND LÖHNE

 Master your phrases

Task 1: The rest is different!

You'll get free	acc..........................	in the guest house.
Remuneration	acc..........................	to performance.
Do you	acc..........................	the terms of the contract?

Task 2: Structure your phrases

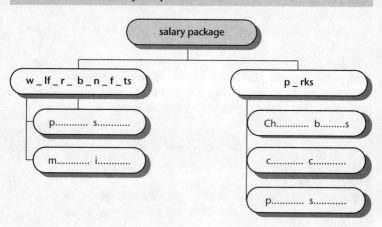

Task 3: Latin words and their Germanic synonyms

formal	informal
increase a wage	.... a wage
reduce wages	.... wages
make an amendment	make a .... (to a contract)
ask for a wage increase	ask for a wage ....

SALARIES AND WAGES 18

Task 4: Replace these phrases by an idiom

1. Try to get a better grip on your life.
2. Only do the minimum work that is required.
3. Work without paying taxes for it.
4. Money is the cause of bad things.

Task 5: Phrases in context

Fill in the gaps with an appropriate phrase, word or idiom:

It's always a bit of a problem when you have to n _ _ _ _ _ _ te your s _ _ _ _ _ or a b _ _ _ _ with your future e _ _ _ _ er. You have to be careful to include the right to a c _ _ _ _ _ y p _ _ _ _ _ y. From the employer's point of view he would like to see that employees are paid according to p _ _ _ _ m _ _ _ _ e and he expects h _ _ d w _ _ k and l _ _ a _ _ y. Neither side wants to t _ _ e s _ _ _ _ e a _ _ _ _ n.

Time for a smile

When I was young I thought money was the most important thing in life. Now that I am old I know that it is.
Oscar Wilde

Money doesn't always bring happiness. A man with twenty million dollars isn't any happier than a man with one million.

The three most beautiful words in the English language are: "Find cheque enclosed."
Dorothy Parker

18 GEHÄLTER UND LÖHNE

Picture your idioms

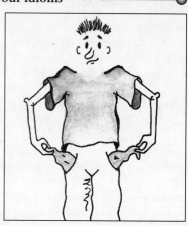

Tom: "I'm ....
As a matter of fact, I haven't got a penny to my name. I'll have to ask the boss for an increase."

Bob: "Don't expect much terms of raises. Our boss's philosophy is that work should be it's own reward."

Bob: "Well, did you ask the boss for a pay raise? How did he react?"

Tom: "He said that the company was not a horn of plenty and that money was the ...."

Time for a smile

A newly married manager went to his boss to ask for a rise.
"I'm sorry to trouble you, sir, but my wife wonders if it might at all be possible for you to raise my salary."
The boss looked at him thoughtfully and said, "Well, in that case I'm going to ask my wife if she thinks I should raise your salary."

SALARIES AND WAGES 18

Lerntip: Wandeln Sie auf Ihren 'Gedankengängen'

Schreiben Sie in die Mitte eines Blattes einen Ausdruck, der Ihnen einfällt. Tasten Sie sich von diesem Wort zum nächsten. Logik und Reihenfolge spielen keine Rolle. Gelangen Sie an das Ende eines 'Gedankenganges', schlagen Sie eine Abzweigung ein oder kehren zum Ausgangswort zurück und beginnen aufs neue. Ihre Gedankengänge erhalten die Form eines Assoziogramms. Die Striche, die Ihre Wörter verbinden, sind echte 'Gedankenstriche'. Manchmal fällt Ihnen nur ein deutsches Wort ein. Schlagen Sie es später nach. In einem zweiten Schritt versuchen Sie, Logik in Ihr Assoziogramm zu bringen. Alle Wörter, die Sie so zu Papier bringen, brauchen Sie sich so schnell nicht vorzunehmen, weil Sie mit beiden Gehirnhälften wiederholt haben.

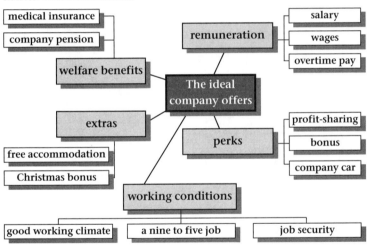

Words of Wisdom

It's true hard work never killed anybody, but why take the chance?
Ronald Reagan

Work is the curse of the drinking classes.
Oscar Wilde

Crossword power

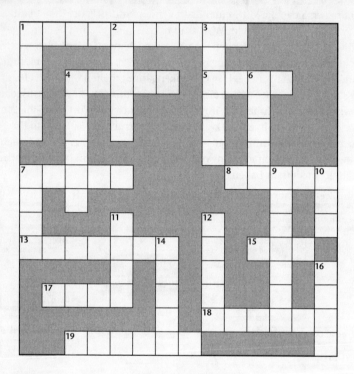

Across

1. Which <s> are you in? 4. What's a synonym for *increase* wages? 5. We don't strike, we just work to <s>. 7. You forgot to sign your tax <s>. 8. *draw up* an employment contract 13. How many workers are on your <s>? 15. They've come out on a wild-<s> strike. 17. We all want a <s> to five job, don't we? 18. Do you belong to any old age provision <s>? 19. I need an advance. I'm out of <s>.

Down

1. It's hard to do <s> work. 2. I'm going to ask the boss for a <s>. 3. I think I've <s> a bonus. 4. demand a salary *Überprüfung*. 6. opposite of *raise* wages. 7. Don't lose your wage <s>! 9. I'd like to ask for an <s> of £200. 10. You can't expect <s> wages the first year. 11. A worker at VMW must work his fingers to the <s>. 12. If he wants to be a manager at Lopy he must have what it <s>. 14. This is the second time he has been on sick <s> this month. 16. The wildcat strike only added <s> to the flames.

ARBEITGEBER UND GEWERKSCHAFTEN

PART 19

EMPLOYERS AND UNIONS

This is a large section. Why? Because it is concerned with people working together. And where people come together there will be friction. This section deals with workers' rights, going to court and all the rest of those unpleasant things around the workplace. Wouldn't the world be beautiful if it weren't for the people in it!

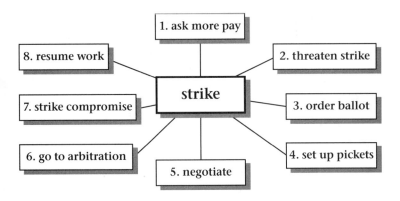

How to put an end to strikes

A company was having a problem with all the employees on a sit-down strike.
A very smart executive told the strikers that they might as well be comfortable, so he provided them with blankets and cases of brandy. When the brandy was half-consumed, the boss sent in ten young women to entertain the sit-downers. Then he brought over the strikers' wives so that they could see how comfortable their husbands were. That ended the sit-down strike.

19 ARBEITGEBER UND GEWERKSCHAFTEN

1. *Gutes Arbeitsklima* / Good working climate

Bei Beziehungen zwischen den Sozialpartnern geht es um ständiges Geben und Nehmen.	Industrial relations is a matter of give and take.
auf weibliche Arbeitnehmer Rücksicht nehmen	make provision for female employees
Tariflohn / -gehalt zahlen	pay the standard union rate / union wage rate
regelmäßige Arbeitszeit	regular working hours
keine Überstunden	no overtime
angemessene Entlohnung	adequate remuneration
zusätzliche Leistungen anbieten	offer perks
Prämien anbieten, um die Arbeitnehmer zu motivieren	offer bonuses to motivate employees
am Gewinn beteiligt sein	participate in profit sharing
ein sicherer Arbeitsplatz	a secure job
Aussicht auf Beförderung	prospect / chance of promotion
gute Zukunftsaussichten	good perspectives for the future
gute Menschenführung	good leadership
ein verständnisvoller Chef	an understanding boss
die Arbeitnehmer einbeziehen	involve employees
das Engagement der Arbeitnehmer fördern	promote employee commitment
selbständig arbeiten	work independently
eine verantwortungsvolle Arbeit	responsible work
Verantwortung übertragen	delegate responsibility
gerechte Beurteilung	fair evaluation
ein offenes Ohr für persönliche Probleme haben	be open for personal problems
Beziehungen fördern / verbessern	promote / improve relations
Verfahrensregeln ausstellen	issue codes of practice
eine großzügige Abfindung erhalten	get a golden handshake

Time for a smile

The only reason my boss never says an unkind remark about anyone is because he only ever talks about himself.

EMPLOYERS AND UNIONS

2. *Schlechtes Arbeitsklima* / Bad working climate

seine Pflichten als Arbeitgeber verletzen	abuse one's rights as an employer
jemanden nicht angemessen beschäftigen	give someone an inadequate job
die Rechte der Mitarbeiter beschneiden	curtail rights of employees
die Arbeitsplatzbestimmungen nicht beachten	fail to observe workplace regulations
Menschen am Arbeitsplatz diskriminieren	discriminate against people at work
jemanden diskriminieren	discriminate against somebody
ungerechtfertigt / willkürlich diskriminiert werden	be a matter of unfair discrimination
willkürliche Behandlung	arbitrary treatment
Sekretärinnen schikanieren	bully secretaries
Mobbing am Arbeitsplatz	bullying at the workplace
Untergebene herumkommandieren	boss subordinates around
jemanden ungerecht behandeln	treat someone unfairly
Privilegien abschaffen	abolish privileges
jemanden ständig kritisieren	constantly criticise somebody
jemanden seelisch quälen	torture someone psychologically
jemanden bei der Beförderung übergehen	pass someone over for promotion
Angestellte in Scheinselbständige umwandeln	convert employees into pseudo-self employed
einen Angestellten auf das Abstellgleis schieben	give someone a dead-end job
Schwarzarbeiter beschäftigen	employ moonlighters
unter Tarif bezahlen	pay below the agreed rates
eine miserable Abfindung erhalten	get a leaden handshake
verschiedene Dienstleistungen nach außen verlagern	outsource various services
eine Firma rationalisieren / abspecken	slim down / rationalise a company
das Unternehmen rationalisieren	delayer the enterprise

ARBEITGEBER UND GEWERKSCHAFTEN

3. *Rechte der Arbeitnehmer* / Workers' rights

Arbeitnehmerrechte schützen	protect employees' rights
die Rechte der Gewerkschaft beschneiden	limit / curtail trade union rights
das Lohngleichheitsgesetz besagt ...	the Equal Pay Act states ...
ein Recht auf Mutterschaftsurlaub haben	have a right to maternity leave
Recht auf Urlaub haben	be entitled to holidays
Recht auf bezahlten / unbezahlten Urlaub haben	have the right to unpaid / paid holidays / vacation
das Recht auf ... ausüben	exercise the right to ...
das Recht auf eine Mindestkündigungsfrist haben	have the right to a minimum period of notice
Das Sozialpartnergesetz besagt ...	It says in the Industrial Relations Act ...
auf Rechte verzichten	waive rights
Arbeitnehmerrechte verletzen	infringe employees' rights
ungerechtfertigte Kündigung	unjustified / unfair dismissal
eine Kündigung zurücknehmen	withdraw notice
die Kündigungsfrist nicht beachten	not to observe the period of notice

It's not easy to please the boss

When I take a long time – I'm slow.
When my boss takes a long time – he's thorough.
When I don't do it – I'm lazy.
When my boss doesn't do it – he's too busy.
When I do something without being told –
I'm trying to be smart.
When my boss does the same – that's initiative.
When I please my boss – that's being a creep.
When my boss pleases his boss – he's co-operating.
When I do well – my boss never remembers.
When I do wrong – he never forgets.

EMPLOYERS AND UNIONS 19

Magic Squares

1. Match the (A, B, C ...) with (1, 2, 3 ...).
If you ...

A. have the right to holidays	B. involve your employees	C. award them a generous compensation
D. make use of your rights	E. rationalise a company	F. take away people's rights
G. get a lousy compensation	H. give up your rights	I. boss your employees around

1. you exercise them	2. you give him a golden handshake	3. you waive them
4. you bully them	5. slim it down	6. you are entitled to them
7. you motivate them	8. they give you a leaden handshake	9. you abolish them

2. Put the numbers in the magic squares.

A =	B =	C =
D =	E =	F =
G =	H =	I =

3. When the answers are correct, all columns and rows will add up to the same number (15).

19 ARBEITGEBER UND GEWERKSCHAFTEN

Master your phrases

Task 1: What it means to have a good job

- 1. a s.........e job
- 2. r.........le work
- 3. an u.........g boss
- 4. good w.........g climate
- 5. p.........s of promotion
- 6. r.........r working hours
- 7. a.........e remuneration

(the ideal job)

---

4. *Vor Gericht gehen* / Going to court

den Rechtsweg beschreiten	take legal action
den Fall vor Gericht bringen	take the case to court
gegen seine Firma prozessieren	take one's company to court
sich an das Arbeitsgericht wenden	appeal to the industrial tribunal
beim Arbeitsgericht Beschwerde einlegen	complain to the tribunal
seine Beschwerde vortragen	present one's complaint
seine Rechte verlangen	demand one's rights
eine Abfindung beanspruchen	claim compensation
Arbeiter ungerechtfertigt entlassen	dismiss workers unfairly
Wiedereinstellung suchen	seek re-employment
gegen den Tarifvertrag verstoßen	infringe / violate the wage agreement
Unterstützung beantragen	claim benefits
von den Dienstjahren abhängen	depend on the length / years of service
den gesetzlichen Mindestlohn fordern	demand the statutory minimum wage

… EMPLOYERS AND UNIONS 19

auf dem Mindestlohn bestehen	insist on the minimum standard of pay
das Arbeitsverhältnis mit oder ohne Kündigung beenden	terminate the contractual relationship with or without notice
aus einem Vorsitzenden und zwei anderen Mitgliedern bestehen	consist of a chairman plus two other members
durch einen Anwalt vertreten werden	be represented by a lawyer
Zeugen benennen	name witnesses
zugunsten von … aussagen	make statements in favour of …
ausreichende Beweise für / gegen … beibringen	provide / supply sufficient evidence for / against …
Haarspalterei betreiben	split hairs
mit einer Sache vor ein Schiedsgericht gehen	go to arbitration with a matter
einen Fall untersuchen	investigate a case
Untersuchungen durchführen	conduct enquiries
durch eine gerichtliche Verfügung erzwingen	enforce by injunction
seinen Prozeß gewinnen / verlieren	win / lose one's case
Gerichtskosten übernehmen	incur court costs

A case of bullying

Unbelievable but true: A Spanish bank clerk who was promoted to managing director, took revenge on his ex-boss by demoting him to the position of office boy. Among his new tasks, the ex-boss had to copy out the local phone book by hand. Fortunately an industrial tribunal forced the new manager to pay compensation.

5. *Arbeitskämpfe* / Labour conflicts

Ein Grund zu streiken / A reason to go on strike

mit der Bezahlung / Arbeitszeit nicht einverstanden sein	disagree over pay / hours
mit den Arbeitsbedingungen unzufrieden sein	be dissatisfied with the working conditions

19 ARBEITGEBER UND GEWERKSCHAFTEN

die Lohnpolitik der Firmenleitung in Frage stellen	question the management's wage policy
die Personalpolitik kritisieren	criticise the personnel policy
ungerechtfertigte Lohnkürzungen befürchten	fear unjustified wage cuts
Gehaltserhöhung verlangen	demand a salary increase
einen Lohnstopp ablehnen	refuse to accept a wage freeze
für höhere Löhne demonstrieren	demonstrate for more pay
auf Lohnfortzahlung im Krankheitsfall bestehen	insist on sick pay
eine 35-Stunden-Woche fordern	demand a 35-hour week
Massenentlassungen ankündigen	announce mass redundancies
Arbeitsplätze wegrationalisieren	rationalise workplaces / jobs
gegen Überstunden protestieren	protest against overtime

A matter of justice

"No way!" said the boss. "I cannot give you two hours off for lunch. Think man, if I did that, I'd have to do the same for every person whose wife had just had twins."

In Verhandlungen eintreten / Enter into negotiations

die Angestellten / Arbeiter vertreten	represent the white collar / blue collar workers
mit dem Gewerkschaftsvertreter / Vertrauensmann die Forderungen erörtern	discuss the demands with the trade union representative / shop steward
mit der Betriebsleitung verhandeln	negotiate with management
Druck ausüben auf ...	bring pressure to bear upon ...
dem Druck der Gewerkschaften standhalten	resist pressure from trade unions
ein Tarifvertrag läuft aus	a collective agreement expires
in Tarifverhandlungen eintreten	enter into collective bargaining
ein Verhandlungsangebot machen	make an offer to negotiate
Das Angebot ist nicht verhandlungsfähig.	The offer is not negotiable.

EMPLOYERS AND UNIONS

eine Lohnanpassung versprechen	promise a wage adjustment
Nachbesserungen verlangen	demand rework / rectification
sich mit einem Angebot nicht zufriedengeben	be dissatisfied with an offer
bessere Konditionen aushandeln	negotiate better conditions
einen Kompromiß vorschlagen	suggest a compromise
bereit sein, Zugeständnisse zu machen	be prepared to make concessions
der Gewerkschaft auf halbem Wege entgegenkommen	meet the unions halfway
einen Kompromiß schließen	strike a compromise
zu einer Einigung kommen	come to an agreement
sich einig werden	establish common ground
ein ausgewogener Kompromiß	a balanced compromise
einen Kompromiß ablehnen	reject a compromise
die Verhandlungen vertagen	adjourn the negotiations
weder Sieger noch Besiegter sein	be neither victor nor vanquished
ein Angebot annehmen / ablehnen	accept / reject an offer
einen Schlichter bestellen	order a mediator
in die Schlichtung eintreten	go to arbitration
in Lohnstreitigkeiten vermitteln	arbitrate / mediate in trade disputes
Auseinandersetzungen an die Schlichtungsstelle verweisen	refer disputes to arbitration / mediation
die Friedensfrist beachten	observe the cooling-off period
annehmbar sein	be acceptable
ein zufriedenstellendes Ergebnis erzielen	reach a satisfactory result
den Arbeitsfrieden wiederherstellen	restore industrial peace
eine Basis für einen Kompromiß finden	find a basis for a compromise

Time for a smile

An employee went to see his boss about an increase in salary.
Employee: "Excuse me, sir, but I think it's time I had a raise. I've been working here for over ten years and doing the work of three men."
Boss: "Well, I must think about it, but what about these three men? Give me their names and I'll fire them!"

19 ARBEITGEBER UND GEWERKSCHAFTEN

In den Streik treten / Go on strike

die Tarifverhandlungen scheitern lassen	allow wage discussions to collapse
die Verhandlungen für gescheitert erklären	declare a breakdown in negotiations
eine Betriebsversammlung anberaumen	call a works assembly
abstimmen lassen	ballot members
durch Handzeichen abstimmen	vote by a show of hands
eine geheime Abstimmung durchführen	conduct a secret ballot (on strike action)
den Sieg davontragen	carry the day
Die militanten Arbeiter trugen einen Abstimmungssieg davon.	The militant workers carried the day at the ballot.
in den Ausstand treten	take industrial action
in den Streik treten	go on strike
die Belegschaft zum Streik aufrufen	call the men out
die Arbeit niederlegen / streiken	down tools
Sie hörten sich das Angebot an. Dann legten sie die Arbeit nieder.	They heard the offer. Then they downed tools.
nicht zur Arbeit erscheinen	fail to turn up at work
in den Streik treten	go out on strike
zum Warnstreik aufrufen	call a warning strike
nach Vorschrift arbeiten	work to rule
Bummelstreik führen	be on a go-slow
mit Aussperrung drohen	threaten a lock-out
Nächste Woche wird die Belegschaft in einen Bummelstreik treten.	Next week the workforce will introduce a go-slow.
zu einem wilden / inoffiziellen Streik aufrufen	call a wild cat / unofficial strike
Streikposten aufstellen	establish / set up pickets
den Zugang zum Betrieb durch Streikposten absperren	picket the company
die Streiklinie durchbrechen	cross the picket line
Streikbrecher verachten	despise the blacklegs / strike-breakers
Streikgelder erhalten	get strike pay
die Produktion stilllegen	bring production to a standstill

EMPLOYERS AND UNIONS

Die Kassen der Gewerkschaft sind gut gefüllt.　　The union's coffers are full.

A box of idioms

den Kopf über Wasser halten	keep one's head above water
Sein eigenes Süppchen kochen	have an axe to grind
ein Hühnchen mit jemandem zu rupfen haben	have a bone to pick with somebody
um den heißen Brei reden	beat about the bush
Reden Sie nicht um den heißen Brei herum. Sagen Sie Ihren Arbeitern, was Sie wirklich meinen.	Don't beat about the bush. Tell your workers what you really think.
stahlhart sein	be as hard as nails
ein Glückskind sein	be born with a silver spoon in one's mouth
sich hocharbeiten	work one's way up
während der Arbeit schlafen	lie down on the job
sich um eine Position rangeln	jockey for position

Time for a smile

A well-known actor decided to have his apartment redecorated from top to bottom, and hired a decorator for the job. In order to get off on the right foot, he presented the decorator with a couple of expensive front-row tickets for his show. After a month he received the bill. One of the items read: Four hours overtime watching customer sing and dance.

19 ARBEITGEBER UND GEWERKSCHAFTEN

Master your phrases

Task 2: Seven steps to re-employment

Match the words to the sentences.
Fill the number of the sentences in the appropriate boxes.

- ❏ represent
- ❏ present
- ❏ make statements
- ❏ enforce
- ❏ supply
- ❏ take
- ❏ costs
- ❏ incur
- ❏ court
- ❏ injunction
- ❏ witnesses
- ❏ evidence

What do you do if your boss has dismissed you unfairly?

1. You .... your case to the industrial tribunal.
2. A lawyer will .... you in ....
3. He will .... your complaint.
4. Make sure you .... sufficient ....
5. Name .... who will .... in your favour.
6. The tribunal will .... re-employment by ....
7. Your company will .... the court ....

Mere child's play? Well, it won't always work out as easy as that.

Task 3: Guided translation – A ritual in nine steps

1. The (*Tarifvertrag*) with the Trade Union (*ist ausgelaufen*).
2. The Union and the employers enter into (*Tarifverhandlungen*).
3. The employers' offer is not (*verhandlungsfähig*).
4. So the Union (*übt Druck aus auf*) the employers and (*ruft zu einem Warnstreik auf*).
5. The employers resist the pressure and the Union (*führt eine Abstimmung durch*).
6. The workers (*legen die Arbeit nieder*) and picket the companies.
7. The (*Lohnstreit*) is referred to (*Schlichtung*).
8. Both parties observe the (*Friedenspflicht*).
9. The employers are ready to (*den Arbeitern auf halbem Weg entgegenkommen*). A (*ausgewogener Kompromiß*) is found.

EMPLOYERS AND UNIONS

Task 4: Correct the following idioms

1. We've got a new manager. He's as hard as steel.
2. Hey. You've been saying bad things about me.
   I've a hen to pluck with you.
3. He's a pushy type. Always commanding me around.
4. He was born with a golden fork in his mouth.
5. What lousy quality! Were you sleeping on the job?

Picture your idiom

Bob: "This is the third time our shop steward has called for a work assembly. What is it about time?"

Tom: "Well, if you ask me, he has his own .... in this matter. He´s very ambitious, you know."

19 ARBEITGEBER UND GEWERKSCHAFTEN

Our working climate has suffered a lot.
There are two colleagues in our department who are .... as chief accountant.

> **Great lies of management**
> - "We're reorganising to better serve our customers."
> - "It's going to be a very tough year."
> - "Don't expect much in terms of raises. Work should be its own reward."
> - "Employees are our most valuable asset."
> - "The future is bright."
> - "Training is a high priority."
> - "We reward risk-takers."
> - "I have an open-door policy."
> *Scott Adams. The Dilbert Principle*

PART 20

DIE WELT DER VERSICHERUNG

THE WORLD OF INSURANCE

We all get afraid of things or worry about future scenarios now and again. And this is the time when the insurance salesman has easy access to us. He can sell us policies to cover us against any risk. He plays on our fears. Nowadays you can insure almost anything. Perhaps we could take out insurance against readers not buying this book?

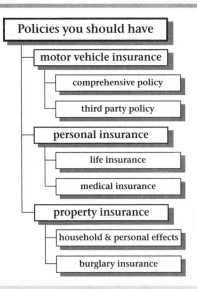

Time for a smile

Life insurance is a bit like fun:
the older you get, the more you pay for it.

Life insurance is something
that keeps a person poor all his life so that he can die rich.

DIE WELT DER VERSICHERUNG

1. *Versicherer* / Insurers

als Versicherungsgeber arbeiten	work as an insurer
ein Versicherungsgeschäft betreiben	transact insurance business
für eine Versicherungsgesellschaft arbeiten	work for an insurance company
eine Versicherungsdirektion leiten	run an insurance head office
Leiter einer Bezirksdirektion sein	be head of a regional head office
ein hauptberuflicher / nebenberuflicher Vertreter	a full-time / part-time agent
als Versicherungsvertreter einstellen	hire an insurance agent
einen Versicherungsmakler beauftragen	commission an insurance broker
in der Schadensabteilung angestellt sein	be employed in the claims department
einen Schadensregulierer hinzuziehen	call in the claim adjuster

2. *Versicherungsaufgaben* / Insurance tasks

ein Risiko versichern	underwrite a risk
eine Versicherungsprämie berechnen	charge a premium
die Prämie festsetzen	fix the premium
den Versicherungsbeitrag festsetzen	fix the premium rates
Policen verkaufen	sell insurance
den Versicherungsnehmer angeben	state the policy holder
eine Versicherungspolice ausstellen	issue a policy
eine Versicherung kündigen	cancel a policy
die Versicherungssumme erhöhen	raise the sum insured
einen Vertrag verlängern	prolong a contract
eine Versicherungsprovision erhalten	get an insurance commission

3. *Was man versichert* / What to insure

Risiken versichern	insure risk / underwrite risks
eine Personenversicherung abschließen	take out personal insurance
eine Lebensversicherung beantragen	apply for life insurance
eine Lebensversicherung mit festem Auszahlungstermin abschließen	take out an endowment insurance

THE WORLD OF INSURANCE 20

gegen Einkommensverlust versichern	insure against loss of income
gegen Unfall versichert sein	be insured against accidental event
ein Gebäude feuerversichern	insure a building against fire
Eigentum / Sachen versichern	insure property
eine Hausratversicherung abschließen	conclude a household & personal effects insurance
eine Diebstahlversicherung unterzeichnen	sign burglary insurance
Waren gegen Verlust / Beschädigung versichern	insure goods against loss / damage
eine Reiseversicherung haben	have a travel policy
Schadensersatz beantragen	claim indemnification

Time for a smile

Agent: "Now that you are married, you should have some insurance."
Lady: "Why? My husband isn't dangerous."

4. *Wie man Versicherungsnehmer wird* / How to become a policy holder

Sind Sie versichert?	Do you have cover?
Die Deckung ist abgelaufen.	Cover has expired.
einen Versicherungsantrag anfordern	request a proposal form
die Versicherungsbedingungen aushandeln	negotiate the terms of the policy
eine Versicherungspolice abschließen	underwrite a policy
einen Versicherungsvertrag abschließen	conclude an insurance contract
einen Versicherungsvertrag unterzeichnen	sign a contract of insurance
einen Versicherungsschein anfordern	request an insurance certificate
die Versicherungsprämie bezahlen	pay the premium
eine abgelaufene Police erneuern / verlängern	renew / extend / prolong a policy
eine Police ergänzen	amend a policy

ein Monat nach Ablauf der Versicherung a month after the date of expiry
Wann läuft die Versicherung aus? When does the policy expire?

5. Was man nicht tun sollte / What you should not do

das Kleingedruckte nicht lesen	ignore the fine print
die Beiträge nicht zahlen	not pay the premiums
etwas absichtlich beschädigen	do deliberate damage
einen Versicherungsbetrug begehen	commit insurance fraud
die Versicherung betrügen	swindle the insurance
falsche Angaben machen	give false information
Schaden absichtlich herbeiführen	bring about damage intentionally
Unfall vortäuschen	pretend there was an accident
Es war höhere Gewalt.	It was an act of God.

6. Schadensregulierung / Settlement of claims

Schadensersatz fordern	claim damages / indemnity
einen Schadensnachweis erbringen	substantiate a claim
einen Schadensfall bearbeiten	handle / process a claim
Schadensersatzansprüche prüfen	check claims
Schadensersatzansprüche nicht anerkennen	reject claims
einen Schaden regulieren	settle a claim
den Schaden feststellen	assess the damage
Wertminderung berücksichtigen	take into account depreciation in value
einen Gutachter beauftragen	commission an assessor
einen Sachverständigen hinzuziehen	consult / call in an expert
Schadensersatz zusprechen	award damages
eine Pauschalentschädigung anbieten	offer a lump-sum settlement

7. Was man erwarten kann / What to expect

Schutz anbieten	offer cover
Versicherungsschutz gewähren	give insurance cover
eine kurze Wartezeit	a short qualifying / waiting period
schnelle Schadensregulierung	prompt settlement of a claim
die Prämie zurückerstatten	refund the premium
Schadensersatz zahlen	pay indemnity / indemnification
Versicherungsansprüche unbürokratisch bearbeiten	process claims without red tape
Schadensersatz leisten	pay out / provide compensation
die volle Haftpflicht übernehmen	incur full liability
den Verlust des Antragstellers entschädigen	indemnify the claimant for loss
für die Folgeschäden aufkommen	compensate / indemnify consequential loss
Schadensersatz erwarten	expect compensation
den Versicherungsnehmer entschädigen	compensate the policy holder
Begünstigte(r) eines Versicherungsanspruchs sein	be the beneficiary of a claim

Time for a smile

An insurance salesman was trying to sell a policy to a factory owner. "I've got all the insurance I need," said the executive. "Fire, accident, employer's liability, the lot, so don't waste your time."
"Are you covered against floods?" asked the salesman. "Floods?" said the businessman with interest. "How do you arrange a flood?"

DIE WELT DER VERSICHERUNG

 Master your phrases

Task 1: Beef up your word power

Find a synonym.

extend a policy	.... a policy
claim damages	claim ....
provide compensation	.... compensation
a short *qualifying* period	a short .... period

Task 2: What to do with a policy

a................ for	c................ e	p................g
a...............d	a policy	r................w
c...............l	e................d	s................n

Task 3: Guided translation

1. Would you please send me the (*Versicherungsschein*)?
2. I'm afraid our company cannot (*dieses Risiko versichern*).
3. You'll have to (*Schaden nachweisen*).
4. It looks as if the damage (*absichtlich herbeiführen*).
5. Committing (*Versicherungsbetrug*) is a serious crime.

Time for a smile

An insurance broker had just tied up a big deal with the boss of a chemical plant, agreeing to insure his warehouse for a large sum. As he signed the contract, the businessman asked jokingly, "And what do I get if the place burns down tonight?"

"At least ten years," said the insurance broker.

THE WORLD OF INSURANCE 20

8. *Das Auto* / The motor car

eine Pflichtversicherung	a compulsory insurance
eine Versicherungsdeckungskarte ausstellen	issue a cover note
eine KFZ-Versicherung abschließen	take out automobile insurance (US) / motor vehicle insurance (GB)
eine Haftpflichtversicherung haben	have third party cover
Teilkaskoversicherung mit Selbstbeteiligung	third party fire & theft policy
Vollkaskoversicherung abschließen	take out a comprehensive policy
eine Verkehrs- / KFZ- / Unfallversicherung haben	have a traffic / motor car / accident policy
eine Unfallmeldung machen	make an accident report
seinen Schadensfreiheitrabatt verlieren	lose one's no-claims bonus

Time for a smile

A certain owner of a department store reported a fire in his establishment the very day he signed a new fire insurance policy. The company suspected fraud, but had no proof. The only thing the manager could do was to write the policy holder the following note:

Sir,
You took out an insurance policy with us at 10 a.m. and your fire did not break out until 3.30 p.m. Will you please explain the delay?

9. *Das soziale Netz* / Social security

Pflichtkrankenversicherung zahlen	pay into compulsory health insurance
eine private Krankenversicherung abschließen	take out private health / medical insurance
Krankengeld beantragen	claim sick pay
Krankengeld beziehen	draw sick pay
Sozial- / Rentenversicherung zahlen	pay social insurance

DIE WELT DER VERSICHERUNG

Sozialversicherung / Altersversicherung / Altersversorgung beziehen	participate in the social insurance system / old-age insurance / old-age pension scheme
Altersrente beanspruchen	claim an old age pension
Zahlung im Todesfall	payable at death
seinen Sozialversicherungsbeitrag zahlen	pay one's national insurance contribution

Time for a smile

An insurance salesman was writing a policy for a zookeeper.
"Have you ever had any accidents?"
"No, not really," said the zookeeper."
"Any injuries?"
"Well, once a rattlesnake bit me and an elephant stepped on my foot."
"Don't you call those accidents?" asked the insurance agent.
"No," replied the zookeeper, "they did it on purpose."

Anspruch auf Rente erheben aus:	claim benefit from a:
Beamtenpension	civil servant's pension
Ruhestandsgeld	retirement pension
Invalidenrente	disablement pension
Arbeitslosenunterstützung	unemployment benefit / dole
Hinterbliebenenrente	dependent's pension
Witwenrente	widow's pension
Waisengeld	orphan's pension

THE WORLD OF INSURANCE 20

A box of idioms

Vorsorgen ist besser als heilen.	An ounce of prevention is better than a pound of care.
die 1000-Dollar-Frage	the $64,000 question
Welches Risiko sollte man versichern? Das ist die 1000-Dollar-Frage.	What risk should you cover? That's the $ 64,000 question.
Vorsicht ist besser als Nachsicht.	Foresight is better than hindsight.
Es kann immer etwas passieren.	Something can always happen.
Vorsicht ist besser als Nachsicht.	Forewarned is forearmed.
Geld rinnt ihm wie Sand durch die Finger.	He spends money like water.
Zu viele Versicherungen. Uns rinnt das Geld wie Sand durch die Finger.	Too many insurance policies. We're spending money like water.
ohne Haken und Ösen	no strings attached
Und hier ist Ihre Police. Alles für £100 und ohne Haken und Ösen.	And here's your policy. All for £100 and no strings attached.

 ## Master your phrases

Task 4: Let's test you on those nasty little words

1. Has he insured the goods .... loss?
2. I think he brought .... the damage intentionally.
3. We have to take the depreciation in value ....
4. Afterwards we'll indemnify the claimant .... loss.
5. Life insurance is only payable .... death.
6. Did he take .... vehicle insurance, too?

20 DIE WELT DER VERSICHERUNG

Task 5: Let's go woggling again

Replace the *woggles* with a suitable word.

1. Do I have third party *woggle*?
2. Will I lose my no-claims *woggle*?
3. Do I participate in an old-age pension *woggle*?
4. May I draw sick *woggle*?

Task 6: Phrases in context

Ron: Hey, Tom, have you t _ _ _ _ o _ _ i _ _ _ _ _ _ _ _ _ for your car?
Tom: Well, I'm still thinking about it. Perhaps I can still use my English one.
Ron: That won't work. You're not on holiday. You should have at least th _ _ _ _ _ _ _ y c _ _ _ _ .
Tom: What sort of pr _ _ _ _ _ do they ch _ _ _ _ here in Germany?
Ron: It's about the same as in England. And that reminds me. I hope you've also arranged m _ _ _ _ _ l _ _ _ _ _ _ _ _ e . Everyone can get ill. And you know you're obliged to p _ _ _ _ _ _ _ _ _ _ e in the s _ _ _ _ l insurance s _ _ _ _ m .

Magic Squares

Match the phrases (1, 2, 3 ...) with the words (A, B, C ...).

Put the numbers in the magic squares. All columns and rows will add up to the same number (15).

1. In the case of an accident you'll lose your ...
2. Foresight is better than ...
3. It was ...
4. An ounce of prevention is better than ...
5. Don't forget to read the ...
6. A policy with ...
7. The insurer suspects ...
8. I'm afraid your policy has ...
9. Forewarned is ...

THE WORLD OF INSURANCE 20

A. expired
B. an act of God
C. a pound of cure
D. no-claims bonus
E. fineprint
F. forearmed
G. no strings attached
H. an insurance fraud
I. hindsight

A =	B =	C =
D =	E =	F =
G =	H =	I =

Lerntip: Die Lernlandschaft – Wortschatz zum Anfassen

Sollten Sie dieses Kapitel gerade an Ihrem Schreibtisch lesen, dann lassen Sie Ihren Blick einmal durch Ihr Büro schweifen. Welche Gegenstände können Sie in der Fremdsprache benennen? Diese Wörter haben Sie damit wiederholt.

Es wird aber eine ganze Reihe von Dingen geben, deren Bezeichnung Sie noch nicht kennen, aber trotzdem wissen möchten. Legen Sie ein Päckchen mit Klebeetiketten oder Haftzetteln auf Ihren Schreibtisch. Wenn Sie ein Wort lernen, das Sie in Ihrer Umgebung sehen, schreiben Sie es auf und kleben es an den betreffenden Gegenstand – am besten mit einem passenden Verb.

Das ist *learning by doing*, Wortschatz zum Anfassen. Sie nehmen den Gegenstand in die Hand und taufen ihn auf seinen fremdsprachigen Namen. Bald tragen die Dinge, die Sie täglich umgeben, ihren englischen Namen. Verfahren Sie so mit dem, was auf Ihrem Schreibtisch steht, dem Inhalt Ihrer Aktenmappe usw.

Wenn Sie nach Vollständigkeit streben, finden Sie den Wortschatz geordnet in den Lernwörterbüchern in Sachgruppen. So holen Sie die Sprache aus den Büchern in Ihren Alltag.

Time for a smile

The life insurance agent thought that his son was marrying into a rather dubious family, but quite how dubious he didn't realise until the wedding when he announced that he was going to give his boy a free life insurance policy.

"Oh, no!" screamed the bride. "Don't do it! I don't want Daddy to set him on fire like the warehouse."

DIE WELT DER VERSICHERUNG

Crossword power

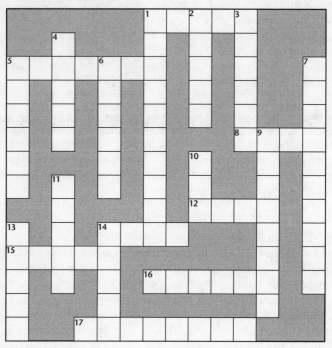

Across

1. I'm afraid your ◈ has expired, sir.
5. We charge you a ◈ of $400 a year.
8. Our company processes claims without red ◈.
12. I want to ◈ out a personal insurance.
14. Never ignore the ◈ print.
15. We can't go on spending money like ◈.
16. When does our policy ◈?
17. In this complicated case we have to call in a claims ◈.

Down

1. The insurance agent gets an insurance ◈.
2. You'll understand that we have to take the depreciation of ◈ into account.
3. What's the opposite of *accept* claims?
4. Are the ◈ of the policy negotiable?
5. I'm afraid your ◈ has expired.
6. I want to ◈ our house against fire.
7. We do not ◈ the risk of bungee jumping.
9. We'll have to call in an assessor who ◈ the damage.
10. This accident was an ◈ of God.
11. Do your cars have third ◈ cover?
13. We cannot ◈ damages before we get the accident report.
14. I suspect Mr Bosy has committed insurance ◈.

GESCHÄFTE MIT DER BANK

PART 21

BANK BUSINESS

We all need to go there from time to time. And sometimes the visits are not so joyful. It depends whether you have money in your account or not. Well, banks should offer you a service, but sometimes you ask yourself what it all means. For example, you deposit a cheque, you have to wait three days to use it, but you can be sure the bank is working with your money.

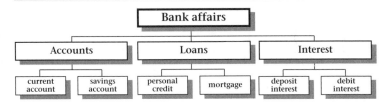

They must have money to burn

An elderly woman in a shabby coat and carrying a large shopping bag walks into a bank. She goes to the vice president, puts the shopping bag on his desk, and says, "I'd like to deposit a million, seven hundred thousand, and thirty dollars."

The vice president counts the money. When done, he says, "I'm sorry, but you only have a million, seven hundred thousand, and eighteen dollars."

"Count it again," the elderly woman says.

After counting it again, the vice president says, "There's only a million, seven hundred thousand, eighteen dollars here."

The elderly woman says, "May I call my husband?"

"Certainly."

The woman dials. When her husband answers, she says, "Idiot, you gave me the wrong shopping bag!"

21 GESCHÄFTE MIT DER BANK

1. *Mensch und Arbeitsplatz* / People and places

in einer Bank arbeiten	work in a bank
als Bankier / Kassierer arbeiten	work as a banker / cashier
Kunden am Schalter bedienen	serve customers at the counter
im gepanzerten Kassenschalter stehen	stand behind the protected counter
eine Ausbildung als Bankangestellter machen	train as a bank clerk
sich in Bankkreisen bewegen	move in banking circles

 Learning by intelligent guessing

Task 1: Banks you might bank with

1. government bank
2. commercial bank
3. mortgage bank
4. municipal bank
5. joint-stock bank
6. savings bank
7. postal savings bank

Can you put the right numbers into the boxes? It's easy.

❏ Sparkasse ❏ Staatsbank ❏ Aktienbank ❏ Handelsbank
❏ Hypothekenbank ❏ Kommunalbank ❏ Postsparkasse

Task 2: Which department would you like to work in?

❏ foreign currency department ❏ bank vault ❏ loans department
❏ international division ❏ investment advice ❏ customer service
❏ teller's cage (US) ❏ account management

1. *Kreditabteilung*
2. *Devisenabteilung*
3. *Auslandsabteilung*
4. *Anlageberatung*
5. *Kontoführung*
6. *Banktresor*
7. *Kundendienst*
8. *Kassenschalter*

BANK BUSINESS 21

2. Mehr über Bankkonten / More about bank accounts

ein Girokonto eröffnen	open a cheque / current account
seine Unterschriftsprobe geben	fill in one's specimen signature
eine Unterschrift überprüfen / bestätigen	check / verify a signature
ein Konto bei einer Bank haben	have an account with a bank
Geld auf ein Konto einzahlen	pay money into an account
Geld auf der Bank haben	have money in the bank
Wie hoch ist mein Guthaben?	What's the balance of my account?
Ich bin bei der Münchner Hypobank.	I bank with Munich Mortgage Bank.
Geld auf ein Sparkonto einzahlen	put in / deposit moncy in a savings account
Beträge ins Sparbuch eintragen	enter figures in the passbook
ein Konto glattstellen / ausgleichen	balance an account
kündigen	give notice
ein Konto schließen	close an account
ein Konto sperren	block an account
Geld von einem Konto abheben	withdraw money from an account
Geld abheben	make a withdrawal
ein Konto überziehen	overdraw an account
im Minus sein	be overdrawn / in the red
einen Überziehungskredit bis zu einem Monatsgehalt einräumen	grant an overdraft facility of one month's salary
Die Überziehungszinssatz beträgt 16 %.	The overdraft charge is 16 %.
Bankgebühren zahlen	pay bank charges

Time for a smile

My bank always makes me feel a bit insecure. If you want to make a withdrawal, you have to stand around the tellers' cage and wait for someone to make a deposit.

21 GESCHÄFTE MIT DER BANK

3. Bargeldloser Zahlungsverkehr / Cashless money exchange

Geld überweisen / Transfer money

Geld auf ein Konto überweisen	have money transferred to an account
den Überweisungsvordruck ausfüllen	fill in the transfer form
die Bankleitzahl einsetzen	fill in the bank sorting code
der Empfänger einer Überweisung	the recipient of a transfer
eine Überweisung aus Deutschland erwarten	expect a transfer from Germany
bargeldloser Zahlungsverkehr	cashless money exchange

Was Sie mit Schecks machen / What you do with cheques

mit Scheck bezahlen	pay by cheque
einen Scheck ausstellen	write a cheque
einen Scheck über $1000 ausstellen	make out a cheque for $1000
einen Scheck auf eine Bank ziehen	draw a cheque on a bank
einen Scheck vordatieren	pre-date a cheque
nur an Empfänger	a/c payee
das Scheckformular ausfüllen	fill in / out the cheque form
der Name des Ausstellers	the name of the drawer
einen Scheck endossieren	endorse a cheque
einen Scheck auf der Rückseite gegenzeichnen	countersign a cheque on the reverse
einen Scheck einzahlen	deposit a cheque
einen Barscheck ausstellen	issue an open cheque
einen Scheck zur Verrechnung ausstellen	cross a cheque / make out a crossed cheque
seine Scheckkarte verlieren	lose one's cheque guarantee card
einen Scheck einlösen	cash a cheque
einen Blankoscheck ausstellen	issue a blank cheque

BANK BUSINESS 21

Was die Bank mit Schecks macht / What the bank does with cheques

Der Scheck ist nicht gedeckt.	The cheque is not covered.
einen Scheck verrechnen	clear a cheque
einen Scheck einem Konto gutschreiben	clear a cheque into an account
den Betrag einem Konto gutschreiben	credit the amount to an account
einen Scheck einlösen	honour a cheque
Ein Scheck wird fällig.	A cheque falls due.
einen Scheck platzen lassen	let a cheque bounce
ein verfallener Scheck	a stale cheque
einen Scheck nicht einlösen	dishonour a cheque

Time for a smile

My bank just sent me a note that my account is overdrawn again.
I'm going to try another bank. They can't all be overdrawn.

4. *Diverse Bankgeschäfte* / Other banking business

Geld im Banktresor aufbewahren	keep money in the bank vault
ein Schließfach mieten	rent a safe-deposit box
Bargeld mit der Kreditkarte abheben	draw cash with the credit card
Geld vom Geldautomaten holen	get money from the cash dispenser
Bankgeschäfte am Schalter	do business over the counter
der Kassierer hinter der Kasse	the cashier in the teller's cage (US) / behind the counter
Geldeinlagen entgegennehmen	accept deposits
den Kontoauszug abholen	collect the bank statement / statement of account
einen Dauerauftrag geben / ändern	place / change a standing order
ein Konto belasten	debit an account
ein Konto entlasten	clear / discharge an account
einem Konto einen Betrag gutschreiben	credit an amount to an account
ein Guthaben bei der Bank haben	have money on one's account / a positive balance

21 GESCHÄFTE MIT DER BANK

Festgeld anlegen	set up a fixed deposit
mit Wertpapieren handeln	deal in securities
den Diskontsatz veröffentlichen	publish the bank rate / discount rate
den Diskontsatz senken	reduce the bank rate
Bankreferenzen erhalten	obtain bank references
Banknoten ausgeben	issue bank notes

Everything is relative

A German businessman entered a Swiss bank. He looked carefully around, went to the reception desk and whispered, "I want to invest 300,000 marks."
"You needn't whisper," said the bank clerk, "poverty is nothing to be ashamed of."

A box of idioms around money

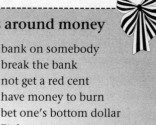

sich auf jemanden verlassen	bank on somebody
pleite gehen, Bankrott machen	break the bank
keinen roten Heller bekommen	not get a red cent
Geld wie Heu haben	have money to burn
sein letztes Hemd verwetten	bet one's bottom dollar
Acht Prozent Zinsen zu bezahlen.	Eight percent interest to pay.
Das ist Wucher.	That's daylight robbery.
es schaffen	be home and dry
Nur noch £ 10 000 zu zahlen, und wir haben es geschafft.	Only another £ 10,000 to pay and we're home and dry.
Bäume ausreißen können	feel like a million dollars
Der Groschen ist gefallen.	The penny's dropped.
Robert hat's verstanden. Endlich ist der Groschen gefallen.	Robert's understood. At last the penny's dropped.
nichts vom Geld verstehen	be penny wise, pound foolish
Bargeld sehen wollen (Bargeld lacht)	see the colour of one's money
Ich will Bargeld sehen.	Let's see the colour of your money.

BANK BUSINESS

Magic Squares

1. Match the phrases (A, B, C ...) ...

A. What's my overdraft facility?	**B.** I'd like to open a savings account.	**C.** I seem to be overdrawn.
D. I'm afraid you've overdrawn your account.	**E.** Who do you bank with?	**F.** I was thinking of applying for a loan.
G. I've lost my credit card.	**H.** I'd like to have money transferred to Germany.	**I.** Where do I collect my bank statements?

... with these phrases (1, 2, 3 ...).

1. How much would you like to pay in?	**2.** Shall we block the account?	**3.** Have you got any security?
4. Please go to counter 7.	**5.** I have an account with the City Bank.	**6.** We'll grant you an overdraft facility of one month's salary.
7. My statement does not show an overdraft.	**8.** I'm afraid you'll have to pay overdraft charges.	**9.** Please fill in the transfer form.

2. Put the numbers in the magic squares below.

A =	B =	C =
D =	E =	F =
G =	H =	I =

When the answers are correct, all columns and rows will add up to the same number (15).

21 GESCHÄFTE MIT DER BANK

 Master your phrases

Task 3: Find the opposite

open an account	.... an account
balance an account	.... an account
deposit money	.... money
increase the bank rate	.... the bank rate

Task 4: Accounts you would wish to have

Can you put the right numbers into the boxes?

1. current account
2. deposit account
3. savings account
4. joint account
5. passbook

❏ Sparbuch ❏ Sparkonto ❏ Girokonto
❏ Depositenkonto ❏ gemeinsames Konto

Task 5: Wordbuilder's corner

Can you find the noun?

close an account	the .... of an account
withdraw money	the .... of money
transfer money	the .... of money
endorse a cheque	the .... of a cheque
publish the bank rate	the .... of the bank rate

Time for a smile

My bank sent me a bank statement last week saying that I was seven hundred pounds overdrawn. I reacted promptly. I immediately wrote them a cheque for the money.

BANK BUSINESS 21

5. *Bankkredite und Darlehen* / Credits and loans

sich von einer Bank Geld leihen	borrow money from a bank
die Kreditwürdigkeit einschätzen	evaluate someone's credit standing
Guthaben / Aktiva und Verbindlichkeiten / Passiva gegenüberstellen	balance assets and liabilities
einen Kredit absichern	secure a loan
Sicherheiten anbieten	offer security
eine Garantie hinterlegen	deposit a guarantee
Wertpapiere als Sicherheit hinterlegen	pledge securities
kreditwürdig sein	be creditworthy
einen Darlehen beantragen	apply for a loan
einen kurzfristigen Kredit benötigen	need a short-term loan
ein zinsloses Darlehen aushandeln	negotiate an interest-free loan
einen Zwischenkredit bekommen	get an interim loan
einen Kreditrahmen einräumen	grant an overdraft facility
einen Kredit gewähren	grant a credit
einen Kredit bestätigen	confirm a credit
einen Kredit / Darlehen vereinbaren	arrange a credit / a loan
einen Darlehensvertrag unterzeichnen	sign a loan agreement
eine Kreditrahmen anbieten	offer a line of credit
einen Kredit in Anspruch nehmen	use / utilise a credit
ein Darlehen aufnehmen	apply for a loan
einen Personalkredit erhalten	obtain a personal loan
einen Kredit aufnehmen	raise a credit
die Laufzeit eines Darlehens	the term of a loan
Wie lang ist die Laufzeit des Darlehens?	What's the term of the loan?
ein Darlehen überziehen	overdraw a loan
einen Kredit einfrieren	freeze a credit
einen Kredit kürzen	reduce a loan
einen Kredit streichen	cancel a loan
einem Schuldner drohen	threaten a debtor
Tilgung eines Darlehens	redemption of a loan
einen Kredit zurückzahlen	redeem a credit
ein Darlehen zurückzahlen	repay a loan

GESCHÄFTE MIT DER BANK

> **Misunderstanding at the Loans Department**
>
> The loan officer checks the application and says to Jones, "Your assets are in good shape. Tell me about your liabilities." Jones says, "That's easy. I can lie with the best of them." (word play on lie and ability)

6. *Hypotheken aufnehmen* / Obtaining mortgages

an ein Finanzierungsinstitut herantreten	approach a financial institution
sich an eine Hypothekenbank / Wohnungsbaugesellschaft wenden	apply to a mortgage bank / building society
ein Wohnungsbaudarlehen beantragen	apply for a housing loan
Baukosten abschätzen	assess building costs
eine erste Hypothek gewähren	grant a first mortgage loan
eine Hypothek aufnehmen	raise / take out a mortgage
ein Grundstück mit einer Hypothek belasten	place / put a mortgage on a property
ein Haus mit einer Hypothek belasten	mortgage a house
eine Hypothek kündigen	call in a mortgage
bei Fälligkeit zurückzahlen	repay at maturity
eine Hypothek zurückzahlen / tilgen	redeem a mortgage
eine Hypothek löschen	discharge a mortgage
Geld in einen Bausparvertrag stecken	put money into a savings agreement
steuerliche Vergünstigungen erhalten	receive a tax concession
Subventionen erhalten	obtain subsidies

7. *Zinsen* / Interest

Zinsen erhalten / Getting interest

Coupons einlösen	cash dividend warrants
Wie hoch ist der Habenzins?	What's the credit interest?
gute Rendite	good return on investment
Zinsen erhalten	get interest
Zinsen tragen	bear interest

Zinsen abwerfen	yield interest
Dividenden laufen auf.	Dividends accumulate.
Kapitalertragssteuer zahlen	pay capital gains tax
Zinsen versteuern	pay tax on interest

Zinsen zahlen / Pay interest

Sollzins zahlen	pay debit interest
Zinsen berechnen	charge interest
monatliche Zinsaufwendung	interest payable per month
mit Zins und Zinseszinsen zurückzahlen müssen	have to repay with compound interest
mit den Zinsen in Verzug sein	be in arrrears with the interest
den Zinssatz erhöhen	increase / raise the interest rate
den Zinssatz senken	lower / reduce the interest rate
Zinsverluste hinnehmen müssen	suffer loss of interest

Time for a smile

Bridget O'Leary was trying to cash a cheque in a Dublin bank. "Can you identify yourself, madam?" asked the clerk. "Certainly," said Bridget, reached into her handbag, took out a little mirror, looked in it and declared confidently,
"Yes, it's me all right. I'd recognise myself anywhere."

21 GESCHÄFTE MIT DER BANK

 Master your phrases

Task 6: Wordbuilder's corner

Say it with a noun.

overdraw one's account	have an ....
repay a loan	.... of a loan
receive a transfer	be the .... of a transfer
redeem a loan	.... of a loan

Task 7: The Credit-ABC

The first one has been done for you.

A *apply for / arrange* a loan
B .... money from a bank
C .... a loan
D .... a guarantee
E .... someone's credit standing
F .... a credit
G .... a credit
and so on

Task 8: Find the opposites

Having *assets* is better	than	having ....
A bank can *grant* a loan	and	.... a loan.
They *raise* the interest rate	and	.... it again.
Lending money is nobler	than	.... money.

What exactly is a bank?

A bank is a place where they lend you an umbrella in
fair weather and ask for it back when it begins to rain.
Mark Twain

Task 9: Say it in other words

repay a loan   .... a loan
put a mortgage on a house   .... a mortgage on a house
lower the interest rate   .... the interest rate
raise the interest rate   .... the interest rate

Task 10: Correct the idioms

1. I've been taking viagra. I feel like a million pounds.
2. Pay £2000 for that old car ? That's daylight burglary.
3. Don't bet on him! He doesn't know what he's doing.
4. When his father died he didn't get a red penny.
5. I think she understands the cash flow now. The penny has fallen.

--- Picture your idiom ---

Tom: Why the hell did you buy all these stocks on the new market. First, they aren't safe. Second, we've exceeded our budget.

Bob: Keep your hair on! It's true, we've overrun our budget. But our investment in Internet stocks won't exactly .... the ....

Correspondence with bankers

My uncle, who had overdrawn his account, received a sarcastic letter from his bank manager.

Dear Mr Johnson,

I have noticed that your account is now overdrawn well over the limit and has been for some time. Can we please return to the original arrangement where you bank with us and not we with you?

21 GESCHÄFTE MIT DER BANK

Lerntip: Fühlen Sie sich zum Sprachenlernen zu alt?

Das Vorurteil von der altersbedingten Abnahme der Lernfähigkeit ist durch viele Untersuchungen korrigiert und in mancher Hinsicht ins Gegenteil verkehrt worden. Was die Fähigkeit der Imitation und die Leistung des Gedächtnisses betrifft, liegt das optimale Lernalter etwa bei 15 Jahren. Aber häufig wird in diesem Alter noch falsch gelernt. Lernpsychologen haben folgendes Experiment durchgeführt. Man gab verschiedenen Altersgruppen Unterricht in Esperanto. Die Gruppe der Teilnehmer bis zu 19 Jahren erhielt doppelt soviel Unterricht wie die 20 bis 25 Jahre alten Lerner. Trotz der Hälfte der Stundenzahl schnitt die ältere Gruppe in einem Vergleichstest erfolgreicher ab als die jugendliche Konkurrenz. Andere Versuche zeigen, daß es zwischen Jugendlichen und Erwachsenen im frühen und mittleren Alter keinen biologisch bedingten Leistungsunterschied gibt. Nachlassende Flexibilität und Anpassungsfähigkeit machen Erwachsene durch Erfahrung und Lernhaltung wett. Sie können sich besser konzentrieren, sich Wissen durch Lesen aneignen und ohne Druck durch Lehrer lernen. Sie haben zwar ein Handikap, was das Gedächtnis und das Nachahmen der Aussprache betrifft. Dafür aber verfügen Sie als Erwachsener über Qualitäten, die Lehrer an jungen Schülern oft vermissen: das Interesse an der Sprache, höhere Konzentrationsfähigkeit, Zuverlässigkeit und Durchhaltevermögen. Außerdem haben Sie Gelegenheit, die Sprache beruflich anzuwenden.

Zwar können Jugendliche besser mechanisch lernen, sie behalten Stoff, selbst wenn sie ihn nicht ganz verstanden haben. Dafür haben Erwachsene die größere Lernerfahrung. Sie lernen anders, nämlich kognitiv, das heißt, sie durchdringen den Lernstoff durch Gliedern und Strukturieren und behalten ihn auf diese Weise besser. Vor allem sind sie bis ins hohe Alter der Jugend im Übertragen des Gelernten auf neue Sprechsituationen (Transfer) überlegen.

Sie werden feststellen, daß sich Ihr Gehirn durch das Lernen langsam verändert. Wie ein Muskel wird Ihr Sprachengedächtnis durch das Training besser. Aber wie im Sport erzielen Sie deutliche Leistungssteigerungen nur durch geeignete Techniken und Strategien. Im geschickten Umgang mit Ihrem Gehirn steigern Sie nicht nur Ihre Gedächtnisleistung, sondern erhalten auch Ihre Intelligenz. Umgekehrt gilt, daß man das Lernen durch Untätigkeit auch wieder verlernt: "Wer rastet, der rostet."

PART 22

DAS GELD ARBEITEN LASSEN

MAKING MONEY WORK

In the old days people used to pay for things with other things. Nowadays we pay with money or with pieces of plastic. Some companies like Siemens seem to have a lot of extra cash to play with. And that is exactly what they do with it. Off to the Stock Exchange where they speculate by buying stocks and shares of companies. If the price of the share rises you can make a lot of money. You can also lose a lot. Other things such as articles and raw materials are bought and sold, too. But it's all a risky business.

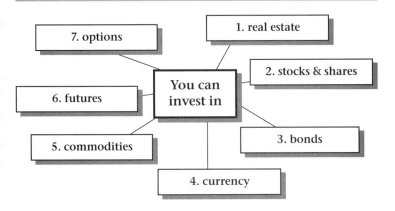

You can invest in
1. real estate
2. stocks & shares
3. bonds
4. currency
5. commodities
6. futures
7. options

Time for a smile

A client gets his bill from his investment adviser. He is stunned by the size. Furious, he calls the adviser and accuses him of trying to squeeze him dry.
The adviser listens for a while and then says, "You're such an ungrateful person! And to think, I named my yacht after you!"

22 DAS GELD ARBEITEN LASSEN

1. *Menschen an der Börse* / People at the stock exchange

ein erfahrener Börsianer	an experienced stock exchange speculator
als Börsenmitglied zugelassen sein	be certified as a member of the stock exchange
eine Börseneinführung beantragen	apply for listing
Börsenmitglied sein	be a member of the stock exchange
ein erfolgreicher Börsenmakler	a successful broker
Ein Terminverkäufer macht Warentermingeschäfte.	A forward seller trades in futures.
eine Ausbildung machen als Freiverkehrshändler	train as a dealer in unlisted securities
als Eigen- / Effektenhändler arbeiten	work as a jobber (GB) / dealer (US)
als Geldhändler / Geldvermittler arbeiten	work as a money-jobber / money-broker
ein Pfandbriefinstitut beauftragen	commission a bond house
einen Anlageberater konsultieren	consult an investment adviser
Aktien gegen Maklerprovision verkaufen	sell shares for a commission
eine Maklergebühr / Provision erhalten	obtain a brokerage / commission
Börsenvollmacht haben	have power of attorney
den Terminkurs notieren	quote the liquidating price
die Kursnotierungen veröffentlichen	publish the quotations
die Börsenordnung einhalten	adhere to stock exchange regulations
Insidergeschäfte sind gegen die Vorschriften des Börsenausschusses.	Insider trading is against the rules of the Securities and Investments Board.
sich an die Börsenaufsicht wenden	appeal to the supervisory body for stock exchanges
die Börsenaufsicht einschalten	call in the Supervisory Board

MAKING MONEY WORK

2. Was tut sich an der Börse? / What goes on at the stock exchange?

Der offizielle Börsenhandel beginnt um ...	Official trading begins at ...
Geschäfte nach Börsenschluß	after-hours trading
an der Warenbörse handeln	trade on the commodity exchange
amtlich notiert werden	be officially quoted / listed
Börsenkurse und -erträge notieren	quote stock prices and yields
einen Kassakurs notieren	quote a cash / spot price
zum Kassakurs kaufen	make a cash purchase
über dem Nennwert verkaufen	sell at a premium
mit Termingeschäften handeln	trade in futures
auf dem Aktienmarkt spekulieren	play the stock market
auf eine Hausse / Baisse spekulieren	speculate on a rise / fall
auf eine Hausse / Baisse spekulieren	speculate on a bull / bear market
Sollen wir auf eine Hausse oder eine Baisse spekulieren?	Shall we bull or bear?
sichere Werte kaufen	buy sound stock
Spitzenwerte halten	keep blue chips
Aktienwerte streuen	spread shares
Risiko vermeiden	avoid risk
das Risiko verteilen	spread the risk
mit Termingeschäften handeln	trade in futures
einen Leerverkauf tätigen	sell short
die Zahlung prolongieren	postpone payment
eine Kaufs- / Verkaufsoption nehmen	place a call / put option
junge Aktien ausgeben	issue new shares
bestens verkaufen	sell at the best price
ein Limit setzen	fix / set a limit
einen Glattstellungsverkauf machen	make a sell-off
mit Termingeschäften spekulieren	speculate in futures
von seinen Dividenden leben	live off one's dividends

22 DAS GELD ARBEITEN LASSEN

3. *Wo kann man investieren?* / What can you invest in?

Immobilien kaufen	buy real estate
mit Freiverkehrswerten handeln	trade in unlisted securities
festverzinsliche Papiere vorziehen	prefer fixed interest stocks
Neuemissionen zeichnen	subscribe to fresh issues
Dividendenpapiere mit guter Rendite	equities with good return on investment
Warentermingeschäfte machen	deal in futures
eine größere Summe investieren	invest a lump-sum
eine einmalige Investition tätigen	make a one off investment

Sie können Handel treiben mit ...	You can trade in ...
Aktien	**Shares**
Stammaktien	ordinary shares
Vorzugsaktien	preference shares
junge Aktien	new shares / stocks
Namensaktien	registered shares
Nachzugsaktien	deferred shares
Optionsscheine	options
Aktienindexfond	tracker funds
Aktien ohne Stimmrecht	non-voting shares
Staatspapiere	**Gilt-edged securities**
Pfandbriefe	mortgage bonds
Wandelanleihen	convertible bonds
Regierungsanleihen	government bonds
Industrieanleihen	**Industrial bonds**
Banken	banks
Brauereien	breweries
Chemiewerke	chemicals
Autoindustrie	automobiles
Stahlindustrie	steel
Textilindustrie	textiles
Papierindustrie	paper
Versicherungen	insurance
Fluggesellschaften	airlines

MAKING MONEY WORK 22

4. *Geschäfte mit Fremdwährung* / Business with foreign currency

in englischer Währung bezahlen	pay in British currency
eine Auslandspostanweisung unterzeichnen	sign a foreign currency order
Auslandsforderungen haben	have foreign debts
Auslandsguthaben besitzen	possess foreign assets
an den Devisenmarkt gehen	go to the foreign exchange market
fremde Währung kaufen	buy foreign currency
den Währungswert überprüfen	check the currency value
in eine Währung investieren	invest in a currency
Der Börsenkurs schwankt täglich.	The exchange rate fluctuates on a daily basis.
Eine Währung verliert an Wert.	A currency depreciates.
Der Euro hat sich gut behauptet.	The euro has held up well.
Der Dollar gibt nach.	The dollar is losing ground.
Das Pfund sackt ab / purzelt nach unten / stürzt.	The pound dives / nosedives / plunges / tumbles.
Die Lira ist eingebrochen / abgebröckelt / abgestürzt.	The lira has collapsed / crumbled / slumped.
Das Pfund fiel im nachbörslichen Handel.	The pound fell in after-hours trading.
Der Schweizer Franken legt zu.	The Swiss Frank is picking up.

Time for a smile

Some people pay their bills when due,
some when overdue,
and some never do.

5. *Währungspolitik* / Monetary policy

eine Münze prägen	stamp a coin
Geld in Umlauf setzen	circulate money / put money into circulation / issue money
die Geldmenge reduzieren	reduce the money supply

22 DAS GELD ARBEITEN LASSEN

aus dem Verkehr ziehen	withdraw from circulation
die Goldwährung aufgeben	abandon the gold standard
zur Goldwährung zurückkehren	return to the gold standard
sich Goldreserven halten	hold gold reserves
die Währung reformieren	reform the currency
Kaufkraft haben	have purchasing / buying power
das Geld knapp halten	keep credit tight
die Währung hart / weich / stabil halten	keep a currency hard / soft / stable
eine Währung überbewerten	overvalue a currency
eine Währung aufwerten / abwerten	revalue / devalue a currency
eine Währung steigt / fällt	a currency appreciates / depreciates
den Wechselkurs einer Währung freigeben	float a currency
ein Währungsabkommen schließen	make a monetary agreement
Preisstabilität erhalten	preserve price stability
die Inflation bekämpfen	counteract inflation
eine galoppierende Inflation erleben	experience runaway / galloping inflation; a hyperinflation
eine Lohn-Preis-Spirale erwarten	expect a wage-price spiral
Was ist die Verrechnungseinheit?	What's the unit of account?
den Wert in Lire ausdrücken	express the value in lira
einen Devisenkurs anbieten	offer a rate of exchange
Wie hoch ist der Briefkurs?	What's the selling rate?
Wie ist der Geldkurs?	What's the buying rate?
die Kurssicherung übernehmen	fix forward rates

Time for a smile

A financial adviser was talking to his ninety-three-year-old, multimillionaire client:
"Mr Goldberg, I have an investment here that will double your money in five years." – "Five years! Are you mad?" shouted Goldberg, ""At my age you don't even buy green bananas."

MAKING MONEY WORK 22

 Master your phrases

Task 1: What's the financial jargon?

1. You buy at a spot price:
   you make a ....
2. You want to sell your company's shares at the exchange:
   you apply ....
3. You wait with selling for rising prices:
   you're speculating on a ....
4. You wait with buying for falling prices:
   you're speculating on a ....
5. You want to avoid risk:
   you'd better .... your shares.

Task 2: You cannot do these things at the same time

lose ground	or	.... ground
abandon the gold standard	or	.... to the gold standard
devalue a currency	or	.... a currency
hold a *soft* currency	or	hold a .... currency
a currency *depreciates*	or	a currency ....

Task 3: Beef up your word power

Find a synonym for the words in *italics*.

The broker obtains a *brokerage*	....
You buy shares at a *cash price*	....
Shares are officially *quoted*	....
The lira has *collapsed*	....

Advice from the experts

There's nothing so disastrous as rational investment
in an irrational world.
John Maynard Keynes

Never invest your money in anything
that eats or needs repairing.
Billy Rose

DAS GELD ARBEITEN LASSEN

6. *Auf und Ab an der Börse* / Ups and downs at the exchange
Eine Hausse / A bull market

Die Kurse werden sich erholen.	Shares will stage a rally.
Die Nachfrage ist gestiegen.	Shares have rallied.
Die Börse ist fest / unverändert.	The market is firm / unchanged.
Die Börse wird fest bleiben.	The market will remain firm.
Die Kurse sind widerstandsfähig.	Prices are resistant.
Die Preise für Kaffee haben sich an der Warenbörse erholt.	The price of coffee rebounded on the commodity exchange.
Aktien höher notieren	mark up shares
Die Aktien ziehen langsam an.	Equities are edging up.
an Boden gewinnen	gain ground
die Kurse steigen	prices appreciate
eine steigende Markttendenz	a climbing market trend
Ein Kursaufschwung ist in Sicht.	An upturn of the shares is in sight.
höher schließen	close higher
5 % über dem Vortageskurs gehandelt werden	trade 5 % above yesterday's price
drei Euro höher schließen als am Tag zuvor	close three euros higher than the day before
Es herrscht Haussestimmung.	It's a bull / bullish market.
von kurzer Dauer sein	be of short duration
die Kurse in die Höhe treiben	push prices up
einen Jahreshöchststand erreichen	reach an annual peak
einen neuen historischen Höchststand erreichen	be at a new all-time high
Der Marktwert ist höher als der Nennwert.	The market value is higher than the face value.

MAKING MONEY WORK

Die Baisse / The bear market

Das Geschäft war uneinheitlich.	Business was irregular.
Die Börse ist uneinheitlich.	The market is unsettled.
Der Handel war schleppend.	Trade was slow.
Die Börse ist unsicher.	Prices are sensitive.
eine Kursschwäche im Börsenverkehr	a weakness in the market
eine Kursanpassung erwarten	expect a price adjustment
die Kurse drücken	push down prices
einem Trend widerstehen	buck a trend
ein Stimmungswandel	a change in mood
eine pessimistische Stimmung gegenüber ...	a bearish attitude towards ...
einen Abwärtstrend erwarten	expect a downtrend
Die Kurse sinken langsam.	Prices are edging down.
an Boden verlieren	lose ground
Die Aktienkurse sind flau.	Share prices are depressed.
Die Börse ist im Stimmungstief.	The market is depressed.
Es herrscht eine Baissestimmung.	The market is all bears.
einen Kursrutsch voraussagen	predict a bear slide
einen starken Kursrückgang erleben	see a sharp fall
auf einen neuen Tiefststand fallen	slip back to a low
einen historischen Tiefstand erreichen	be at an all-time low
dem Baissedruck widerstehen	resist the bear squeeze
ein Baissemanöver vermuten	suspect a bear raid
einen Börsensturz befürchten	fear a crash
Die Börse bricht zusammen / stürzt ein.	The exchange crashes / collapses.

22 DAS GELD ARBEITEN LASSEN

 Master your phrases

Task 4: Let's go woggling again

Replace the *woggles* with a suitable word.

Tom: I told you the shares would *woggle*.
Bob: You were right. Siemens is *woggling* 5% above yesterday's price.
Tom: However, insiders expect a price *awogglement*. The market is *wogglish*.
Bob: But I'm sure Siemens will resist the bear *woggle*.
Tom: I'm not so sure. The market is de*woggled*.
Bob: At least the euro closed three cents *woggler* than the day before.

Task 5: Yes or No?

	Yes	No
1. When business is irregular the market is unsettled.		
2. When shares rally the market is bullish.		
3. When your shares buck the trend it's a positive sign.		
4. When experts suspect a bear raid, should you sell?		
5. When prices depreciate they are edging up.		

7. Gewinn und Verlust machen / Making profit and loss

Schwarze Zahlen schreiben / Being in the black

bares Geld haben	have ready cash / money
bar bezahlen	pay (in) cash
schwarze Zahlen schreiben	be in the black
Profit machen	make profit
gut bei Kasse sein	be in the money
Geld adelt	money talks
im Geld schwimmen	be coining money in / rolling in money
sich reich verheiraten	marry money
Geld wie Heu haben	have money to burn
Seit dem Tod ihres Vaters hat sie Geld wie Heu.	Since the death of her father she has money to burn.
Geld beschaffen / aufbringen	find / furnish / procure money

MAKING MONEY WORK 22

Rote Zahlen schreiben / Being in the red

knapp bei Kasse sein	be short of / pushed for money
pleite sein	be broke
in finanziellen Schwierigkeiten sein	be in financial trouble
sich verspekulieren	speculate on the wrong side
kurz vor dem Ruin stehen	be almost ruined
sein Vermögen an der Börse verlieren	lose one's fortune on the stock exchange
Konkurs anmelden	file for bankruptcy
gepfändet werden	be pledged / seized as security
versteigert werden	be up for auction
den Gerichtsvollzieher im Haus haben	have the bailiff in the company
Verluste ausgleichen	offset losses
Geld / Schecks fälschen	counterfeit / falsify money /cheques
eine feindliche Übernahme befürchten	fear a hostile take-over

A box of idioms

nicht alles auf eine Karte setzen	not put all one's eggs into one basket
mit leeren Händen dastehen	come away empty-handed
das Terrain sondieren	test the water
Wir sollten noch nicht unser ganzes Geld investieren. Sondieren wir zuerst das Terrain.	We shouldn't put all our money in yet. Let's test the water first.
keinen Pfennig in der Tasche haben	not have two pennies to rub together
Geld investieren? Ich habe keinen Pfennig in der Tasche.	Invest money? I haven't got two pennies to rub together.

Time for a smile

I once knew a Japanese gentleman who was so wealthy that he was considering buying himself what he called 'a place down South'. It was Australia.

22 DAS GELD ARBEITEN LASSEN

 Master your phrases

Task 6: What's the phrase?

1. Which kind of paper can you change into other forms?
   ....
2. What is business done after official business hours called?
   ....
3. What is the money earned on buying and selling?
   ....
4. What does a company have to do if it wants to offer its shares on the stock market?
   It has to ....

Task 7: Phrases in context

Everybody plays the Stock Exchange now and again. What sort of things can you t _ _ _ _ in ? Well, you could buy g _ _ _ _ _ _ _ _ _ t b _ _ _ s , or g _ _ _ -e _ _ _ d s _ c _ _ _ _ _ _ s . And if you prefer there are stocks and shares in the automobile and chemical industries. You could invest in some b _ _ _ c _ _ _ s . They're probably the safest. But just take my advice and don't t _ _ _ _ in f _ _ _ _ _ s or op _ _ _ _ s or anything like that. You'll come away e _ _ _ _ -h _ _ _ _ _ _ .

> ### Time for a smile
>
> A friend once asked me for some investment advice. I asked him if he had any liquid assets. He said he did – three bottles of Scotch and a can of fizzy orange.

MAKING MONEY WORK 22

Picture your idioms

Invest money? It's all very well for you to say so. You're rolling in money, whereas I Haven't got .... together.

Bob: "We should put all our money into this company. It's up for grabs."
Tom: "Isn't that a bit too risky? Let's .... the .... first."

Tina: "There's a fortune in Internet shares. We should ...."
Toni: "Careful! I'm afraid we might be backing the wrong horse again."

22 DAS GELD ARBEITEN LASSEN

Lerntip: Wortschatz aufschnappen

Sie haben Kontakt zu "native speakers"? Sie wollen von ihnen lernen? Wenden Sie folgende Lernstrategie an:

1. **Fragen:** What exactly do you mean by 'bull market'?
2. **Wiederholen:** I see. A 'bull market' is when prices rise sharply.
3. **Assoziieren:** Prägen Sie sich den Ausdruck zusammen mit der Situation und dem Gesicht des Partners ein. Wortschatz haftet besser, wenn er mit kompletten Situationen assoziiert wird.

Magic Squares

1. Match the phrases (1, 2, 3 ...) with the words (A, B, C ...).

1. It's safe as ...
2. It means taking a ...
3. I fear a ...
4. It means bucking a ...
5. Let's test the ...
6. They're trying for a ...
7. I suspect a bear ...
8. He has money to ...
9. It's Hobsons ...

A. burn	B. houses	C. take-over
D. crash	E. water	F. raid
G. trend	H. choice	I. risk

2. Put the numbers in the magic squares.

A =	B =	C =
D =	E =	F =
G =	H =	I =

3. Check yourself. When the answers are correct, all columns and rows will add up to the same number (15).

JOB LIST

A list of the typical jobs in a company

GERMAN	ENGLISH
Abteilungsleiter	department leader
Abteilungsreferat	department specialist
angelernter Arbeiter	semi-skilled worker
Angestellte im Büro	white-collar workers
Arbeiter	blue collar workers
Arbeitslose	jobless / unemployed
Arzthelferin	medical assistant
Aufsichtsrat	supervisory board
Auftragsabwicklung	order processing
Ausbilder	trainer
Aushilfe	auxiliary worker
Auszubildender	apprentice
Bauingenieur	civil engineer
Berater für DV-Bürosysteme	DP office systems consultant
Berater für Personalentwicklung	personnel development consultant
Betreuer der Systemsoftware	system software support
Betriebsrat	staff representative / works council
Buchhalter	accountant
Büroassistent	office assistant
Bürokraft	clerk
Chefingenieur	chief engineer
Chefsekretärin	secretary to the Director
Chemiker	chemical engineer
Chemietechniker	chemical technician
Controller	contoller
Disponent	managing clerk / planner
Einkäufer	buyer / purchasing clerk / agent
Einkaufssachbearbeiter	purchasing clerk
Elektriker	electrician
Empfangsdame	receptionist
Entwickler	design / development engineer
Entwicklungsingenieur	research engineer
Erfinder	inventor
Ersatzteile	spare parts
Facharbeiter	skilled worker
Fahrer	driver

JOB LIST

Fahrzeugingenieur	automotive engineer
Fertigungsingenieur	production engineer
Fotograf	photographer
Fuhrpark	car pool
Führungskraft	executive
Geschäftsführer	C.E.O. (Chief Executive Officer) / managing director (M.D.)
Grafiker	graphic designer
Großkundenbetreuer	key account manager
Industriekaufmann	commercial clerk
Instrukteur	instructor / trainer
Jurist	lawyer / legal specialist
Konstrukteur	designer
Krankenschwester	nurse
Laborassistent	lab assistant
Labortechniker	lab technician
Lagermeister	store foreman
Leiter der Werbeabteilung	head of advertising
Leiter ...	head of ...
Monteur	fitter
Normen	standards
Öffentlichkeitsarbeit	public relations
Patente und Warenzeichen	patents and trade marks
Patentingenieur	patent engineer
Personalleiter	head of personnel
Personalsachbearbeiter	personnel clerk
Pförtner	security guard
Praktikant	placement student
Pressesprecher	press spokesman
Produktmanager	product manager
Produktspezialist	product specialist
Programmierer	programmer
Projektkoordinator	project coordinator
Projektleiter	project leader
Rechnungsprüfer	invoice controller
regionaler Außendienstverkäufer	area sales manager
Regionalleiter	head of region
Sachbearbeiter / Bürokraft	clerk
Softwareentwickler	software engineer

JOB LIST

stellvertretender Leiter	deputy leader
Systemanalytiker	systems analyst
Techniker	technician
technischer Autor	technical text writer
technischer Zeichner	technical draftsman
Teilzeitbeschäftigter	part-time worker
Telefonist	telephonist
Trainee	management trainee
Übersetzer	translator
Umweltschutz	environmental pollution
ungelernter Arbeiter	unskilled worker
Verkäufer	salesman
Verkaufssachbearbeiter	sales clerk
Versuchsmeister	test lab supervisor
Vorarbeiter	foreman
Vorstand	Board of Management
Vorstandsassistent	assistant to the Board
Wareneingang	goods inward / incoming goods
Wartungsmechaniker / Techniker	maintenance fitter / technician
Werbekaufmann	advertising clerk
Werbetexter	copywriter
Werksarzt	company doctor
Wirtschaftsprüfer	auditor
Zeitarbeiter	temporary worker

JOB LIST

ENGLISH	GERMAN
accountant	*Buchhalter*
advertising clerk	*Werbekaufmann*
apprentice	*Auszubildender*
area sales manager	*regionaler Außendienstverkäufer*
assistant to the Board	*Vorstandsassistent*
auditor	*Wirtschaftsprüfer*
automotive engineer	*Fahrzeugingenieur*
auxiliary worker	*Aushilfe*
blue collar worker	*Arbeiter*
Board of Management	*Vorstand*
buyer	*Einkäufer*
C.E.O. (Chief Executive Officer)	*Geschäftsführer*
car pool	*Fuhrpark*
chemical engineer	*Chemiker*
chemical technician	*Chemitechniker*
chief engineer	*Chefingenieur*
civil engineer	*Bauingenieur*
clerk	*Bürokraft / Sachbearbeiter*
commercial clerk	*Industriekaufmann*
company doctor	*Werksarzt*
contoller	*Controller*
copywriter	*Werbetexter*
department leader	*Abteilungsleiter*
department specialist	*Abteilungsreferent*
deputy leader	*stellvertretender Leiter*
design engineer	*Entwickler*
designer	*Konstrukteur*
development engineer	*Entwickler*
DP office systems consultant	*Berater DV-Bürosysteme*
driver	*Fahrer*
electrician	*Elektriker*
environmental pollution	*Umweltschutz*
executive	*Führungskraft*
fitter	*Monteur*
foreman	*Vorarbeiter*
goods inward	*Wareneingang*
graphic designer	*Grafiker*

JOB LIST

head of ...	*Leiter ...*
head of advertising	*Leiter der Werbeabteilung*
head of personnel	*Personalleiter*
head of region	*Regionalleiter*
incoming goods	*Wareneingang*
instructor / trainer	*Instrukteur*
inventor	*Erfinder*
invoice controller	*Rechnungsprüfer*
jobless / unemployed	*Arbeitslose*
key account manager	*Großkundenbetreuer*
lab assistant	*Laborassistent*
lab technician	*Labortechniker*
lawyer / legal specialist	*Jurist*
maintenance fitter / technician	*Wartungsmechaniker / Techniker*
management trainee	*Trainee*
managing clerk	*Disponent*
managing director (M.D.)	*Geschäftsführer*
medical assistant	*Arzthelferin*
nurse	*Krankenschwester*
office assistant	*Büroassistent*
order processing	*Auftragsabwicklung*
part-time worker	*Teilzeitbeschäftigter*
patent engineer	*Patentingenieur*
patents and trade marks	*Patente und Warenzeichen*
personnel clerk	*Personalsachbearbeiter*
personnel development consultant	*Berater Personalentwicklung*
photographer	*Fotograf*
placement student	*Praktikant*
planner	*Disponent*
press spokesman	*Pressesprecher*
product manager	*Produktmanager*
product specialist	*Produktspezialist*
production engineer	*Fertigungsingenieur*
programmer	*Programmierer*
project coordinator	*Projektkoordinator*
project leader	*Projektleiter*
public relations	*Öffentlichkeitsarbeit*
purchasing clerk	*Einkaufssachbearbeiter*
purchasing clerk / agent	*Einkäufer*

JOB LIST

receptionist	*Empfangsdame*
research engineer	*Entwicklungsingenieur*
sales clerk	*Verkaufssachbearbeiter*
salesman	*Verkäufer*
secretary to the Director	*Chefsekretärin*
security guard	*Pförtner*
semi-skilled worker	*angelernter Arbeiter*
skilled worker	*Facharbeiter*
software engineer	*Softwareentwickler*
spare parts	*Ersatzteile*
staff representative	*Betriebsrat*
standards	*Normen*
store foreman	*Lagermeister*
supervisory board	*Aufsichtsrat*
system software support	*Betreuer der Systemsoftware*
systems analyst	*Systemanalytiker*
technical draftsman	*technischer Zeichner*
technical text writer	*technischer Autor*
technician	*Techniker*
telephonist	*Telefonist*
temporary worker	*Zeitarbeiter*
test lab supervisor	*Versuchsmeister*
trainer	*Ausbilder*
translator	*Übersetzer*
unskilled worker	*ungelernter Arbeiter*
white-collar worker	*Angestellte im Büro*
works council	*Betriebsrat*

GLOSSARY: UNDERSTANDING THE JOKES

accessible	*zugänglich*
accuse	*beschuldigen, anklagen*
add up	*addieren, zusammenzählen*
advice	*Rat*
age	*Alter*
alike; be / look ~	*sich gleichen*
amass a fortune	*ein Vermögen anhäufen*
amplifier	*Verstärker*
apart; fall / take apart	*auseinanderfallen / -nehmen*
apology	*Entschuldigung*
applicant	*Bewerber*
approach someone	*jemanden ansprechen*
art	*Kunst*
assemble	*zusammenbauen, montieren*
asset	*hier: Trumpf, Vorteil*
attend a congress	*einen Kongreß besuchen*
auditor	*Wirtschaftsprüfer*
avoid	*vermeiden*
bald	*glatzköpfig, kahl*
bargain; strike a good ~	*ein gutes Geschäft machen*
blade	*Klinge*
blame someone	*jemandem die Schuld geben*
bloke	*Bursche*
body; only over my dead ~	*nur über meine Leiche*
boost sales	*den Absatz ankurbeln*
booth	*Marktbude, Messestand; Fernsprechkabine*
brain	*Gehirn*
breathtaking	*atemberaubend*
broom	*Besen*
business administration	*Betriebslehre*
by mistake	*zufällig*
candle	*Kerze*
case	*Kiste; Rechtsfall*
cast pearls before swine	*Perlen vor die Säue werfen*
cheque enclosed	*Scheck liegt bei*
claim to power	*Machtanspruch*
concerned; be ~	*betroffen, besorgt sein*

GLOSSARY

conform to	*entsprechen, passen zu*
conform to the theory	*der Theorie entsprechen*
confront someone with a problem	*jemanden vor ein Problem stellen*
consider	*erwägen; betrachten*
consider	*bedenken*
consignment	*Lieferung; Sendung*
consumer report	*Verbraucherbericht*
contain	*enthalten*
cover up mistakes	*Fehler vertuschen*
coward	*Feigling*
crawl	*kriechen*
creep; be a ~	*ein Radfahrer sein*
crook	*Schurke*
cruise ship	*Kreuzfahrtschiff*
curse	*Fluch*
decide	*sich entschließen, entscheiden*
degree	*hier: Diplom*
delicate	*zart, zerbrechlich*
demand	*Forderung, Nachfrage*
demote	*degradieren*
destination	*Ziel; Bestimmungsort*
destiny	*Schicksal*
disappear	*verschwinden*
disastrous	*katastrophal*
discard	*wegwerfen*
drawback	*Nachteil, Handicap*
drop	*fallen lassen*
dubious	*zwielichtig*
due; be ~	*fällig sein*
education	*Erziehung; Ausbildung*
embark on a career	*eine Karriere starten*
encourage	*ermutigen*
encouraged	*ermutigt*
enemy	*Feind*
entertain	*unterhalten; bewirten*
entrepreneur	*Unternehmer*
equal	*gleich*
essentially	*im wesentlichen*

UNDERSTANDING THE JOKES

experience	*Erfahrung*
expire; a warranty ~s	*eine Garantie läuft aus*
fail someone	*jemanden im Stich lassen, enttäuschen*
fare	*Fahrpreis*
fed; be ~ up with	*die Nase voll haben*
file a document	*ein Dokument archivieren, zu den Akten legen*
firm handshake	*fester Handschlag*
fizzy orange	*Orangenbrause / -limonade*
flood	*Überschwemmung*
fool around	*herumschäkern*
fool the public	*die Öffentlichkeit täuschen*
fortune teller	*Wahrsager*
forwarding agent	*Spediteur*
found	*gründen*
funding	*finanzielle Ausstattung*
gadget	*Gerät; Schnickschnack*
get along with someone	*mit jemandem auskommen*
gossip	*Klatsch*
grant someone something	*jemandem etwas zugestehen, gewähren*
handkerchief	*Taschentuch*
honesty	*Ehrlichkeit*
hoodwink someone	*jemanden reinlegen, hinters Licht führen*
horrify someone	*jemanden entsetzen, erschrecken*
identical parts	*identische Bauteile*
improper	*unanständig*
include	*mit einschließen, beinhalten*
increase in salary	*Gehaltserhöhung*
injury	*Verletzung / Beleidigung*
insist upon	*bestehen auf*
invariably	*hier: stets, immer; unverändert*
irreplaceable	*unersetzlich*
item	*Artikel, Ware*
join someone	*sich jemandem anschließen*
kit	*Bausatz*
laundry	*Wäscherei*
lazy	*faul*
library	*Bibliothek*
liquid assets	*flüssiges Geld*

GLOSSARY

lisp	*lispeln*
lorry driver	*LKW-Fahrer*
loss	*Verlust*
maim	*verstümmeln*
marvel	*Wunder*
Master of Business Administration (M.B.A.)	*Diplom in Betriebswirtschaft*
memorable	*denkwürdig*
merchandise	*Ware*
merit pay system	*Bonus- / Prämiensystem*
nod	*mit dem Kopf nicken*
occurrence	*Ereignis; Vorkommnis; Gelegenheit*
opportunity	*günstige Gelegenheit*
overdue; be ~	*überfällig sein*
owe money	*Geld schulden*
own	*besitzen*
own; be on one's ~	*auf sich allein gestellt sein*
pale; go ~	*blaß werden*
pan	*Pfanne*
paper-shredder	*Aktenvernichter*
part	*sich verabschieden, trennen*
particular; a ~ word	*ein besonderes, spezielles Wort*
peaks of inactivity	*Arbeitsflauten*
pen	*Bleistift*
performance	*Aufführung, Vorstellung; Leistung*
pile of files	*Aktenstoß*
plant	*Werk, Fabrik; Pflanze*
plug something in	*etwas in die Steckdose stecken*
pour something back	*etwas zurückgießen*
proof	*Beweis*
propagate gossip	*Klatsch verbreiten*
prove	*beweisen*
purchase	*Kauf, Einkauf; einkaufen*
purpose; on ~	*absichtlich*
put something off	*etwas verschieben*
quotation	*Zitat*
raise	*Gehaltserhöhung*
rate "best buy"	*als Testsieger einstufen*

UNDERSTANDING THE JOKES

razor	*Rasierer*
redecorate a house	*ein Haus renovieren*
redundant	*sich wiederholend; arbeitslos*
references	*Empfehlungsschreiben*
relieved	*erleichtert*
remark	*Bemerkung; bemerken*
remote control	*Fernbedienung*
reproach someone with something	*jemandem etwas vorwerfen*
require	*benötigen; fordern*
retire	*in Pension gehen*
reveal a secret	*ein Geheimnis preisgeben*
revenge; take ~	*Rache nehmen*
ruse	*List*
rush	*Hetze; eilen, hetzen*
sad(ly)	*traurig*
safety clamp	*Sicherheitsklammer*
schedule	*Plan, Terminkalender*
screen off	*abschirmen*
senior executive	*leitender Angestellter*
sense; make ~	*Sinn machen*
service manual	*Bedienungsanleitung*
shareholder	*Aktionär*
sheet	*Bettlaken*
sigh	*seufzen*
sign	*Schild, Hinweis, Zeichen*
sit-down strike	*Sitzstreik*
smoothly; go ~	*glattgehen*
smoothly; run ~	*ruhig laufen (Motor)*
snappy quotations	*pfiffige Zitate*
solve a problem	*ein Problem lösen*
spare time	*Freizeit*
speech	*Rede*
squeeze someone dry	*jemanden wie eine Zitrone ausquetschen*
stagger	*stolpern, straucheln, taumeln*
stone deaf	*stocktaub*
straight	*gerade, direkt*
strikers	*Streikende*
strings	*Streicher (Musik)*

GLOSSARY

stunned; be ~	bestürzt sein
succeed	erfolgreich sein
suggestion	Vorschlag
suit the occasion	dem Ereignis angemessen sein
supersonic transport	Überschall-Lufttransport
support a theory	eine Theorie stützen
surprised	überrascht
survey	Überblick; Studie
survive	überleben
suspect fraud	Betrug vermuten
sweep the floor	den Boden fegen
tear, tore, torn	zerreißen
temper	Stimmung, Laune
thorough	gründlich
tie up a deal	ein Geschäft abschließen
time-and-motion co-ordinator	REFA-Fachmann
tiptoe	auf Zehenspitzen gehen
tool	Werkzeug
tough; a ~ year	ein schwieriges Jahr
treat someone badly	jemanden schlecht behandeln
twins	Zwillinge
ungrateful	undankbar
unit	Einheit; Gerät
unless	wenn nicht, es sei denn
untidy	unordentlich
urgent(ly)	dringend, eilig
utter something	etwas äußern, sagen
vice	Laster
wafer-thin	hauchdünn
waitress	Kellnerin
warranty	Garantie
wealthy	wohlhabend
wedding	Hochzeit
whether	ob
whine	jammern
wisdom	Weisheit
worried	besorgt
worthwhile	der Mühe wert

KEY TO THE EXERCISES

1. Rund um die Firma / Around the company

Task 1: Translate the German into English

1. go *bust / bankrupt / broke*
2. have spirit of enterprise / have entrepreneurial spirit
3. have a limited partnership
4. have joint liability

Task 2: Complete the idioms

1. go down the *drain*
2. The firm is up for *grabs*
3. *bite* on the bullet.

Task 3: Beef up your word power

found a company	*establish* a firm
form a business	*start* an enterprise
shut up shop	*close down*
finance an enterprise	*fund* an enterprise
go to the wall	go *bust*

Task 4: Find the opposite

a free enterprise economy	a *state-controlled* economy
privatise a company	*nationalise* a company
establish a company	*close down* a company
join a partnership	*withdraw from* a partnership

Task 5: Which phrase is the opposite

let prices float	*fix* prices
keep your money safe	*speculate* with your money
sell a company	*acquire / buy / take over* a company
this contract is legal.	this contract is *illegal / null and void*

Task 6: Which idioms could you use to mean …?

1. *Your days are numbered.*
2. *Buy a pig in a poke.*
3. *It's peanuts / chicken feed.*

KEY TO THE EXERCISES

Task 7: Beef up your word power

manage a firm
expand a company
delayer a company
acquire a concern

run a firm
enlarge an enterprise
slim down an enterprise
take over a concern

Task 8: Fill in the missing letters

So what do we do when we want to get into business? The normal way is to *found* a company. But what sort of company? A *partnership* can be a dangerous thing. If we get the wrong structure the whole business could go *down* the *drain*. Then we'll have to *shut up shop*. And that's no good for anybody. And if you have a partner and even if the business is a *success*, but he wants to leave anyway, you have to *buy* him *out*. It's not so easy to *dissolve* a partnership.

Picture your idiom

I'm afraid we've backed the wrong horse.

Crossword power

KEY TO THE EXERCISES

2. Im allgemeinen Büro / At the General Office

Task 1: Let's go woggling

1. We work in an open-*plan* office.
2. Please *confirm* the appointment by fax.
3. Sorry we haven't *received* your fax.
4. Clip the documents together with a *stapler*.
5. No private calls during *office* hours.

Task 2: Phrases in context

It's a bit old-fashioned, but never mind. They still do good work. Often the general office is *open-plan* where all the desks are located in one room. One of the tasks of the general office is to *order stationery* for the other offices.
They could probably order things such as *ballpoints, paper clips* etc.
So what goes on in the general office? People play with simple equipment. They sharpen their *pencils* with a *pencil sharpener*, *staple* sheets of paper together, and put *stamps* on letters. If they want to survive as an office, they have to work hard. The general office must keep its *nose* to the *grindstone*.

Picture your idiom

They have to keep their noses to the grindstone.
I'm snowed under with work.

KEY TO THE EXERCISES

Crossword power

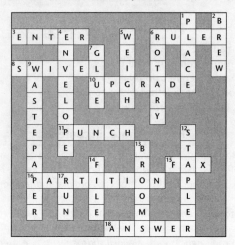

3. Die oberen Etagen / Rooms at the top

Task 1: Beef up your wordpower

call a general meeting	*convene* a meeting
take part in a meeting	*participate* in a meeting
go to a meeting	*attend* a meeting
put off a meeting	*postpone* a meeting
have real power	*possess* real power
fire / sack an employee	*dismiss* an employee

Task 2: Find the noun

resign as CEO	submit one's *resignation* as CEO
promote an employee	give *promotion* to an employee
delegate tasks	the *delegation* of tasks
decide something	take a *decision* on something
develop strategies	the *development* of strategies
be *responsible* for a company	have *responsibility* for a company
succeed as a businessman	have *success* as a businessman

KEY TO THE EXERCISES

Task 3: What might you do with the following?

You might
1. *prepare / sign / check* a balance sheet
2. *call / convene / postpone* a meeting
3. *perform / delegate / distribute* tasks
4. *report to* the Supervisory Board

Task 4: What does the Board not do?

☑ report to the staff representative
☑ write the profit & loss account
☑ club together to buy things

Task 5: Phrases in context

Dr Cautert was *appointed* to the *board* at Low Valley Photocopiers. Now at last he had the chance to do some real *strategic planning*. He still had to *report* to the *supervisory* board, but that was no problem. Now Dr Cautert was really *responsible* for the company. And there certainly were a lot of *tasks* to complete. Cautert's first idea was to *restructure* the company and even sell *off* parts of it. And there were one or two employees who he wanted to get *rid* of. They could *pack* their *bags* in any case.

Task 6: Find the lively idioms

1. He's a big cheese.
2. He has money to burn.
3. Roll out the red carpet.
4. It's peanuts / small beer / chicken feed.

Picture your idiom

You can't *teach* an *old dog* new *tricks*.
Tom's got money to burn. Half a million is just *chicken feed* for him.

KEY TO THE EXERCISES

Crossword power

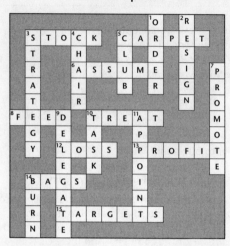

4. Das Rückgrat der Firma / The company's backbone

Task 1: Better phrases for the words in italics

1. Would you like to leave a *message*?
2. Could you *draw up a draft* of this report?
3. Please *audiotype* these letters.
4. The office *is working like clockwork*, isn't it?

Task 2: Four verbs for the better letter

1. *type*   2. *lay*out   3. proof-*read*   4. *correct*

Task 3: What do you do?

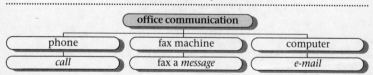

270

KEY TO THE EXERCISES 5

Task 4: How would you react?

1. Is Brian taking the minutes?
   B. Yes, his shorthand is better than mine.
2. May I ask what it is concerned with?
   C. It concerns the copier I bought the other day.
3. Miss Read is always papering over the cracks.
   A. Yes, she is a loyal secretary.

Task 5: What does a secretary do?

1. *organise* the day of her boss so well that he can make the best use of his working day;
2. *screen* him from unnecessary callers and problems;
3. *set* his priorities, but in a discreet way;
4. *bring* important matters to his attention when necessary;
5. *handle* those trivial and unimportant details in his life which become very important when not dealt with;
6. *deputise* for him and handle his problems in a sensible way when he is out of town;
7. *be* a valve when he is under pressure and needs to let off steam;
8. *act* as a link between him and his staff so he does not get out of touch.

5. Einstellung und Entlassung / Recruitment and Dismissal

Task 1: Definition exercise

1. all the employees of the company: *workforce*
2. job to be filled: *vacancy*
3. place for hanging information: *notice board*
4. practical period at a company: *placement*

Task 2: Preposition time

Put the applicant	*at*	ease!
Would you agree	*to*	a probationary period?
Don't forget to put	*in*	your application!
I'm afraid Tom's not	*up to*	the mark.
When did you sign	*on at*	the company?

5 KEY TO THE EXERCISES

Task 3: Guided Translation

1. He's a social *climber*, always wanting to move up.
2. £3,000 ? Not so good ! That was a *leaden handshake*.
3. Jim got the *boot / sack / axe / chop* for being unreliable.

Task 4: Complete the idioms

1. No priority. Put it on the *back burner*.
2. Tom's not reliable. I'm going to give him his *walking papers*.
3. You've got no problems. You're holding all the *aces*.

Task 5: Phrases in context

You've got to find the right man, but before that happens, personnel has to do some *manpower planning*. The boss has to decide how many new men to *take on*. What do you do if you want to fill a *vacancy*? There are various tasks. For example, when we need a new man we have to *place* an *advertisement*. In the advert we have to list his *responsibilities*. If we can't find anybody we should contact a *head-hunter*. His candidate will certainly have *practical knowledge* of the subject.

Picture your idiom

You can't make a *silk purse* out of a *sow's ear*.

Crossword power

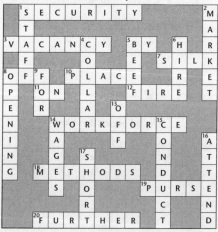

KEY TO THE EXERCISES

6. Personnel Development / Personalentwicklung

Task 1: Find the opposite

basic training	*advanced* training
identify weak points	identify *strong* points
my weaknesses	my *strengths*
he is lazy	he is *hardworking*
fail an exam	*pass* an exam

Task 2: Complete the cluster

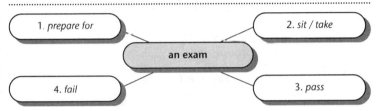

Task 3: Fill in the missing prepositions

1. He didn't perform *up to* par.
2. We gave him hands *on* training.
3. Daimler have invested millions *in* their employees.
4. Twenty candidates. We have to sift *out* the best.

Task 4: Fill in the missing letters

1. Further education costs a *pretty penny*.
2. The company is holding an *employee appraisal*.
3. I've checked. He's got an excellent *track record*.
4. It's not a special job. Clerks are *ten a penny*.

Task 5: Written versus spoken English

Written English	Spoken English
provide training	*give / offer* training
conduct a training course	*hold* a training course
attend a seminar	*go* to a seminar
select the best	*sift* out the best
allocate an assignment	*give* an assignment
embark on a career	*launch* a career

KEY TO THE EXERCISES

Task 6: Step by step

1. *request* the examination documentation
2. *register* for the exam
3. *prepare* the subject
4. *cram* for the exam
5. *take* the exam
6. *pass* the exam with distinction
7. *get* a good report

Picture your idiom

Our books are so successful that Rowohlt's competitors have been trying to *head-hunt* us for years.

Bob Small hasn't got a *snowball's* chance *in hell* of getting a professorship at university.

Crossword power

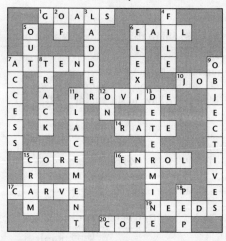

KEY TO THE EXERCISES

7. In der Einkaufsabteilung / At the Purchasing Department

Task 1: Find the easier synonym

Latin word	Germanic word
attend trade fairs	*go* to trade fairs
initiate business relations	*start* business relations
replenish stocks	*fill* up stocks
grant a *quantity* discount	grant a *bulk* discount
purchase from a regular supplier	*buy* from a regular supplier

Task 2: Find the opposite

buy *retail*	buy *wholesale*
reject an offer	*accept* an offer
revoke a quotation	*confirm* a quotation

Task 3: Fill in the prepositions

draw	up	a short list of suppliers
check	out	suppliers
operate	on	higher mark-ups
take supplies	into	stock
impose conditions	on	suppliers

Task 4: The verbs begin with the same letter

place an order	and	*process* it
accept an order	and	*attend* to it
cancel the order	or	*confirm* it
land an order	or	*lose* it

Task 5: Can you guess the verb?

1. You can do it with Goethe and prices:	quote
2. You can do it with glasses and contracts:	break
3. You can do it with ships and orders:	land
4. You can do it with a fast car and a hard bargain:	drive

Task 6: Correct the idioms

1. The works council at the trade union is working hand in *glove* to trick management.

KEY TO THE EXERCISES

2. Put your money into S.U.P. The company is as safe as *houses*.
3. The market is flooded. All our prices are at *rock bottom*.

Task 7: Phrases in context

S: So we thought we might *negotiate* a new *contract* to fit the new *conditions*.
T: Maybe you're right. When we *struck* our *bargain* together last year things were different. This year we're buying a lot more from you. Let's talk about you *granting* us a *bulk discount*.
S: But our costs have risen for all our *raw materials*.
T: And where do you purchase?
S: All over Germany.
T: Aha! Have you never heard of *global sourcing*? You can *source* your *raw materials abroad*. It's much cheaper.

Picture your idiom

He's *as safe as houses*.

8. Forschung und Entwicklung / Research and Development

Task 1: Let's go woggling again

1. Who is *running* the R&D department?
2. Who is in *charge* of the project?
3. Have you already *raised* funds for the project?
4. Our company *looks* forward into the future.
5. We try to *keep* up with the times.

Task 2: Say it in colloquial English

We mustn't *exceed* the budget.	We mustn't *overrun* the budget.
We've got to *adhere* to the budget.	We've got to *keep within* the budget.
I'm afraid they'll *reduce* the budget.	I'm afraid they'll *cut* the budget *back*.
When will you *generate* new ideas?	When will you *come up* with new ideas?

KEY TO THE EXERCISES

Task 3: Find the misprints

Have you arised enough funds for the project?	Have you *raised* enough funds for the project?
When will we get rerunts on our layout?	When will we get *returns* on our *outlay*?
Who is sopsernible for the testing pnalt?	Who is *responsible* for the testing *plant*?
It's high time we reengeined a new ductrope.	It's high time we *engineered* a new *product*.

Task 4: Find idioms for these definitions

1. be careful about what you spend: *watch every penny*
2. find no solution even though you tried: *draw a blank*
3. try to be up-to-date in what you do: *keep up with the times*

Task 5: Complete the following idioms and phrases

1. The R&D department got their figures wrong.
   The company really *came* a *cropper* with that product.
2. R&D is building a new *test lab* to check the quality of their machinery.
3. You can't just spend money. You have to *negotiate* a *budget* with the Board.
4. There's too much competition in this area. We have to *open* up new *fields* if we want to survive.

Task 6: Phrases in context

Everybody's *cutting* costs and that applies to the R&D department, too. They have to *keep* within certain *budgets*. The company needs to get *returns* on *outlay* for any new products designed. The next problem is the documentation. For every product developed and sold the company is obliged to *compile technical documentation*. At the beginning of a project the engineers have to *work out specifications*. Later they will *produce* a *prototype* which will be tested at a *testing plant*.

Picture your idiom

If the departments don't *keep up with the times*, the products will soon be out of date.

With this research project, I think we're *beating* our *heads* against a *stone wall*.

KEY TO THE EXERCISES

Crossword power

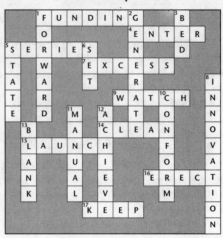

9. Die Produktionsabteilung / The Production Department

Task 1: The first letter is an 'R'

eine Fabrik leiten	*run* a factory
die Produktion erhöhen	*raise* production
Ausfallzeiten erfassen	*record* down time
Produktion wiederaufnehmen	*resume* production
die Lagerkapazität verringern	*reduce* storage space

Task 2: Beef up your word power

work on the conveyor belt	work on the *assembly line*
supply parts	supply *components*
streamline production	*optimise* production
produce goods	*manufacture* goods

278

KEY TO THE EXERCISES

Task 3: What is the idiomatic phrase?

production in another country	*offshore* production
production at the customer's location	production *at the customer's site*
production out of town	production on a *green-field site*

Task 4: Two words for one word

liaise with Marketing	*link up* with Marketing
a problem in the machine shop	a *hold-up* in the machine shop
assemble a machine	*put together* a machine
finish a part	*turn out* a part
start production	*take up* production

Task 5. They all begin with 're'

für Serienfertigung freigeben	*release* for series production
schlechte Qualität ablehnen	*reject* poor quality
Ausschuß verschrotten	scrap *rejects*
die Werkzeugmaschinen ersetzen	*replace* the tooling machines

Task 6: Complete the phrases

1. How long does it take to *assemble* a *machine*?
2. The works manager has to plan the *production schedules*.
3. The *machine engineer* is responsible for the repair of machines.

Task 7: What's the opposite of ...?

curb production	*raise / increase* production
check every 20 items	do a *random* sampling
produce it by automation	produce it *manually / by hand*
use customised methods	use *standard* methods

Picture your idiom

If our company puts bad products on the market,
it's our department that'll *carry the can*.

KEY TO THE EXERCISES

Crossword power

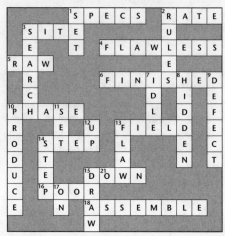

10. Die Marketingabteilung / The Marketing Department

Task 1: Fill in the missing words in the phrases:

1. Your offer's very interesting. Could you show me your complete *product portfolio*.
2. If we want to survive we have to *enter new markets*.
3. A lot of variety. We must give the customer the correct *product mix*.

Task 2: Find the correct preposition

1. carry	*out*	marketing planning
2. decide	*on*	the portfolio
3. apply	*for*	trade mark
4. deal	*in*	consumer goods
5. sell	*on*	a world-wide scale

KEY TO THE EXERCISES

Task 3: Find idioms for the words in italics

1. Okay, I'll deal with the question of advertising.
   This is right up my street.
2. The plan's failed. *Back to square one / to the drawing board*.
3. I think we have to *branch out*.

Task 4: Translate the German phrases

1. Sometimes I feel like I do the I do the *donkey work* while others play sport.
2. With advertising from „Show It" I think we'll *reach our target group*.
3. MacRenRob have failed, so it's *back to the drawing board / to square one*.

Task 5: Phrases in context

The danger of the marketing department is that they look into the future and make prognoses. They tend to think they have sold before they actually have. It's a question of don't *count* your *chickens* before they're *hatched*. Well, what does the marketing specialist have to do first? He has to *identify* a *potential* market and then *attack* it. It's important to *grab* a big market *share*. To do this you've got to research the market, prepare the appropriate product and *launch* it. Maybe if it's good it'll be a *money spinner*.

11. In der Werbeabteilung / At the Advertising Department

Task 1: Find a phrase that suits the definition

1. carry out a consumer survey
2. do the artwork
3. write a catch-phrase
4. address a market segment

Task 2: Let's go woggling again

1. Lupy has to *attract* new customers if it wants to survive.
2. If we want to survive on the market we have to *counter* the competition.
3. Lupy has to hire a good *copy*-writer for their advertising department.
4. *Comparative* advertising used to be forbidden in Germany.

KEY TO THE EXERCISES

Task 3: The verb that does the job

1. *apply* for the post of advertising director
2. *report* to the account director
3. *decide on* the brand name
4. *launch* an advertising campaign
5. *calculate* advertising expenditure
6. *keep within* the advertising budget

Task 4: Beef up your word power

launch an advertising *campaign*	*start* an advertising *drive*
select a headline	*choose* a headline
emphasise customer benefits	*highlight* customer benefits
offer an *introductory* price	offer a *knock-down* price

Task 5: Phrases in context

To get the information to the public, to potential buyers, the *advertising* department has to work out advertising *campaigns*. This means they have to get the right advertising *mix* in order to *gain* new *customers*. To survive, a company must *expand* its *markets*. Part of all this activity is to create a positive image of the company among the *general public*. This is the area of *public relations*. And how should we do all this? We can go to an advertising *agency* and let them do. But whatever strategy the company chooses it should always remember to be *customer-oriented*.

Picture your idiom

Comparative advertising in Germany – that's opening a can of worms.

KEY TO THE EXERCISES 12

Crossword power

12. In der Verkaufsabteilung / At the Sales Department

Task 1: Remember the prepositions

hold	*down*	the job of sales manager
meet	*with*	fierce competition
proven	*in*	many tests
tested	*under*	extreme conditions

Task 2: Find the missing twin

hire	and	*fire*
supply	and	*demand*
wear	and	*tear*
buying	and	*selling*
hard sell	or	*soft sell*
sale	or	*return*

283

KEY TO THE EXERCISES

Task 3: Say it in other words

prepare a sales *campaign*	prepare a sales *drive*
submit a *bid*	submit a *tender*
call on major customers	*visit* major customers
attend a sales training course	*participate* in a sales training course

Task 4: Beef up your word power

1. The following *items* are missing. — *articles*
2. Some of the *parts* are defective. — *components*
3. I have to *make* a serious complaint. — *register*
4. You have not *kept* the deadline. — *met*

Task 5: Say it the other way round

1. The quality is *unsatisfactory*.
2. This kind of thing is *unacceptable*.
3. The shipment is *incomplete*.
4. The printing press is *unreliable*.

Task 6: What do the following idioms mean?

1. strike while the iron's hot
   C. act immediately
2. make a comeback
   B. begin over again
3. sell like hot cakes
   C. sell extremely well

Task 7: Phrases in context

T: I've just heard they've *appointed* James Dean *sales director*. I hope he can *hold* the job *down*.

J: No problem there. He worked in sales and *distribution* in Australia and our equipment is *selling* like *hot cakes* there.

T: I've heard he'll probably hire a new *sales manager* straight away. Actually did you know that sales have been *falling off* here in Europe?

J: Of course I did. But I also know we've got something that's completely different from everything on the market. This Dean will help us to act quickly. We have to *strike* while the *iron's* hot.

Picture your idiom

It's always the reps who *do* the *donkey work*, don't they?

KEY TO THE EXERCISES 13

13. Im Warenlager / At the warehouse

Task 1: Find a synonym

run low on stock	run *short* on stock
replenish stock	*fill up / refill* stock / *restock*
retrieve stock levels *from* a computer	*call up* stock levels *from* a computer

Task 2: Find the opposite

goods *outward*	goods *inward*
overstock goods	*understock* goods
fill the shelves	*clear / empty* the shelves

Task 3: Improve the following idioms and phrases

1. Before we make a decision we'd better *take stock of the situation*.
2. We have our own *storage facilities*.
3. It's all too much stress. *I'm at the end of my tether*.
4. Bad management ! We've *overstocked* the goods.

Task 4: Phrases in context

R: What does your work in the warehouse consist of?

D: Well, it's not just a matter of *storing* goods. There are other things. For example, every six months we have to do our *stocktaking*.

R: Do you ever manage to *clear* stock completely?

D: We certainly do, and then we have to *replenish* stock so that we're always able to satisfy customers' wishes.

R: So it never happens that you *run out* of stock?

D: Rarely. There is one bottleneck in the warehouse. That's where parts come in *goods inward*. Then the boss is under pressure and shouts at me until I'm at the *end* of my *tether*, too.

KEY TO THE EXERCISES

14. In der Versandabteilung / At the Despatch Department

Task 1: Can you complete the table?

By rail	By air	By water
goods / freight train	freight plane	cargo steamer
railway	airways / flight path	water way / route
station	airport	sea port / harbour
platform	runway	docks
driver	pilot	captain

Task 2: Chosing the right transport

These goods should go

perishable goods	by *refrigerator* van
bulky goods	by *barge*
urgent documents	by *overnight courier*
crude oil	by *tanker*
diamonds	in an *armoured* van

Task 3: Beef up your word power

Latin English	Germanic English
What *mode* of *carriage* do you *require*?	What *manner* of *shipment* do you *need*?
Shall we *convey* the goods by air?	Shall we *forward* the goods by air?
I *prefer* using public *conveyance*.	*I'd rather* use public *transport*.
Please *despatch* the *consignment* by water.	Please *move* the *shipment* by water.

Task 4: Fill in the missing words

Some tasks in the *despatch* department:
First you must *decide* on the mode of *transport*. You might need to *select* a *haulage company*. If it's going by sea or air, it will be necessary to *book* some *freight* space. It's expensive.
Don't forget to *calculate* the costs of *delivery*.

Task 5: Guided translation

Paul: We've been asked to *send a delivery* of electrical DXII components.
Fred: Well, we'd better be careful this time. They *refused to accept delivery* of the last consignment.

KEY TO THE EXERCISES 14

Paul: They *checked through the terms of delivery* and found we were late and there were other discrepancies as well.

Fred: Right, then we'd better *group the consignment* and *load* the lorry.

Task 6: Phrases in context

I work in the *shipping department* of a large manufacturing company in the sector of mechanical engineering. One of our tasks is to *forward* the *goods* to customers as soon as they are ready. Sometimes we use private carriers but often we *send* goods by *public conveyance.* The job is difficult sometimes. It's not easy to *handle freight* which *bulky* or heavy. Then there's the question of documents. In addition to dealing with carriage you have to *fill* in the *customs documents*.
And we need to watch costs. In this world it's *dog eat dog*!

Picture your idiom

I'm afraid we can't deliver the products before January. It's Christmas season and we are *up to our ears* in work as usual.

Crossword power

KEY TO THE EXERCISES

15. Beim Kundendienst / At Customer Service

Task 1: Where do these adjectives belong?

1. The customer has the right to return *unsatisfactory* products or *damaged* articles.
2. The customer may expect *consistent* quality and *professional* advice.

Task 2: Put the verbs in their places

1. *assess* customers' needs
2. *provide* good customer service
3. *create* a customer base
4. *comply* with the customers' wishes

Task 3: Find words that have the same meaning

Our company is customer *orientated*.	Our company is customer *driven*.
We try to *meet* customers' needs.	We try to *fulfil* customers' requirements.
We'll get in *contact* with you regularly.	We'll get in *touch* with you regularly.
We have a team of *competent* mechanics.	We have a team of *able* mechanics.
We service your machines *locally*.	We service your machines *on site*.

Task 4: Find the opposite

patronise a company	*withdraw* one's custom
accept a shoddy product	*reject* a shoddy product
start a conversation	*close* a conversation

Taks 5: Fill in the prepositions

1. Calm the angry customer *down*.
2. Take the complaint *down*.
3. Clear misunderstandings *up*.
4. Try to sort the problem *out*.
5. Fix *up* a service call, if necessary.

KEY TO THE EXERCISES

Task 6: Explain the following phrases

1. assess customers' needs
   B. check what the customer wants
2. place the caller on hold
   A. ask the caller to wait
3. placate the customer
   A. calm him down
4. register a complaint
   A. take a complaint down

Task 7: Spot the mistakes

1. Our company takes accurate documentation for *granted*.
2. I don't believe a word I *hear*.
3. That was easy money. *Money* for old rope.
4. In simple English we're *facing bankruptcy*.

Task 8: Complete the idioms

1. We don't want to air our *dirty* linen in *public*.
2. The personnel department doesn't really mean it. They're just *going* through the *motions*.
3. We've got so many problems. I'm at the *end* of my *tether*.

Task 9: Phrases in context

Jan: Customer service is quite a good department to work in, but I don't like working on the *hotline desk*.

Tom: Why not ? I find the work okay.

Jan: That's because you're an extrovert and your English is better than mine. Nowadays it's difficult to *comply* with all the *customers' wishes*, so they often *complain* about the *service*.

Tom: Don't worry, Jan. They're people too, you know. The hotline is one way of *keeping* in *touch* with customers. And *handling* people is more interesting than filing documents. Whatever happens, *stay calm!*

Picture your idioms

To put it in a nutshell, we're totally disappointed with your service.

KEY TO THE EXERCISES

Crossword power

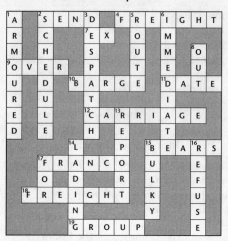

16. Die Rechtsabteilung / The Legal Department

Task 1: Verbs around a contract:

award annul	a contract	arrange amend
cancel contest	a contract	conclude countersign

Task 2: Word builder's corner

The verb	and its noun
amend a contract	make an *amendment*
extend the contract	add an *extension*
penalise someone	levy a *penalty*
sign a contract	put a *signature* to a contract

KEY TO THE EXERCISES

Task 3: Guided translation

1. After two years the patent was finally *granted*.
2. Our competitor refused to *pay royalties*.
3. They tried to *get round the patent*.
4. However, they didn't succeed. They *infringed our patent*.
5. We had to *take legal steps / take proceedings*.
6. But nevertheless we *lost the patent ligitation*.

Task 4: Beef up your word power

take legal *proceedings*	take legal *steps*
file a patent	*take out* a patent
issue a patent	*grant* a patent
display a trademark	*bear* a trademark

Task 5: Phrases in context

The first thing you need for this work is a *university* degree. With the help of this you can learn how to draft or *finalise contracts*. The company lawyer has to make sure contracts are *fulfilled* to the *letter*. There should also be some lawyers working in the patent department. Here they *file* patents and *apply* for *trademarks*. And when a competitor *infringes* on a patent they must fight a patent *ligitation*. It's very tiring and detailed work.

Picture your idiom

Sorry, but *my hands are tied* in this case.

KEY TO THE EXERCISES

Crossword power

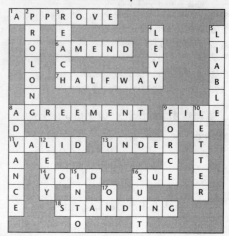

17. Finanzen und Buchhaltung / Finance and Accountancy

Task 1: Fill in the preposition

1. write something *off* after 5 years
2. keep *within* the budget
3. apply *for* a loan
4. fill *in* the tax forms
5. arrange *for* the auditing of the company

Task 2: The A, B, C of books

Books should (not) be

| *audited* | *balanced* | *cooked* |

Task 3: Find opposites for the following

prices *shoot up*	prices *slump / dip / are at rock bottom*
increase fixed costs	*reduce* fixed costs
keep within the budget	*exceed / overrun* the budget
gain value	*lose* value

KEY TO THE EXERCISES

Task 4: Find the words for the following definitions

1. do a course involving working out costs of things: *study cost accounting*
2. send customers a bill: *invoice them*
3. the value of a country's money goes down: *it depreciates*
4. check the accounts of a company: *do an audit / audit the company*

Task 5: Fill in the missing words

1. Customers must pay in *advance*.
2. First rule in finance: don't *exceed* the budget.
3. A bad purchase: It was money down the *drain*.

Task 6: Fill in the missing letters

The financial men in the company have to know where to invest the *profits*. They can take the capital to the *stock market* in order to *invest* in *shares* or *equities*. It's a risky business. The company itself may go *public*. In order to create more liquidity, more available money, the board may decide to *float* the company's *shares*. But who is it that checks the company's business? This, of course, is done by a new unloved tribe of *consultants*. They *monitor* everything. Some people argue they have no vision.

Picture your idiom

We'd better start *cooking the books*

KEY TO THE EXERCISES

18. Gehälter und Löhne / Salaries and Wages

Task 1: The rest is different!

You'll get free	*accommodation*	in the guest house.
Remuneration	*according*	to performance.
Do you	*accept*	the terms of the contract?

Task 2: Structure your phrases

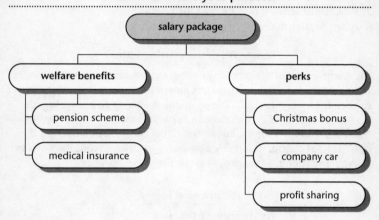

Task 3: Latin words and their Germanic synonyms

formal	informal
increase a wage	*raise* a wage
reduce wages	*lower* wages
make an *amendment*	make a *change* (to the contract)
ask for a wage *increase*	ask for a wage *raise / rise*

Task 4: Replace these phrases by an idiom

1. Try to get a better grip on your life: *Pull your socks up*
2. Only do the minimum work that is required: *Work to rule*
3. Work without paying taxes for it: *moonlight / go moonlighting*
4. Money is the cause of bad things: *Money is the root of all evil*

KEY TO THE EXERCISES 18

Task 5: Phrases in context

It's always a bit of a problem when you have to *negotiate* your *salary* or a *bonus* with your future *employer*. You have to be careful to include the right to a *company pension*. From the employer's point of view he would like to see that employees are paid according to *performance* and he expects *hard work* and *loyalty*. Neither side wants to *take* strike action.

Picture your idioms

I'm out of pocket.
He said that the company was not a *horn of plenty* and that money was the *root of all evil*.

Crossword power

¹P	A	Y	B	²R	A	C	K	³E	T		
I				A				A			
E		⁴R	A	I	S	E		⁵R	U	⁶L	E
C		E		S				N		O	
E		V		E				E		W	
		I						D		E	
⁷S	H	E	E	T				⁸D	R	⁹A	F	¹⁰T
L		W								D		O
I			¹¹B				¹²T			V		P
¹³P	A	Y	R	O	L	¹⁴L	A		¹⁵C	A	T	
			N			E	K			N		¹⁶F
	¹⁷N	I	N	E		A	E			C		U
						V	¹⁸S	C	H	E	M	E
		¹⁹P	O	C	K	E	T					L

KEY TO THE EXERCISES

19. Arbeitgeber und Gewerkschaften / Employers and Unions

Task 1: What it means to have a good job

1. a *secure* job
2. *responsible* work
3. an *understanding* boss
4. good *working* climate
5. *prospects* of promotion
6. *regular* working hours
7. *adequate* remuneration

Task 2: Seven steps to re-employment

2 represent	6 enforce	7 costs	6 injunction
3 present	4 supply	7 incur	5 witnesses
5 deposit	1 take	2 court	4 evidence

1. You *take* your case to the industrial tribunal.
2. A lawyer will *represent* you in *court*.
3. He will *present* your complaint.
4. Make sure you *supply* sufficient *evidence*.
5. Name *witnesses* who will *make statements* in your favour.
6. The tribunal will *enforce* re-employment by *injunction*.
7. Your company will *incur* the court *costs*.

Task 3: Guided translation – A ritual in nine steps

1. The *collective agreement* with the Trade Union *has expired*.
2. The Union and the employers enter into *collective bargaining*.
3. The employers' offer is not *negotiable*.
4. So the Union *brings pressure to bear upon* the employers and *calls a warning strike / wild cat strike*.
5. The employers resist the pressure and the Union *conducts a ballot*.
6. The workers *down tools* and picket the companies.
7. The *wage dispute* is referred to *arbitration*.
8. Both parties observe *the cooling-off period*.
9. The employers are ready to *meet the workers halfway*. A balanced *compromise* is found.

KEY TO THE EXERCISES 20

Task 4: Correct the following idioms

1. We've got a new manager. He's as hard as *nails*.
2. I've a *bone* to pick with you. You've been saying bad things about me.
3. He's a pushy type. Always *bossing* me around.
4. He was born with a *silver spoon* in his mouth.
5. What lousy quality! Were you *lying down* on the job?

Picture your idiom

Well, if you ask me, he has his own *axe to grind* in this matter. He's very ambitious, you know.

Our working climate has suffered a lot. There are two colleagues in our department who are *jockeying for position* as chief accountant.

20. Die Welt der Versicherungen / The world of insurance

Task 1: Beef up your word power

extend a policy	*prolong* a policy
claim *damages*	claim *indemnity*
provide compensation	*pay* compensation
a short *qualifying* period	a short *waiting* period

Task 2: What to do with a policy

apply for	conclude	prolong
amend	**a policy**	renew
cancel	extend	sign

Task 3: Guided translation

1. Would you please send me the *insurance certificate*?
2. I'm afraid our company cannot *underwrite this risk*.
3. You'll have to *substantiate the claim*.
4. It looks as if the damage *has been brought about intentionally*.
5. Committing *insurance fraud* is a serious crime.

KEY TO THE EXERCISES

Task 4: Let's test you on those nasty little words

1. Has he insured the goods *against* loss?
2. I think he brought *about* the damage intentionally.
3. We have to take the depreciation in value *into account*.
4. Afterwards we'll indemnify the claimant *for* loss.
5. Life insurance is only payable *at* death.
6. Did he take *out* vehicle insurance, too?

Task 5: Let's go woggling again

1. Do I have third party *cover*?
2. Will I lose my no-claims *bonus*?
3. Do I participate in an old-age pension *scheme*?
4. May I draw sick *pay*?

Task 6: Phrases in context

Ron: Hey, Tom, have you *taken out insurance* for your car?

Tom: Well, I'm still thinking about it. Perhaps I can still use my English one.

Ron: That won't work. You're not on holiday. You should have at least *third party cover*.

Tom: What sort of *premium* do they *charge* here in Germany?

Ron: It's about the same as in England. And that reminds me. I hope you've also arranged *medical insurance*. Everyone can get ill. And you know you're obliged to *participate* in the *social* insurance *system*.

KEY TO THE EXERCISES

Crossword power

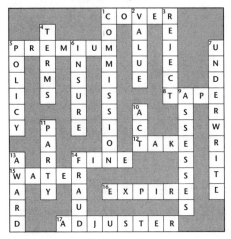

21. Geschäfte mit der Bank / Bank operations

Task 1: Banks you might bank with

1. *Staatsbank*
2. *Handelsbank*
3. *Hypothekenbank*
4. *Kommunalbank*
5. *Aktienbank*
6. *Sparkasse*
7. *Postsparkasse*

1. government bank
2. commercial bank
3. mortgage bank
4. municipal bank
5. joint-stock bank
6. savings bank
7. postal savings bank

Task 2: Which department would you like to work in?

1. *Kreditabteilung*
2. *Devisenabteilung*
3. *Auslandsabteilung*
4. *Anlageberatung*
5. *Kontenführung*
6. *Banktresor*
7. *Kundendienst*
8. *Kassenschalter*

1. loans department
2. foreign currency department
3. foreign exchange department
4. investment advice
5. account management
6. bank vault
7. customer service
8. counter / teller's cage

KEY TO THE EXERCISES

Task 3: Find the opposite

open an account	*close* an account
balance an account	*overdraw* an account
deposit money	*withdraw* money
increase the bank rate	*reduce* the bank rate

Task 4: Accounts you would wish to have

1. *Girokonto* — current account
2. *Depositenkonto* — deposit account
3. *Sparkonto* — savings account
4. *gemeinsames Konto* — joint account
5. *Sparbuch* — passbook

Task 5: Wordbuilder's corner

close an account	the *closure* of an account
withdraw money	the *withdrawal* of money
transfer money	the *transfer* of money
endorse a cheque	the *endorsement* of a cheque
publish the bank rate	the *publication* of the bank rate

Task 6: Wordbuilder's corner

overdraw one's account	have an *overdraft*
repay a loan	*repayment* of a loan
receive a transfer	be the *recipient* of a transfer
redeem a loan	*redemption* of a loan

Task 7: The Credit-ABC

A *arrange / apply for* a loan
B *borrow* money a from bank
C *cancel* a loan
D *deposit* a guarantee
E *evaluate* someone's credit standing
F *freeze* a credit
G *grant* a credit
   and so on

KEY TO THE EXERCISES

Task 8: Find the opposites

Having *assets* is better	than	having *liabilities*.
A bank can *grant* a loan	and	*cancel* a loan.
They *raise* the interest rate	and	they *lower* it again.
Lending money is nobler	than	*borrowing* money.

Task 9: Say it in other words

repay a loan	*redeem* a loan
put a mortgage on a house	*take out* a mortgage on a house
lower the interest rate	*reduce* the interest rate
raise the interest rate	*increase* the interest rate

Task 10: Correct the idioms

1. I've been taking viagra. I feel like a million *dollars*.
2. Pay £ 2000 for that old car? That's daylight *robbery*.
3. Don't *bank* on him! He doesn't know what he's doing.
4. When his father died he didn't get a red *cent*.
5. I think she understands the cash flow now. The penny has *dropped*.

Picture your idiom

It's true, we've overrun our budget. But our investment in Internet stocks won't exactly *break* the *bank*.

Hans made a typical mistake: *Bench* ist die Bank, auf der man sitzt! Die kann zwar auch brechen, aber die Bank, bei der man sein Geld hat, ist *the bank*.

KEY TO THE EXERCISES

22. Das Geld arbeiten lassen / Making money work

Task 1: What's the the financial jargon?

1. You buy at a spot price:
   you make a *cash purchase*.
2. You want to sell your company's shares at the exchange:
   you apply *for listing*.
3. You wait with selling for rising prices:
   you're speculating on a *bull market*.
4. You wait with buying for falling prices:
   you're speculating on a *bear market*.
5. You want to avoid risk:
   you'd better *spread* your shares.

Task 2: You cannot do these things at the same time

lose ground	or	*gain* ground
abandon the gold standard	or	*return* to the gold standard
devalue a currency	or	*revalue* a currency
hold a *soft* currency	or	hold a *hard / stable* currency
a currency *depreciates*	or	a currency *appreciates*

Task 3: Beef up your word power

The broker obtains a *brokerage*	commission
You buy shares at a *cash price*	spot price
Shares are officially *quoted*	listed
The Lira has *collapsed*	slumped

Task 4: Let's go woggling again

Tom: I told you the shares would *rally / rise*.
Bob: You were right. Siemens is *trading* 5 percent above yesterday's price.
Tom: However, insiders expect a price *adjustment*. The market is *bearish*.
Bob: But I'm sure Siemens will resist the bear *squeeze*.
Tom: I'm not so sure. The market is *depressed*.
Bob: At least the euro closed three cents *higher* than the day before.

KEY TO THE EXERCISES

Task 5: Yes or No?

1. When business is irregular the market is unsettled.	Yes
2. When shares rally the market is bullish.	No
3. When your shares buck the trend it's a positive sign.	Yes
4. When experts suspect a bear raid, should you sell?	Yes
5. When prices depreciate they are edging up.	No

Task 6: What's the phrase?

1. Which kind of paper can you change into other forms?
   convertible bonds
2. What is business done after official business hours called?
   after-hours trading
3. What is the money earned on buying and selling?
   commission
4. What does a company have to do if it wants to offer its shares on the stock market?
   It has to *go public / be listed*.

Task 7: Phrases in context

Everybody plays the Stock Exchange now and again. What sort of things can you *trade* in? Well, you could buy *government bonds*, or *gilt-edged securities*. And if you prefer there are stocks and shares in the automobile and chemical industries. You could *invest in* some *blue chips*. They're probably the safest. But just take my advice and don't *trade* in *futures* or *options* or anything like that. You'll come away *empty-handed*.

Picture your idioms

I haven't got *two pennies to rub* together
Let's *test* the *water* first.
We should *put all our eggs into one basket*.

Com-be-nations

Communication between nations

Personal Executive Language Consultants

Improve your Business English
with the authors of this book.

A language seminar
customized to your company.

Contact

Dr. René Bosewitz
Com-be-nations
Communication between nations

Czernyring 22/12
69115 Heidelberg
Tel.: 0 62 21 2 75 90
Fax 2 75 13